View and Window Controls

Action	Press
Full Screen View On/Off	W
Labels On/Off	L
Activate *or* Open View 1	1
Activate *or* Open View 2	2
Activate *or* Open Map View	M
Instrument Panel On/Off	I
Cycle through Cockpit, Chase, and Assigned Views	S
Switch between Panning and Tracking Modes	D
HUD On/Off	H
Choose Map origin	O
Choose Reference Object	Alt R
Choose Tracking Object	T
Cycle through Tracking Objects	. *or* ,
Change Chase Craft Distance	Alt – *or* Alt +
Switch between Relative/Absolute Chase View	B
Change Assigned View Location	A
Zoom In	+
Zoom In Fast	Shift +
Zoom Out	–
Zoom Out Fast	Shift –
Return to Normal Magnification	0
Pan Up	Alt ↑
Pan Down	Alt ↓
Pan Left	Alt ←
Pan Right	Alt →
Center View	Alt Keypad 5

Space Simulator Strategies & Secrets

Nick Dargahi

SYBEX®

San Francisco

Paris

Düsseldorf

Soest

Acquisitions Editor: Kristine Plachy
Developmental Editor: Gary Masters
Editor: Vivian Perry
Project Editor: Neil Edde
Technical Editor: Aaron Kushner
Series Designer: Ingrid Owen
Technical Art: Nick Dargahi and Cuong Le
Page Layout/Desktop Specialist: Thomas Goudie
Proofreader/Production Assistant: David Nash
Indexer: Ted Laux
Cover Designer: Archer Design
Cover Illustrator: Don Dixon

Library of Congress Card Number: 94-68875
ISBN: 0-7821-1504-7

Manufactured in the United States of America
10 9 8 7 6 5 4 3 2 1

ACKNOWLEDGMENTS

I wish to thank my family, including Xenia Lisanevich, Milou and Kira Ivanovsky, Ali, and Alec for having given me all the opportunities in life I have been blessed with. Special commendation goes to Adriene for patiently listening to me babble on and on about "gravity assists," and other technical jargon. This proved helpful in convincing myself that I actually knew what I was talking about.

The faculty at Merritt College gave me my start in the world of science, and I salute their dedication and devotion to educating new generations of students.

I also wish to acknowledge the work of Professors Jerry E. White, Roger R. Bate and Donald D. Mueller, authors of the fascinating book, *Fundamentals of Astrodynamics*. Their book is a veritable gold mine of information on space flight. Francis J. Hale's book, *Introduction to Space Flight,* was another inspirational book that kept surprising me with things I didn't know.

At Microsoft, Jon Solon and Harry Emil assisted me by promptly delivering the latest betas of the software the minute they became available. Charles Guy, the genius who created Space Simulator, provided me with fresh insights into the inside workings of the program that were very helpful.

Vivian Perry, my editor, surgically excised unneeded text and expertly trimmed my florid writing to a manageable length. Thanks go also to Aaron Kushner, Neil Edde, Gary Masters, and all the production staff at Sybex.

CONTENTS AT A GLANCE

TABLE OF CONTENTS

PART TWO: ASTRODYNAMICS FOR ASTRONAUTS 137

APPENDICES

INTRODUCTION

Never has a moment so captivated the world's attention as when astronauts Neil Armstrong and Edwin (Buzz) Aldrin landed their Apollo 11 Lunar Module on the Moon's Sea of Tranquillity. "Houston, Tranquillity Base here. The Eagle has landed," Armstrong radioed NASA's Mission Control on July 30, 1969, as a spellbound worldwide audience of more than a half-billion people listened and watched. When Armstrong descended the ladder and made that first momentous step on the Moon, he said, "That's one small step for a man, one giant leap for mankind." Orbiting above the Moon and maintaining a lonely vigil, Michael Collins piloted the Command Module. Five more successful landings—and one near fatal failure—followed before the Apollo missions ended in 1972.

Since that time, however, no human has returned to the Moon, and it is doubtful that in our generation anyone will. This was a defining moment in history, perhaps humanity's brief flash in the pan, yet it was an incredible achievement. No one could deny that this single act of putting a man on the moon was a stunning accomplishment of daring, genius, and courage. Scientists visiting a remote Stone Age culture in the New Guinea highlands, one almost unknown to Western civilization, noted that the people were ignorant of wristwatches, soft drinks, and frozen food. They knew about Apollo 11, though. They knew that people had once walked on the Moon. A thousand years from now, people may little remember the petty wars, dictators, and other miseries of the twentieth century, but they will remember one thing: humans first set foot on another world in 1969.

It is a fitting tribute to the Apollo 11 landing that 25 years later we can re-enact their mission on a personal computer running software that realistically simulates space travel. Though Apollo 11 once gave us confidence in the future, we seem to have dropped the torch, forgetting that better and brighter time ahead. At long last, those dreamers among us can now allow our imaginations to soar where Apollo 11 left off.

WHAT SPACE SIMULATOR OFFERS

Space Simulator is the most advanced and complex simulation program ever created for the PC. The program combines the awesome photorealistic graphics engine of Flight Simulator 5.0 with a newly created orbital dynamics simulation, so that you can actually recreate the motion of spacecraft in outer space. Spacecraft can rotate and move in three dimensions, planets can rotate along their axes and move in their assigned orbits. Well-known comets, such as Halley's, Swift-Tuttle, Kohoutek, and West are plotted accurately, as are some of the larger asteroids of the solar system. Twenty-one nearby star systems have been recreated with imaginary planetary systems that you can visit with your spacecraft. It is also possible to take intergalactic trips to visit 21 deep space objects, including galaxies, nebulae, star clusters, and black holes. Because even at light speed, or 300,000,000 meters per second (186,000 miles per second), journeys of such vast distances can take thousands of years, Space Simulator gives you the option of accelerating and decelerating the passage of time. This means that you can fly to the heart of the Milky Way Galaxy after breakfast and return to Earth in time for lunch.

Other new graphics innovations have been incorporated in Space Simulator 1.0 as well. Space Simulator supports an 800x600 pixel (800 picture elements horizontal by 600 picture elements vertical) 256-color Super VGA (also called SVGA) graphics resolution. At this high resolution, objects and scenery have a photorealistic appearance. Images of the Earth, moon, planets, and their satellites have been texture-mapped onto 3-D objects that move and rotate in space. For example, photorealistic imagery of the Earth is smoothly wrapped around a three-dimensional sphere that revolves in space just as the Earth does. Lighting and shading effects from the Sun are realistically rendered so that the Earth appears to have seasons.

Using Newtonian equations of motion, Space Simulator simulates actual spacecraft motion with a fair degree of realism. Unfortunately, due to the heavy number crunching that is going on beneath the hood of your computer, some accuracy is sacrificed when time is accelerated or velocities are high. This drawback in the program precludes accurate targeting of spacecraft for interplanetary missions, but it is not so severe that you can't demonstrate some really interesting orbital dynamics principles. Due to special algorithms that govern the motions of the planets, their plotted positions are much more accurate than that of spacecraft at any given time.

OTHER FEATURES OF THE PROGRAM

Program features include:

- Choice of spacecraft and space stations
- Astronomical observatory
- External Chase and internal Cockpit 3-D View windows with auto-tracking and panning capabilities
- Video recordings/ space photographs/ situation recorder
- Autopilot
- Flight computer to link together Autopilot commands
- Space missions: Space Shuttle and Apollo 17 LEM landing

HARDWARE REQUIREMENTS

Due to the complex calculations and high Super VGA graphics overhead, if you don't have at least a local bus 80486DX-based CPU running at 66MHz with a local bus video SVGA accelerator card, you are likely to experience annoying performance problems, such as choppy animation. Pentium processors are, of course, much better suited for the high-end processing demands of Space Simulator, but you'll still need an accelerated PCI or local bus SVGA video card to absorb the huge graphics data stream from your computer to your monitor.

On a 66MHz DX2 486 with a local bus SVGA accelerator card you should expect a frame rate of at least 4–5 frames per second with a quarter-sized 3-D View window (half the size of the opening default screen) and at least 2–3 frames per second with your View window set to full screen.

SPACE SIMULATOR CRITIQUE

It's hard to be critical of Space Simulator, since there are no competing space simulations that even come close to its capabilities. Yet, after spending many hours learning the program, I've become an armchair quarterback, annoyed at missing features and elements that I feel weaken the simulation. For example, there is no display of your spacecraft's positional vector coordinates or its velocity vector components. Without this information it is impossible to calculate the six orbital elements that define all orbits. Thus, you cannot determine your orbit's angle of inclination, nor can you pinpoint its exact location in space. More information is needed on the Map display to indicate where your spacecraft is in space (for example, is it behind a planet or in front of it?), and the coordinate axis should be displayed (vernal equinox is not displayed—and it should be). It would be nice to have your orbital elements calculated for you and updated on screen, such as your true anomaly, eccentricity, angle of inclination, semimajor axis, longitude of the ascending node, and argument of periapsis.

But Space Simulator's worst fault is the gross inaccuracy in the plotted position of spacecraft when time is accelerated beyond a few hours per second. This one flaw destroys any possibility of realistically coasting on a Hohmann intercept trajectory to other planets. Another nuisance is that the gravitational sphere of influence for each planet and moon is incorrect, in some cases by as much as 10 times. This means that your spacecraft will encounter a planet's gravitational field at a different distance than would be the case if it were really in space.

Despite these flaws, Space Simulator is well worth the price of admission. This is the first generation software of this type, and we can expect that future versions will correct these and other deficiencies.

Some people may be disappointed with the lack of "entertainment" features in Space Simulator 1.0. Be forewarned, Space Simulator is not a typical computer game. It is a serious science simulation of orbital dynamics, one that will serve to challenge and stimulate your interest in space. If you are looking for a "shoot 'em up" arcade game, you will be sorely disappointed with this program. If, on the other hand, you are curious about how spacecraft actually fly in space and are wondering how it is possible to travel between planets, then Space Simulator is the program for you. The principles and theory behind orbital dynamics are not easy to grasp, but once demonstrated they become obvious. If you take the time to go below the surface of this program, you will be rewarded with a deeper understanding of how our universe works. What's more, for the first time you'll be able to experience the thrill of piloting your own spacecraft, using real space flight equations of motion.

THE PURPOSE OF THIS BOOK

The main purpose of this book is to teach you how to navigate and fly your spacecraft, as well as to give you a basic understanding of orbital mechanics. Examples are provided throughout the book to illustrate key concepts, and you are encouraged to experiment and have fun by making up your own orbital situations. After reading this book, you'll be able to precisely position your spacecraft in any orbit around any planet and have fun changing orbits yourself.

This book is not designed to replace the Microsoft manual; it is intended to give you new skills and knowledge to help you get the most out of Space Simulator. If this book encourages a few budding rocket scientists out there, then it will have done its job. And for those non-rocket scientists who just want to experience the excitement of space travel, the examples provided herein will hopefully be as entertaining as they are informative.

Using a Scientific Calculator Is Helpful

Although no formal mathematical training is required in Space Simulator, the use of a scientific calculator with trigonometric functions will prove useful for performing some of the calculations found in this book. If you don't want to be bothered by the math or by using a calculator, you can still perform the examples in the book (which all have solutions accompanying them) and still have fun watching your spacecraft do new tricks that it could not do before.

Sidebar Notes, Tips, and Warnings

Throughout the book, special tip, warning, and note boxes are used to aid in understanding the text. The special sidebar notes delve into more detail on subjects that are dealt with in a more general way in the text.

How This Book Is Organized

The book is divided into three parts and concludes with several useful reference appendices:

One: Mastering the Simulator

Two: Astrodynamics for Astronauts

Three: Missions You Can Fly Manually

Part One: Mastering the Simulator The first five chapters cover how to control and customize the simulation. Chapter 1 is an introduction to the basics of Space Simulator. Chapter 2 takes you on your first space flight, where you'll dock with a space station, undock, then fly your spacecraft so close to the Earth you might even get dizzy. Chapter 3 discusses the instrumentation found in your cockpit. You'll master spacecraft thrust and rotation controls in Chapter 4, while in Chapter 5 you'll learn how to customize and use many of the simulator's special features.

Part Two: Astrodynamics for Astronauts The second part of the book deals with the theoretical underpinnings of astrodynamics. In Chapter 6, you'll be introduced to Kepler's Three Laws of Planetary Motion, Newton's Three Laws of Motion and his Law of Universal Gravitation. You'll also learn that all orbits are based on a family of curves called conic sections, and that the geometrical shape of any conic orbit is either a circle, ellipse, parabola, or hyperbola. Chapter 7 discusses the coordinate systems that are used in celestial mechanics, the concept of sidereal versus solar time, and how to figure out the six classical orbital elements of your spacecraft's orbit.

Part Three: Missions You Can Fly Manually The third part of the book deals with learning how to make changes in your orbits and fly missions to other planets. In Chapter 8, you'll learn how to create circular, elliptical, parabolic, and hyperbolic orbits, and see your spacecraft fly the trajectory you've chosen for it. You'll also learn how to perform basic orbital maneuvers such as making in-plane and out-of-plane orbit changes. Chapter 9 teaches you how to plot a lunar trajectory to the Moon, while Chapter 10 shows you how to plot a trajectory to Mars and other interplanetary destinations.

Appendices Appendix A is a refresher review of algebra, vectors, and geometry for those interested in studying the mathematical explanations found in the text. Appendix B contains a table of useful physical constants, including metric-to-English conversions. Appendix C presents principal orbital and physical data for the solar system's planets and moons. Appendix D shows you how to determine your spacecraft's position and velocity vector components in Space Simulator so that you can determine your orbital elements.

I hope you find Space Simulator as fascinating as I do. The simulation of spacecraft moving in three-dimensional orbits on a personal computer using advanced modeling, texturing, and rendering of 3-D graphics is an incredible technical accomplishment. Because much of what is found buried in Space Simulator is not readily apparent on the surface, this book will help guide you on your journeys through the universe.

Questions and comments are welcome, and can be sent to me via e-mail on CompuServe at {72772,2673}, or on the Internet at Dargahi@ix.netcom.com. My WWW home page on the Internet is at ftp://ftp.netcom.com/pub/dargahi/nick.html.

PART ONE

MASTERING THE SIMULATOR

Space Simulator Academy: Ground School

ONE

In this chapter you'll be introduced to many of Space Simulator's amazing new features. After you've finished this chapter, you will have grasped the essentials of Space Simulator and will be able to make your way around the program on your own. If you are eager to fly, or have already mastered the basics of Space Simulator, you may want to skip ahead to the next chapter where you'll pilot your first space flight.

ACCESSING MENUS AND COMMANDS

Space Simulator comes with a complete menu system that allows you to access all commands from drop-down menus and dialog boxes. Each menu groups similar commands into a list that you can open by using the mouse or keyboard. To open a menu using the mouse, position the mouse pointer over the menu name and then click the left mouse button. You can also open any menu from the keyboard by holding down the Alt key and then pressing the key which matches the underlined letter of the menu's name. You access commands that are displayed in each menu much the same way: click the name of the command with the mouse, or from the keyboard press the key which matches the underlined letter of the command name. Any menu command that is followed by an ellipse (...) opens a dialog box. If you prefer to use the keyboard, most of the dialog boxes can also be accessed by direct keyboard commands, thereby obviating the need to use the menus.

NOTE

There are two mouse modes in Space Simulator: Pointer mode and Yoke mode. When the mouse pointer is on screen you are in Pointer mode and can click the left mouse button to choose menus and commands. If the mouse pointer has vanished from the screen, you are in Yoke mode and your mouse controls the rotation, thrust, or panning controls of your spacecraft, depending on which control is active on your instrument panel. To switch back and forth between modes, simply click the right mouse button.

To close any menu, press the Esc key or, with the mouse, click anywhere outside of the menu. To close any dialog box, press the Esc key, or with the mouse click the OK or Cancel button.

Keyboard Conventions

Space Simulator uses many keys from the keyboard in different ways. For example the number 1 on the *main keyboard* is used to call up the View 1 window, while the number 1 key (also known as the End key) on the *numeric keypad* can be used to alter your view direction or increase thrust to maximum, depending on whether you are in Panning or Thrust mode. To avoid confusion between the number keys, whenever you are asked to press or use the numeric keypad keys, we use the word Keypad. For example "press Keypad 1" means to press the *numeric keypad* number 1 key, while "press the 1 key," means to press the 1 key on the *main keyboard*.

> **WARNING**
>
> **Whenever you type numbers into dialog boxes or other option text fields in Space Simulator, you *must* use the number keys on the main keypad, not the numeric keypad. Because the numeric keypad is used to control the spacecraft, using these keys could affect the way your spacecraft flies when you return to the simulation.**

STARTUP SITUATION

To start Space Simulator, change to the directory where it is stored, then type **ss1**. After a few moments, you'll see the Microsoft Home logo on screen, followed by the opening introduction screen for Space Simulator. Next, the simulation's cockpit and view window will open up, as in Figure 1.1, and you'll see a space station revolving on your left. If you have a sound card and have installed the sound drivers in the Space Simulator setup, you'll hear Johann Strauss' *Blue Danube* waltz playing. If you've heard the waltz before and can't remember where, think back to 1970 and you'll remember Stanley Kubrick's classic movie *2001: A Space Odyssey*. This music was used for a spectacular scene at the beginning of the movie where a PanAm Spaceplane docks with a revolving space station.

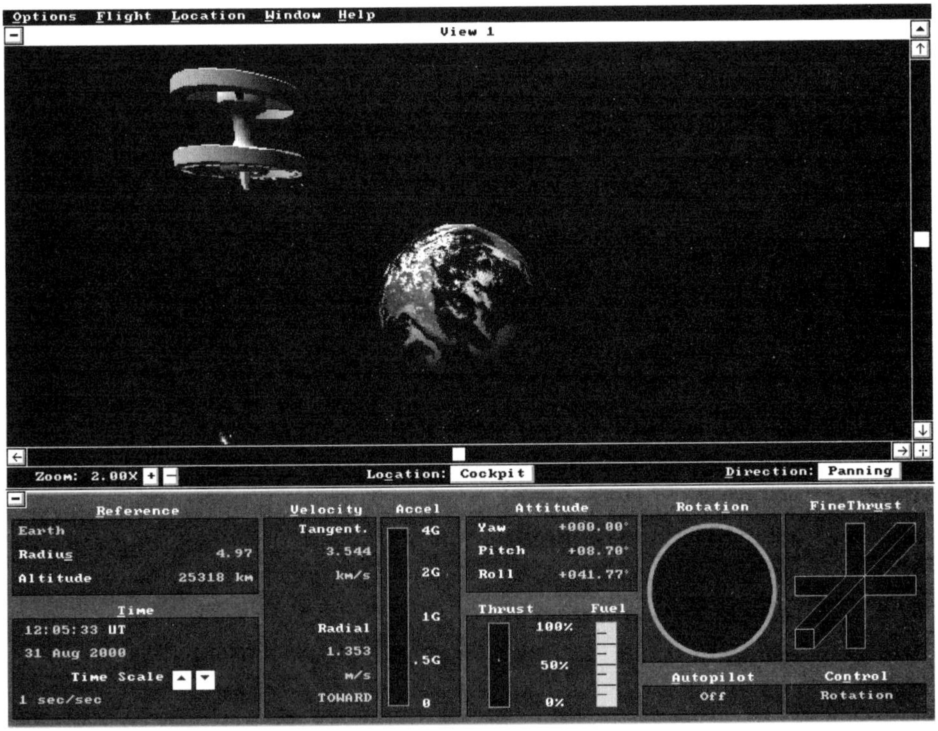

FIGURE 1.1 *Initial Cockpit view in Space Simulator*

Initially your Galactic Explorer spacecraft is in a 31,696 km *parking orbit* circling the Earth. A parking orbit is a transition orbit between launch from the surface of the Earth and a new trajectory or orbit. The use of parking orbits increases launch flexibility and the number of *launch windows,* which are the opportunities during which you can accelerate your spacecraft.

All the characteristics of this initial situation are stored in special *situation* files. A situation file stores such things as the time, date, spacecraft in use, location, speed, acceleration, 3-D view window size and position, and many other preferences. You can save your situation the way you like it and have Space Simulator store it as a new situation that you can open at any time or as the default situation that will always open when you start the program.

The default startup for Space Simulator always begins with the **Flight** situation, unless you change it to a new default situation. Let's take a look at how you change your situation by opening a new pre-existing situation called **1999.** This situation starts you out near the newly constructed Space Station Freedom in low Earth orbit.

1. With the mouse, click the Options menu (from the keyboard, press Alt O).
2. When the Options menu opens, click the mouse on the Open Situation command (from the keyboard press the O key, since *O* is underlined in the command name).
3. In the Open Situation dialog box, scroll the File Name list box up until you see the **1999** situation. To scroll the list box, click on the arrow buttons, or use your ↓ or ↑ keys on the keyboard until you've highlighted the **1999** situation.
4. Press the ↵ key, or click the OK button. You should see the Space Station Freedom in low Earth orbit.

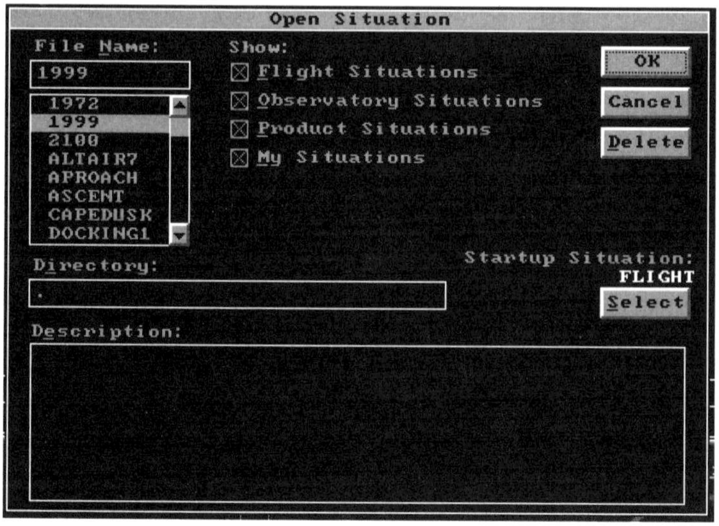

Restarting a Situation

Now that **1999** is your new situation, you can reset or restart your situation to the beginning by selecting the Reset command from the Options menu. Try this, and note that the time on the instrument panel clock reverts to the original time that the situation was started.

Creating a New Default Startup Situation

Even though **1999** is your currently selected situation, if you were to exit Space Simulator and restart the program, your startup situation would revert to **Flight**. If you prefer to have a different situation load up each time you start Space Simulator, you need to change the Startup Situation **Flight** file name that is listed in the Open Situation dialog box.

SELECTING YOUR VIEW

Space Simulator comes with two three-dimensional view windows which allow you to see unobstructed 360° views of space from inside or outside your spacecraft. These windows, called View 1 and View 2, can be configured to display different views at the same time. You can have one view window show your Cockpit view, while at the same time a second view screen can show an external Chase view of your spacecraft from behind. Each view screen can be independently controlled from the keyboard so that you can easily change view angles by using special keyboard commands, or alternatively, by using the on-screen View Tools in the Vertical and Horizontal Panning Bars. Also, Space Simulator has a new "power panning" feature which allows you to scroll your view by rolling your mouse in the direction you want to pan.

A separate map window can be displayed which shows your spacecraft's location in space. Both the view and map windows can be zoomed in or out, but the view windows can also be assigned different camera locations and camera angles. Each of the view windows and the map window can be repositioned or resized on screen and can even be expanded to fill the whole screen. What's more, each of the view windows can be set to automatically track any object in space, so that the object will always remain centered in the window, even as you move.

Using the On-Screen Viewing Tools

The view windows have on-screen view tools which allow you to customize your viewing environment quickly and easily. Let's try using some of these tools to see what they do. Figure 1.2 shows the View 1 window and the name of each tool along with a short description.

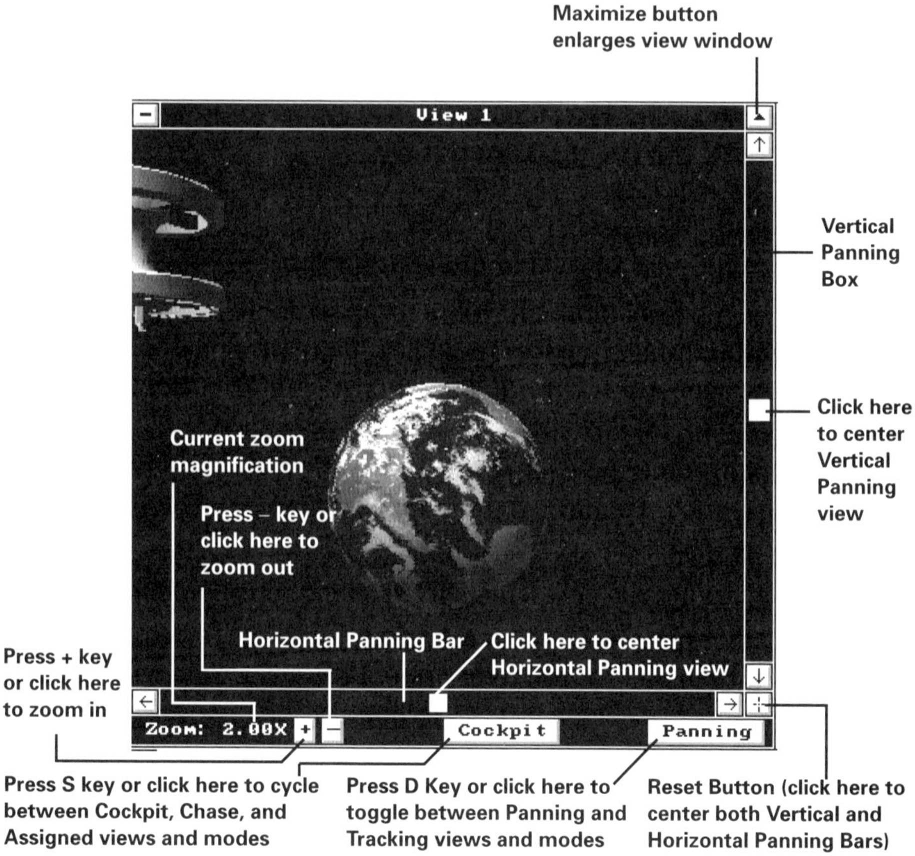

FIGURE 1.2 *The View Tools (Cockpit view)*

There are three possible choices for each view window: Cockpit, Chase, and Assigned. With each of these choices, you have the option of keeping your view locked on a particular object (called *tracking*), or of manually panning your view via the mouse or keyboard (called *panning*). To switch between Cockpit view, Chase view, and Assigned view, click the Location button, noticing as you do that the button's name changes to reflect the changed view location.

Table 1.1 describes the three view choices for the View windows.

TABLE 1.1: *The Three View Choices for the View Windows*

View	View Description
Cockpit	View of the universe from the perspective of being inside your spacecraft.
Chase	View of your spacecraft from an external observer spacecraft that is "chasing" you.
Assigned	View from any planet, moon, star, spacecraft, comet, or asteroid you assign as your viewing location, even if your spacecraft is far away

Choosing Your View Try experimenting with the three view perspectives. First press the S key. You should see a view of your Galactic Explorer spacecraft from the vantage point of a "chaser" craft behind you. At first, the view will pan slightly as the chaser craft moves into the correct viewing angle, but you can change the viewing position at any time by panning the screen. Press S once more to obtain an Assigned camera view of your ship from the vantage point of the Ring Station 1 Space Station. Press S a third time, and you will return to your Cockpit view. Now repeat the above steps, but this time click the Location button just below the Horizontal Panning Bar. Back in Figure 1.2 we saw the Cockpit view. Figures 1.3 and 1.4 show the Chase view and Assigned view respectively.

> **TIP**
>
> **You can quickly toggle between Cockpit view, Chase view, and Assigned view, by pressing the S key on the keyboard.**

Panning Your Cockpit View Panning allows you look in many directions around your spacecraft in Cockpit mode, or to look at your spacecraft from many locations in Chase mode. You can pick your panning directions using the keyboard or on-screen View Tools.

To pan your Cockpit view, make sure that your current view selection mode is set to Cockpit, as indicated inside the Location button on the

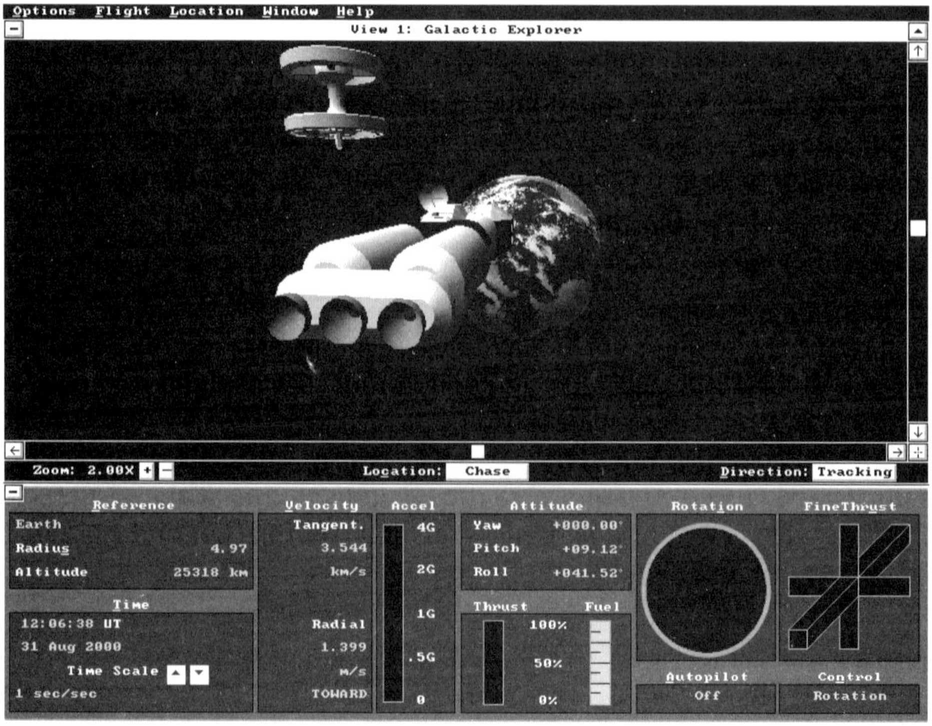

FIGURE 1.3 *External Chase view of your spacecraft*

Horizontal Panning Bar. If you are not in Cockpit mode, click the Location button or press the S key until the Cockpit label appears.

You can use the on-screen Vertical and Horizontal Panning Bars to smoothly transition your view to any angle outside your ship. For example, to pan upward or downward, click the Up or Down Arrow on the Vertical Panning Bar. Similarly, to pan left or right, click the Left or Right Arrow on the Horizontal Panning Bar. To quickly jump to a new pan location, drag the light gray colored Panning Box to a new location on either the Vertical or Horizontal Panning Bar.

If you prefer to use the keyboard, you can pan your view by using the Alt key in combination with the cursor keys. For example, to pan left, press Alt ←; to pan right, press Alt →. To pan up, press Alt ↑, to pan down, press Alt ↓.

FIGURE 1.4 *Assigned view of the Galactic Explorer from the Ring 1 Space Station*

Power Panning Your View Windows Space Simulator offers a new innovation in simulator technology in what is known as *power panning*. This feature allows you to smoothly pan your view in all directions by moving your mouse in the direction you wish to view. To power pan your view windows, first enter Yoke mode (click the right mouse button so that the pointer disappears), then click the Control indicator on your instrument panel until the Panning indicator lights up. Next, roll your mouse in the direction you want the view screen to pan.

TIP

To quickly center your view, click the blue Panning Box in the center of the Horizontal or Vertical Panning Bar. You can center both Panning Bars simultaneously by clicking the Reset button, located at the lower right corner of the View windows (or by pressing Alt Keypad 5).

WARNING

Make sure that the Instrument Panel Control indicator displays *Panning* before clicking your right mouse button to enter Yoke mode. If you don't check this, and your Control indicator is on *Thrust* or *Rotation,* your ship will rotate or thrust to the movements of your mouse instead of panning!

You can quickly jump to any of eight power pan angles using the keyboard. To do this, hold down the Shift key and press the 7, 8, 9, 6, 3, 2, 1, or 4 key on the numeric keypad. Each number will shift your view in the direction that points away from or toward the 5 key, as shown in Figure 1.5.

TIP

To quickly center your pan view, press the Reset button at the lower right corner of the view window, or press Alt Keypad 5.

Panning Your Chase View

To pan your Chase view, switch the view to Chase mode by clicking the Location button or pressing the S key until *Chase* appears inside the Location button.

To pan up or down, use the Vertical Panning Bar just as in Cockpit panning. Note that you can only pan up or down by 90°, or a quarter circle, around the ship. You can pan farther than this and see the front of your ship only if you first scroll sideways to the front by using the left or right panning tools.

To pan the view window left, click the left arrow on the Horizontal Panning Bar. Notice as you do that your view shifts to a sideways perspective of your spacecraft and then moves around to a frontal view. Notice that when using the left or right panning tools you can pan 180°, or a half-circle, around your ship, but you can't do a complete 360° tour.

You can also quickly cycle through any of eight power pan angles using the keyboard. To do this, hold down the Shift key and press the 7, 8, 9, 6, 3, 2, 1, or 4 key on the numeric keypad. The Chase view direction will shift to the direction indicated in Figure 1.5. When you are finished, return to a centered view of the Galactic Explorer by clicking on the blue Panning Box in the center of the Horizontal Panning Bar.

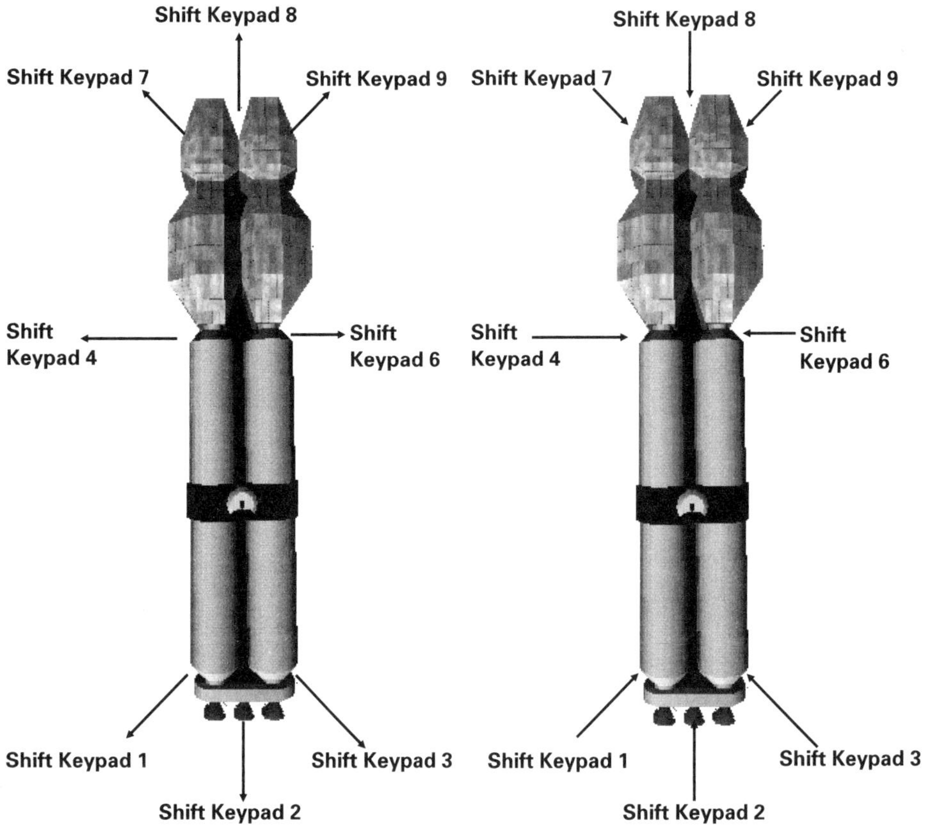

FIGURE 1.5 *Power panning angles for Cockpit view and Assigned view (on left) and Chase view (on right)*

Enlarging the Size of Your Windows

Space Simulator allows you to enlarge any window to full screen size, allowing more detail to fit into the available space. There are two ways to do this:

- Press the W key to fill the whole screen without the View Tools or Panning Bars.

- Click the Maximize button, located on the right upper corner of the view window. This maximizes the view to full screen, but includes the View Tools and Panning Bars.

TIP

To display the menu bar while in full screen view, press the Alt key or click the mouse pointer at the top of the screen.

To return the window to its normal size, press the W key or click the Restore button (which replaces the Maximize button when the window is enlarged).

NOTE

The larger your view window, the slower the frame rate will be.

NOTE

The more windows you display, the slower the graphics frame rate will be.

Activating a View Window

To bring up, or activate any view window on screen, press the 1 or 2 key on the main keyboard, or select the Window menu and then choose Show View 1 or Show View 2. To close a window, click the Close Box, located at the upper right corner of the view window. You can also close a window by pulling down the Window menu and choosing Hide View 1 or Hide View 2.

Zooming a Window

In Space Simulator, zooming a window causes the view to be increasingly magnified, with an effect like that of a telescope. You can increase the magnification of a window to view far-off objects that would not otherwise be visible. You can see what your current zoom magnification is by looking at the number that is displayed next to the + or - button. A magnification of 2.0 is normal, while a magnification much below this will cause a fish-eye distortion, similar to very myopic vision. Higher zoom numbers indicate increased magnification, while lower zoom numbers indicate decreased magnification. Zoom magnification values range from 0.1X to 32,767X.

Before zooming a window, make sure that the window you want to zoom is the active window. To activate a window, click anywhere inside the window so that the Title Bar at the top of the window turns light gray. A blue Title Bar indicates an inactive window.

To zoom in a window, click on the plus sign button located just below the Horizontal Panning Bar. To zoom out, click on the minus sign located next to the plus sign. From the keyboard, you can zoom a window by pressing the + or – keys.

Tracking

In addition to panning a view window, you can instruct the view windows to lock on and *track* a target that may or may not be moving. This is called Tracking mode. To toggle between Tracking and Panning, simply click the Direction button in the 3-D window. The current mode will be displayed on the button. You can use the Vertical and Horizontal Panning bars to scroll Tracking view just as you did Panning view.

> **TIP**
>
> **You can quickly toggle between Tracking and Panning modes by pressing the D key.**

Let's try using the Tracking mode to track the Earth. Press the 2 key to open the View 2 window. If needed, click the Direction button to change the view from Panning to Tracking. Since for this situation, Tracking view is set to follow the Ring 1 Space Station, the title of the View 2 window will be Ring 1 Station. To change the tracking object to the Earth, press the T key to bring up the Select Tracking Object dialog box. Click the Planets radio button, then highlight the Earth in the list box. When

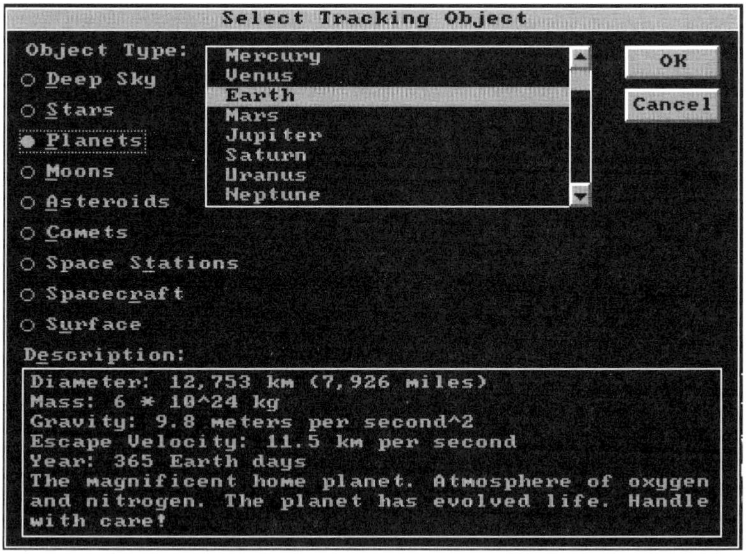

you are finished, click the OK button to continue. When you return to the main screen, the Earth should be the center of attention for the View 2 window, as shown in Figure 1.6.

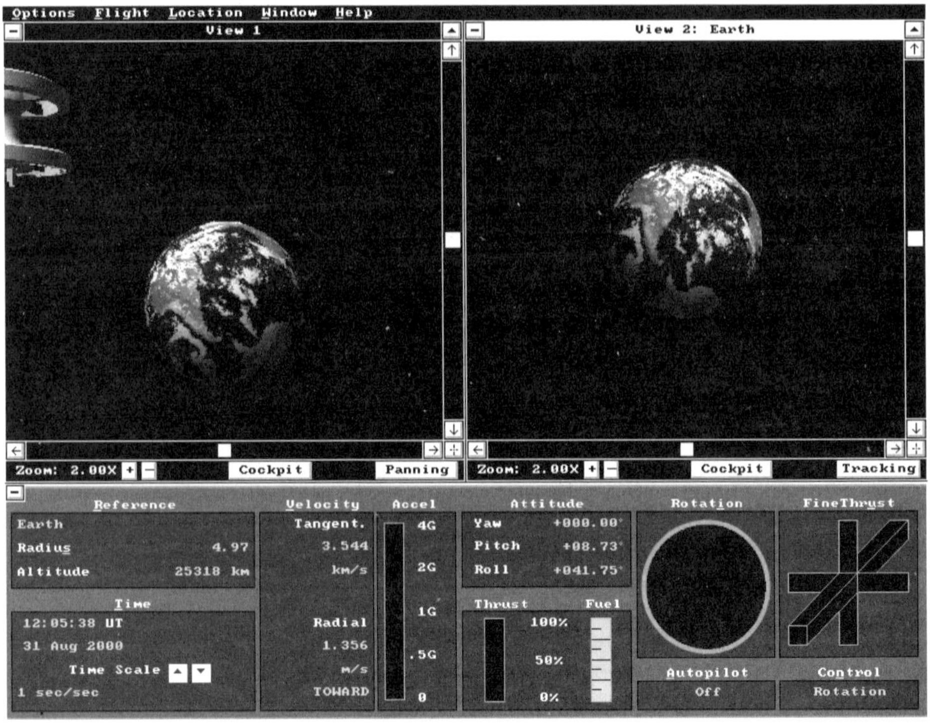

FIGURE 1.6 *After setting the tracking object to Earth for the View 2 window, no matter where your spacecraft is, the View 2 window will track and display the Earth. The View 2 window is the active window, as shown by the highlighted title bar.*

Now, whenever your ship moves or changes its attitude (orientation) in space, the View 2 window will track the Earth and keep it centered on the screen.

SUMMONING THE MAP WINDOW

To call up a map view of your spacecraft, press the M key. You can make the map disappear by pressing the M key, so don't worry about the on-screen clutter for now. You will see a screen that looks like Figure 1.7.

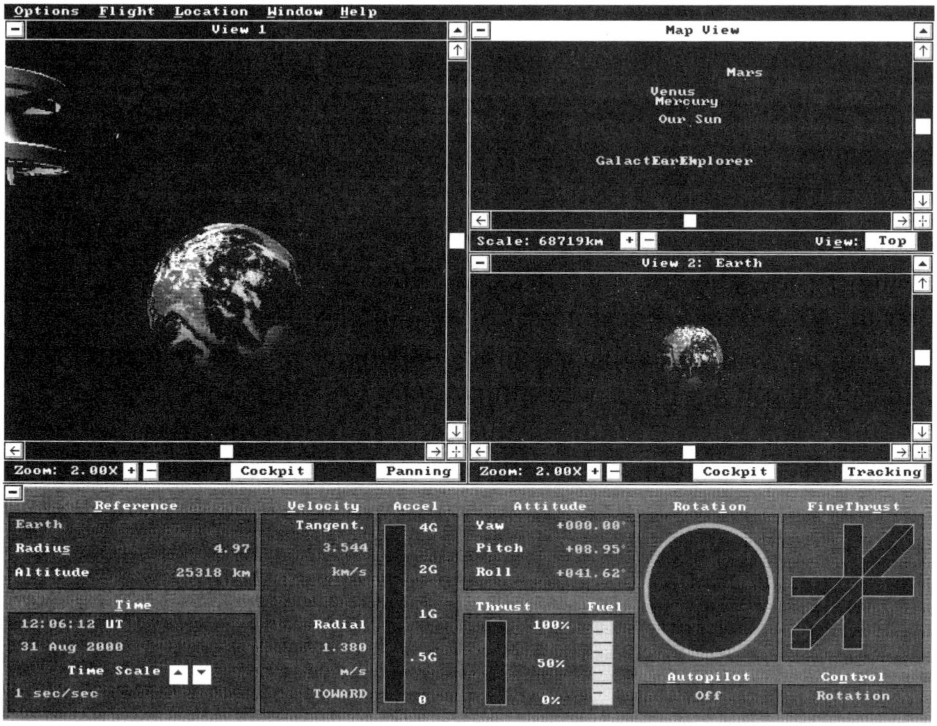

FIGURE 1.7 *The map window displayed concurrently with the View 1 and View 2 windows*

The map looks a little like the two view windows, but it has no scenery or views of space. Instead, you'll see moving dots representing planets and spacecraft. Each object is labeled, but because the spacecraft, Earth, and Ring 1 Station are so bunched up together, the text overlaps and is almost impossible to read. There are the usual zoom, panning, and view window tools, most of which you use in a similar way. The zoom control, however, works a little differently. In map view, when you press the plus key on the zoom control, or press the + key on the main keyboard, the map zooms closer to the center of the map. Zoom is measured in kilometers, and the closer you zoom in, the smaller the radius to the map center. The current zoom factor is displayed alongside the zoom magnification buttons and kilometers are abbreviated by the characters *km* on screen. To zoom out press the minus key on the zoom control, or press the - key on the main keyboard. You can enlarge the map to full screen size by clicking the Maximize button located at the top right corner of the map window. Maximizing your window has no effect on zoom.

Changing the Map Orientation to an Earth-Centered View (Geocentric)

Since you are in orbit around the Earth and the current map view is Sun-centered, or *heliocentric*, you'll want to change your map orientation to an Earth-centered, or *geocentric*, map view. Follow these steps:

1. Press O to open the Map Origin dialog box.
2. Click the Planets button and select the Earth.
3. Return to the simulation and press M to open the map.

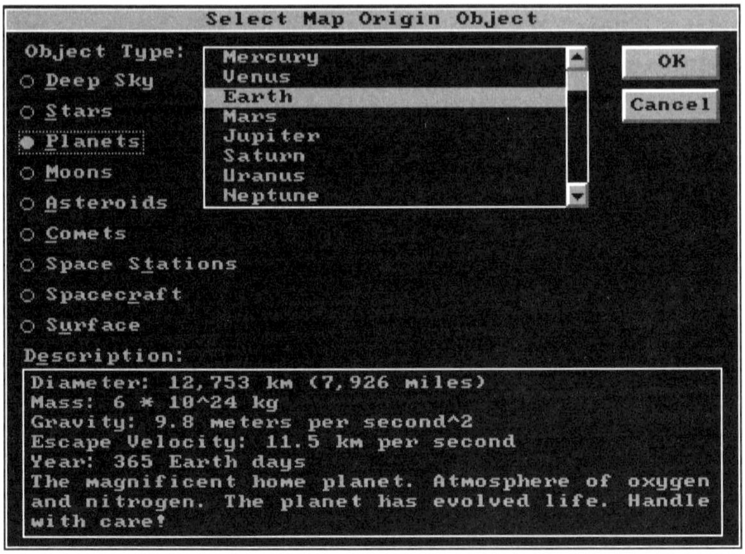

To see your spacecraft more clearly, you will have to zoom the map in to a higher magnification and increase the size of the map window. Just click the + key until the map zoom shows the radius of the display from the Earth's center as 68,719 km. At this point, you'll see the Galactic Explorer circling the Earth, which is shown on the map as a large circle.

Because you have limited screen space, however, the map window is so small that it's hard to see the true scale of things. To enlarge the map, click the Maximize button at the upper right corner of the map window. When you are finished looking at the map, you can shrink the map window back to its original size by clicking the Restore button, which replaces the Maximize button.

Choosing a Map View: Top, Side, or Front

You can change your map view to one that shows a Side, Front, or Top view. Your current map perspective is indicated by the label inside the View button inside the map window. To change perspectives, click the View button to cycle between Top, Side, and Front.

> **TIP**
>
> **There is a terrific keyboard shortcut which avoids the bother of using the menus. Simply press the letter O key, and the Select Map Origin Object dialog box will open. Then you can click on the Planets radio button and choose Earth. Memorize this command; you'll use it over and over to avoid the irritation of using the cumbersome menu commands.**

ROTATING AND FLYING YOUR SPACECRAFT

In space, there is no up or down. Your normal sense of direction is disrupted because of the lack of visual cues, such as the horizon, sky and ground. What's more, you won't be able to tell which direction you are moving in or, in some cases, whether you are moving at all! Looking out your view windows is no help, because all you'll see are stars and perhaps a planet or two looking like faint dots of light. These problems are partially solved by using the Autopilot and the Head Up Display (HUD) to orient your spacecraft.

There are two principal modes of movement in space travel: *translation* and *rotation***.** Translation occurs when you move your spacecraft from one location to another. You can translate the spacecraft small distances up and down, left and right, or backward and forward using the fine thrust controls. For traveling longer distances, or when making orbital changes, you use your Main Thrusters, which are much more powerful.

Rotation is the revolving or turning motion that occurs around one of the spacecraft's axes. Unlike translation, during rotation the spacecraft's position in space does not change. There are rotation thrusters mounted on your spacecraft that allow you to yaw, pitch, or roll your spacecraft to any orientation, or *attitude*. Attitude is a term that refers to your spacecraft's current orientation in space relative to some coordinate system.

Rotating Your Spacecraft

There are three axes of rotation: pitch, yaw, and roll.

- Pitch refers to rotation about the spacecraft's lateral axis.
- Yaw refers to rotation about the spacecraft's vertical axis.
- Roll refers to rotation about the spacecraft's longitudinal axis.

Let's try rotating the spacecraft using the keyboard. Press the key on the numeric keypad corresponding to the rotational direction you wish to rotate.

Figure 1.8 illustrates the rotation controls on the numeric keypad. You can also use the mouse to rotate your spacecraft as shown in Figure 1.9. Simply click the Control indicator until it displays *Rotation*, then click the right mouse button to enter Yoke mode. Roll the mouse to rotate the spacecraft.

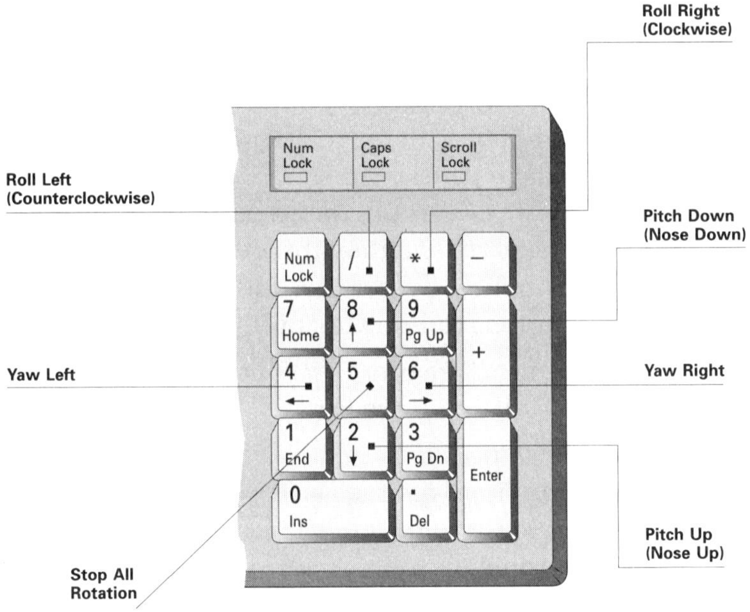

FIGURE 1.8 *Keyboard rotation controls on the numeric keypad*

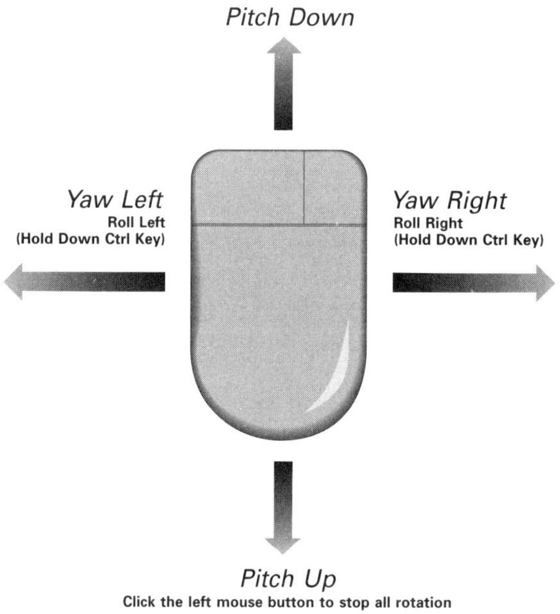

FIGURE 1.9 *Mouse rotation controls*

Notice that as you play with these rotation controls, not only does your View 1 change in response to the rotation, but the digital Attitude display on your Instrument panel changes as well. For example, as you rotate clockwise by pressing Keypad *, the scenery and stars inside the View 1 window will rotate *left*, and the Attitude display's Roll readout will change. You might notice that the Yaw and Pitch readings change as well during the roll. To stop rotation you must press Keypad 5.

All rotation measurements are based on your *reference object,* which in the case of the **Flight** situation is the Earth.

When the current reference object is the Earth, for example, a 0° yaw is the direction pointing directly at the Earth, while 180° is the direction pointing directly away. The 0° pitch mark is centered on the Earth, while the +90° or -90° mark would mean that your spacecraft is oriented perpendicular to the Earth. (Note that if you are yawed at 180°, you can be pitched at 0° and be pointed directly away from the Earth. We'll cover this in later chapters.)

REFERENCE POINTS FOR DISTANCE AND VELOCITY READINGS

Your spacecraft's distance and velocity readings, displayed on the Instrument Panel, are *relative* to the current *reference object*. To choose a new reference, open the Reference Object dialog box by clicking on the Reference Box inside the Instrument Panel (or pressing Alt R), then select the new reference object. To see how far you are from the Moon, for example, you would open the Reference Object dialog box, select the Moons radio button and highlight the Earth's Moon listing. When you return to the simulation, the distance readings and velocities you see displayed will be relative to the Earth's Moon, no matter where you are in the Universe.

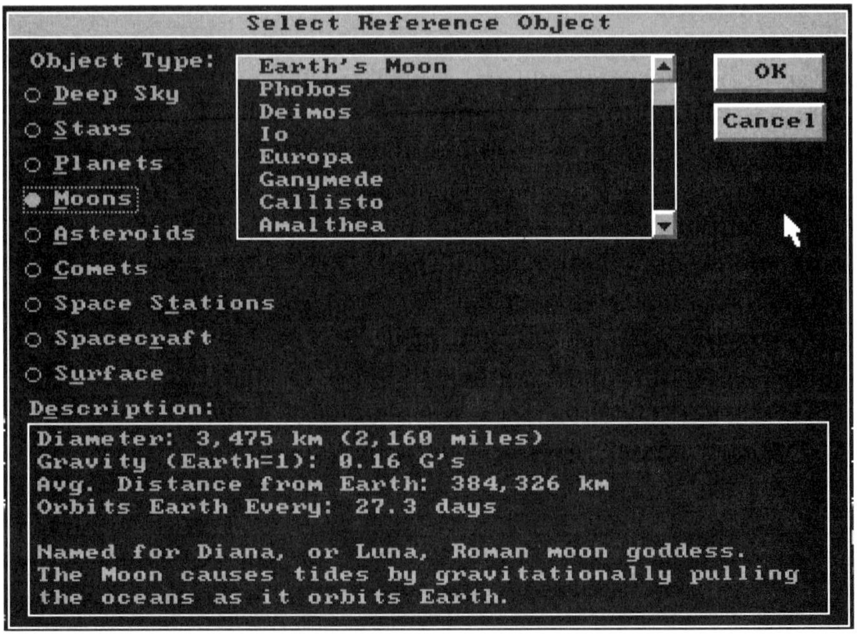

Translating (Flying) Your Spacecraft

For small changes in your spacecraft's position, you use the Fine Thrust controls to translate your spacecraft. For large changes, such as when changing orbits, you use the Main Thrusters. Remember that for translation, as opposed to rotation where your position remains fixed, your spacecraft actually gains velocity in a new direction and changes position. And once you apply thrust, your spacecraft will continue to move, unless you reverse thrust or use the special cut velocity command (press F4 to have the spacecraft automatically zero all previous velocity, relative to your current reference object). Also note that when you fire your thrusters, they will continue firing until you press Keypad 7.

Translation Using Fine Thrusters To move, or translate your spacecraft, using the Fine Thrusters from the keyboard press the key on the numeric keypad which corresponds to the translational direction you wish to move. To stop translation, press Keypad 7 to cut your thrusters off, and then press F4 to stop all velocity.

Figure 1.10 identifies the keys which are assigned translational thrust on the numeric keypad.

You can also use the mouse to translate your spacecraft up or down, and left or right, using the Fine Thrusters. Unfortunately, you can't use the mouse to translate forward or backward.

To translate your spacecraft using the mouse, simply click the Control indicator until it displays *Thrust*, then click the right mouse button to enter Yoke mode. Roll the mouse to apply thrust as shown in Figure 1.11.

You can see the current level of thrust in the Fine Thrust Indicator on screen, as shown in Figure 1.12.

Using Your Main Thrusters For Large Translational Movements The Main Thrusters of your spacecraft only allow you to accelerate forward along the spacecraft's longitudinal axis. To fly in a particular direction, you must rotate the spacecraft

> **TIP**
>
> **To cut all thrust, press the Keypad 7 key. To cut all velocity relative to the current Reference Object displayed on your Instrument Panel, press the F4 key.**

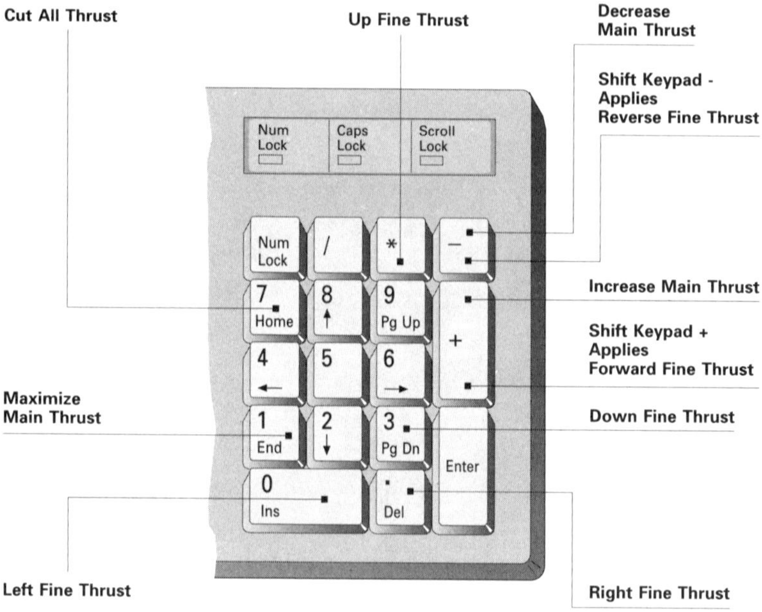

FIGURE 1.10 *Keyboard translational thrust controls on the numeric keypad.*

to face the direction you wish to go. And, if you want to slow down you must reverse the spacecraft, so that the tail is facing your forward *velocity vector*, and then fire your Main Thrusters. A velocity vector simply refers to the magnitude of speed and the direction your spacecraft is currently traveling. Vectors can be broken up into components which describe motion or position based on an X Y Z Cartesian coordinate system. We will cover this topic in later chapters.

How do you determine which direction you're traveling? Well there is no simple way to do this visually, since Space Simulator does not provide you with vector velocity components, such as $\mathbf{V_X}$, $\mathbf{V_Y}$, $\mathbf{V_Z}$. But, using the Autopilot, you can *retrograde* or *prograde* your spacecraft so that it will automatically orient your spacecraft in the proper direction for firing your thrusters. When you *retrograde* your spacecraft, your spacecraft faces tail first towards your present velocity vector and firing your Main Thrusters will *decrease* your velocity. When you *prograde* your spacecraft, you face forwards and firing your Main Thrusters will *increase* your velocity.

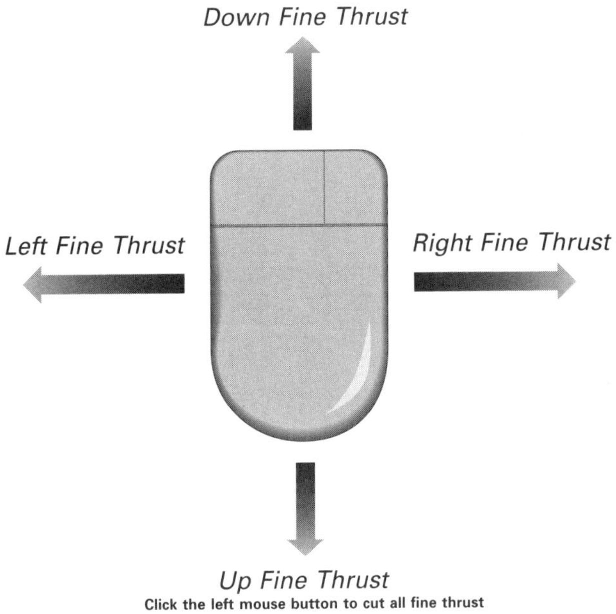

FIGURE 1.11 *Mouse translation controls*

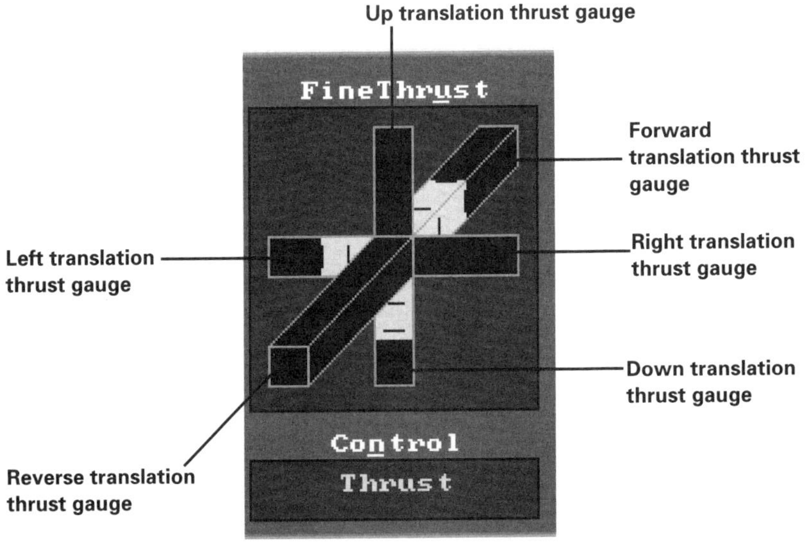

FIGURE 1.12 *The Fine Thrust indicator tells you how much Fine Thrust is being applied in a particular direction.*

Another autopilot command, called *turnover,* comes in handy when you are performing small translational movements that are sideways to your orbital velocity vector. After firing your thrusters, you can use *turnover* to flip the spacecraft around 180°, and then fire your thrusters again to cancel your original acceleration.

To increase thrust from your Main Thrusters, you press Keypad +. To decrease thrust, press Keypad –. Also, you can instantly increase thrust to maximum by pressing Keypad 1, and cut all thrust by pressing Keypad 7.

Now that you understand how your thrust controls work, let's learn how to orient the spacecraft using the Earth as an orientation point. Reset the **Flight** situation before proceeding to the next section.

Orienting Your Spacecraft Toward Earth

To orient your spacecraft toward the Earth, first check to make sure that your Reference Object display on your Instrument Panel is assigned to the Earth. Once the Earth is selected as your Reference Object, all you need to do is rotate the spacecraft to face the Earth, using your attitude indicators to help guide your ship. The spacecraft will face the Earth when the Digital Attitude Display shows 0° Yaw, 0° Pitch.

Using Autopilot to Orient Your Spacecraft If you don't want to bother with manually orienting your spacecraft, there's a really fast way to have your Autopilot do the work for you.

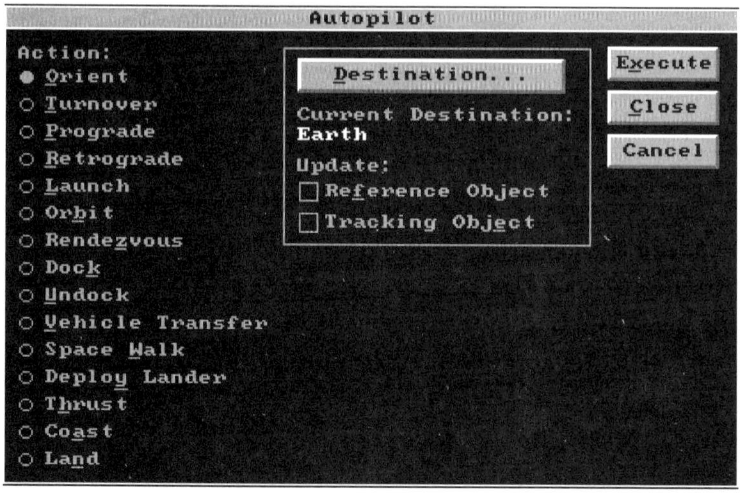

To do this, press Alt A to open the Autopilot dialog box, then click the Orient button. Choose your destination then, before exiting the Autopilot, click the Execute button.

ACCELERATING TIME

Space Simulator comes equipped with a time display on the Instrument Panel that not only displays the current time and date, but allows you to accelerate or slow down the passage of time. The current time shown is displayed in *Universal Time (UT)*, which is based on Greenwich, England mean solar time. Since the Earth is divided into 24 time zones approximately 15° of longitude apart, the local mean solar time in each time zone differs from neighboring zones by one hour.

Changing the Time and Date Affects Lighting Conditions and Planetary Positions

Lighting conditions and planetary positions are accurately portrayed according to time and date. Thus, when the vernal equinox occurs on March 21 each year, at exactly noon UT the Sun will be in the constellation of Aries and will cross the Earth's equator on its way to the Tropic of Cancer (where the Sun's most northerly position occurs on the summer solstice, June 21). If your spacecraft were to fly over the Earth, you would notice that it is still dark in San Francisco, but that dawn is just breaking in New York.

Time is displayed in 24-hour format. To change the time or date, follow these steps:

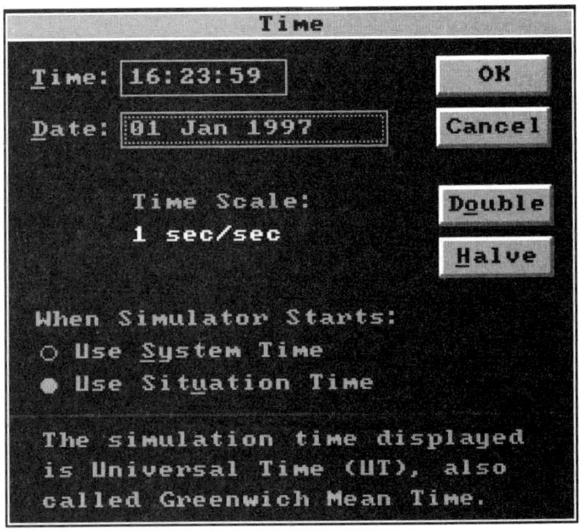

1. Click the Time display on the Instrument Panel, shown in Figure 1.13.
2. When the Time dialog box opens, type in the new time. Make sure that you enter the time in 24-hour format, and that you separate minutes from hours and seconds with a colon. To enter 4:23:59 p.m., type **16:23:59** in the Time text entry box.
3. Type in the new date, making sure that you abbreviate the month to three characters. The proper format is **01 Jan 1997.** Click the OK button to return to the simulation.

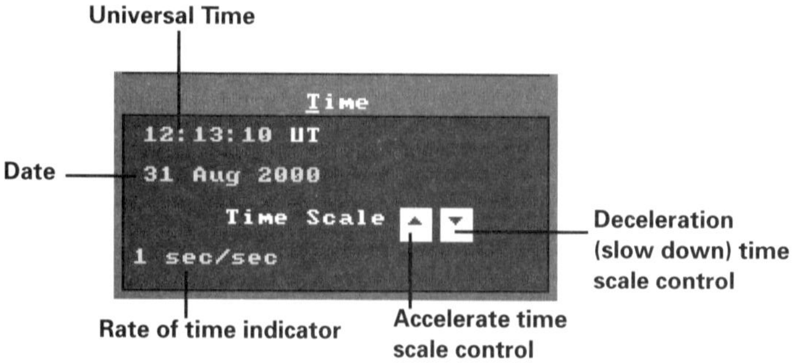

FIGURE 1.13 *Time controls*

NOTE

When you change the time or date in Space Simulator, the positions and lighting conditions of the planets will change to reflect the new time. However, your spacecraft will maintain the *same relative position* in space to the nearest planetary object. It will not advance in its orbit to a new position. But when you *accelerate* time, your spacecraft *will* move, as will the planets, moons and other celestial objects.

WARNING

If you accelerate time more than 1 day/second (in some cases even changing your time to more than 17.1 minutes/second will affect your orbit!), your orbit will change and deviate from the path it would have taken if time had been left at a normal rate of 1 second/second. This is because Space Simulator cannot calculate trajectories with high precision when time is accelerated.

When you exit the dialog box, the planets and moons will move to their new positions and will also rotate to face the Sun properly for the new epoch you have chosen.

Accelerating Time To Rapidly Traverse Orbits

Accelerating time allows you to see what your orbit looks like very rapidly. It also allows you to get from one place to another very quickly. However, the higher the rate of time, the more imprecise your orbit will be due to time approximation errors that accumulate. Eventually, with the time control cranked up to more than a day per second, your orbit will be only a crude approximation of what it would really be if you were flying in real time. With even higher time accelerations, your orbit will deviate so far from its original parameters that, in essence, you will have created an entirely new orbit!

WHY YOUR SPACECRAFT SEEMS TO POINT IN DIFFERENT DIRECTIONS WHILE ORBITING

Whenever you accelerate time, you should *always* set your View 1 window to Tracking mode and select a planet or other object to track. This way, your view window will always point at the planet/object, even though your spacecraft may be pointing in an entirely different direction as it traverses its orbit. Keep in mind that unless you rotate your spacecraft, it will always point in the *same* direction relative to the stars, regardless of what kind of orbit you are in. So when your spacecraft orbits the Earth, for example, and it is oriented toward the star Polaris, no matter where your spacecraft is in its orbit, it will *always* point toward

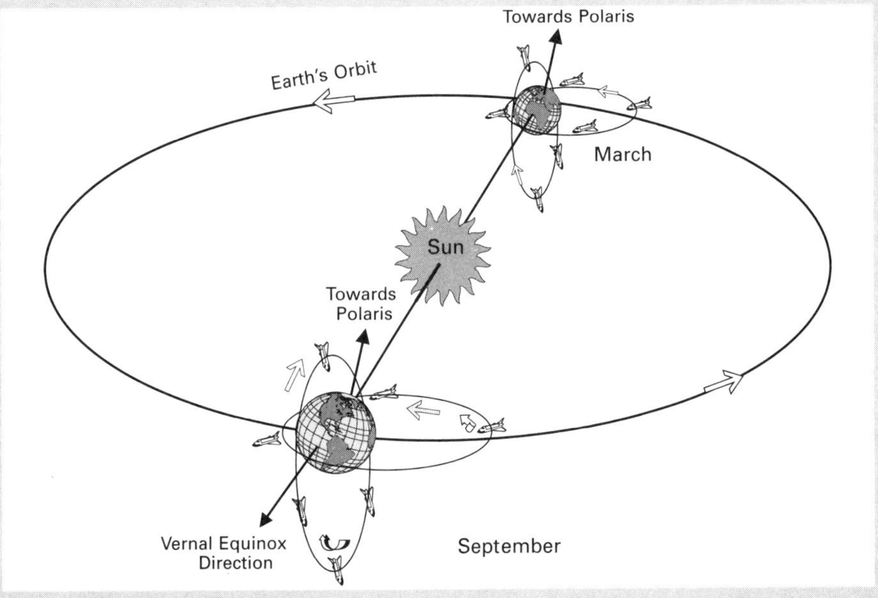

Polaris! Your Earth orbiting spacecraft never seems to keep the Earth in view while in Panning mode because it is moving around the Earth. If your ship is initially pointing *toward* the Earth, after a half orbit it will be pointing *away* from the earth. After one entire orbit, the spacecraft will again be pointing toward the Earth. The nose of the ship always remains fixed relative to the stars.

Let's try accelerating time to 17.1 minutes for each second of elapsed real time in the opening **Flight** situation, and then watch as the spacecraft rapidly orbits the Earth.

To resume normal time, click the Decrease Time Scale button in the Time Control box inside the Instrument Panel, until the current time scale displays 1 second/second.

Now that you've learned the basics of Space Simulator, it's time to take the Galactic Explorer spacecraft out for a spin. The next chapter will get you going on two space flights where you'll rendezvous and dock with the Ring 1 Space Station, and then undock and fire your Main Thrusters for a breathtakingly close encounter with the Earth.

Piloting Your First Space Flight

TWO

Even though you may never have set foot in a real spacecraft, this chapter will teach you how to dock your Space Simulator spacecraft and how to change orbits. You will first dock the Galactic Explorer at the Ring 1 Space Station. Then you'll disembark from the station and retrofire your Main Thrusters to create a new elliptical orbit. This orbit will swing your spacecraft so close to the Earth that it will fill your view screen at *perigee*, or the point of closest approach to the Earth. The new orbit will return you to the your current location, although the Ring 1 Space Station will not be there. The a*pogee* of the new orbit, or point farthest from the Earth, will thus be at the location you are right now.

DOCKING AND IN-PLANE ORBIT CHANGES

Although you can use Space Simulator's Autopilot to perform most orbital maneuvers, including docking and in-plane orbit changes, you'll have a lot more fun and learn much more if you do it yourself. The next section teaches you how to manually dock with a space station, and the section following it instructs you how to manually perform an in-plane orbital change. In the docking procedure, you'll eyeball your position in space and rendezvous with the Ring 1 Space Station before docking. After undocking, you'll pilot your spacecraft toward the Earth. You'll swing by the Earth at a *perigee* of 1000 km, and your spacecraft will return to its present *apogee* distance of 31,696 km from the center of the Earth.

Setting Space Simulator's Precision to Maximum

Before beginning any high precision orbital maneuver, you *must* set Space Simulator's Precision setting to its highest level. To do this:

1. Select the Options menu.
2. Choose Preferences.
3. Click the Precision button.
4. Drag the Precision slider to the highest setting (8).
5. Click OK to return to the simulation.

RENDEZVOUS AND DOCKING WITH THE RING 1 SPACE STATION

Before beginning the rendezvous, first reset the **Flight** situation, assuming that it is the currently loaded situation. From the Options menu, select Reset, and you'll be ready to go.

> **TIP**
>
> **To pause the simulation at any time, press the Pause key on your keyboard. To resume the simulation from where you left it, press the Pause key again.**

Whenever you rotate your spacecraft, to stop the rotation you must press Keypad 5, and when you translate the spacecraft, you must cut the thrusters by pressing Keypad 7 followed by the F4 key.

Follow these steps to initiate the docking sequence:

1. Switch to Chase view by pressing the S key.
2. Open the Reference Object dialog box. Click Space Station and highlight Ring Station 1. Click OK. The Instrument Panel will display the distance to the Ring Station 1 and the velocity of the Galactic Explorer with respect to the space station (before it showed distance and velocity of your spacecraft relative to the Earth).
3. If your display shows Radius and Altitude data for the Ring Station, click either Radius or Altitude to change the readout to Distance. The space station should be about 2.349 km away. Note

also that your radial velocity towards the space station is 0 meters/second (m/sec). You needn't concern yourself with tangential velocity.

4. Yaw the spacecraft by pressing Keypad 4 until the Digital Attitude display shows 0°. To stop yawing, press Keypad 5.
5. Pitch the spacecraft up by pressing Keypad 2 until the Digital Attitude display shows –10°. To stop pitching, press Keypad 5. Once you arrive at this pitch angle, don't worry if it strays.
6. Press Shift Keypad + to accelerate forward with the Fine Thrust controls.
7. When you reach 10 m/sec, press Keypad 7 to reduce the Fine Thrust to zero.
8. Accelerate time by clicking on the Increase Time Scale button, inside the Time controls on the Instrument Panel. A good rate is 4 seconds/second. When you get within 500 meters of the space station, reduce the time scale to 1 second/second.

Keep watching the distance display to see how close you can bring the Galactic Explorer to the space station. The distance to the station should be getting smaller; if it isn't or if you notice that the distance indicator suddenly reverses course and starts getting larger, you should immediately press F4 to stop all velocity.

Aligning the Docking Hatches

At this point, you should be within 416 meters of the Ring Station. Don't worry if you've overshot this distance or are a little farther away.

Drag the Vertical Panning Box all the way down. Your view should look something like Figure 2.1, where you are looking upwards at the bottom of the Galactic Explorer. The space station is revolving counterclockwise, and your goal is to attach the orange docking hatch to the hexagonal-shaped docking mechanism protruding from the space station.

Press the B key to change to Absolute view in your Chase view window. This will keep your Chase view of the spacecraft fixed while the

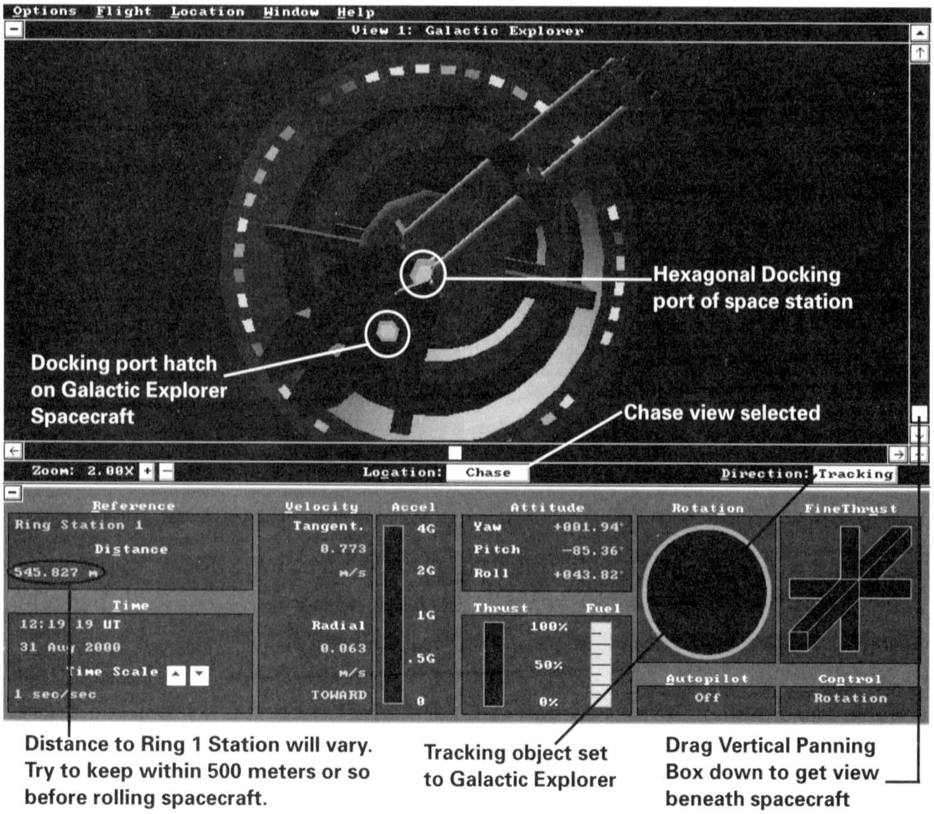

FIGURE 2.1 *Chase view prior to docking*

spacecraft rotates and moves for the final docking sequences. When you press the B key, the view will shift slightly. Now you are ready to dock:

1. Since your orange docking hatch is facing away from the docking port on the space station, you must roll the spacecraft 180° to bring it around to the opposite side. Press the Keypad / key (or Keypad *) to begin rolling the spacecraft.
2. Continue the roll until your pitch readout on the Digital Attitude display shows +80° (you started the roll at –80°). When you reach +80°, quickly press Keypad 5 to stop the roll. Note that even though you are rolling the spacecraft, it is the pitch readout that

you are concerned with, not the roll readout (this point will be explained in later chapters). Figure 2.2 shows the Galactic Explorer in the midst of the roll maneuver.

3. Press Keypad 3 to translate toward the space station until your spacecraft's radial velocity increases to slightly less than 1 m/sec. Press Keypad 7 to cut the thrust to zero when you reach this speed. (Although the Keypad 3 key thrusts you downwards, don't get confused by your directions here: The hatch on the spacecraft is on the bottom of the spacecraft, but since you have rolled the spacecraft over, the bottom faces the space station. Applying down translation thus moves you closer to the space station).
4. Accelerate time to 4 seconds/second. When you close to within 320 meters of the space station, as indicated on the Distance display, press F4 to stop all velocity. Note that the actual docking occurs at 294 meters from the space station, a mere 26 meters from your present position!
5. Reduce the time scale to 1 second/second.

Evaluate your current docking hatch position in relation to the docking port. Drag the Vertical Panning Box of your Chase view window upward to see several positions around your spacecraft. You'll get a better idea of which direction you need to move, or rotate, to align the docking ports. Figure 2.3 shows one vantage point that helps you see how far apart the docking ports are. You can drag the Horizontal Panning Box to get different side views as well.

Last Minute Docking Maneuver

To zero in on the docking hatch follow these steps:

1. If needed to align the docking ports, yaw left or right by pressing Keypad 4 or Keypad 6 respectively. To stop the yaw, press Keypad 5.
2. Pitch the spacecraft up (Keypad 2) or down (Keypad 8) as needed, until the Pitch readout displays 88° or 89°. If you can't pitch the spacecraft any closer than 85° or so, just get it as close as you can

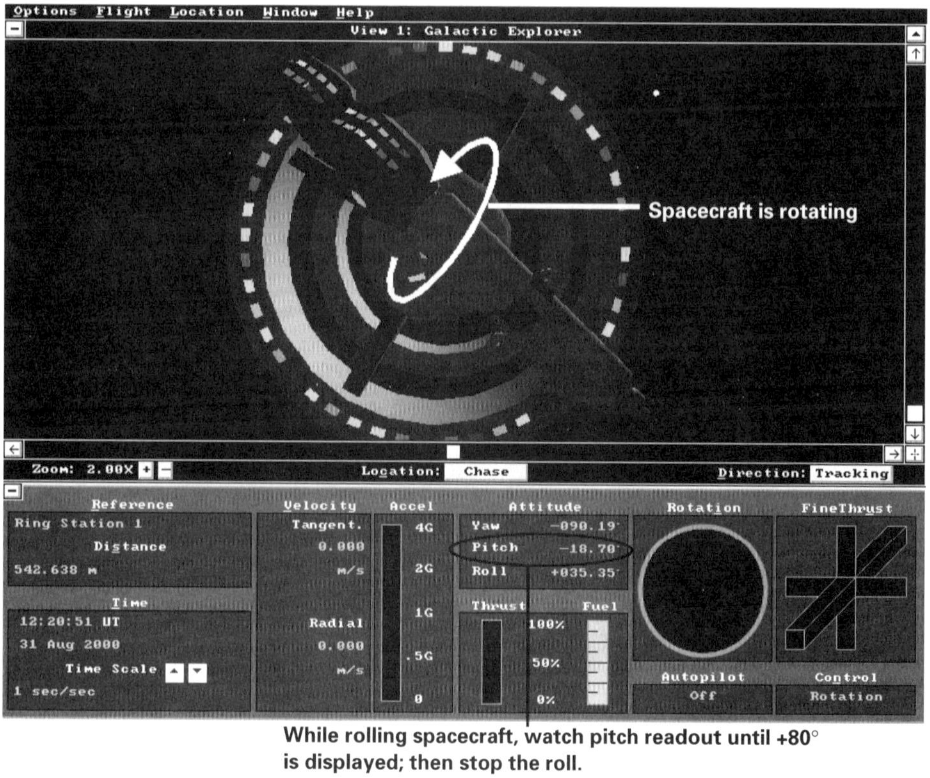

FIGURE 2.2 *Rolling the spacecraft 180° to align the orange docking hatch with the Ring 1 Space Station's docking port*

to 90°. Your goal here is to try to orient the spacecraft at right angles (i.e., perpendicular) to the space station so that the hatches will align properly. To stop the pitch, press Keypad 5.

3 Drag the Vertical Panning Box to the top of the Vertical Panning Bar. This gives you a view looking down at your spacecraft's docking hatch.

4 Translate the ship backward (Shift Keypad –) or forward (Shift Keypad +), left (Keypad 0) or right (Keypad .) as necessary to align the docking ports. Before each translation, make sure you press the 7 key to cut thrusters, and make *doubly sure* you press F4 to cut your velocity.

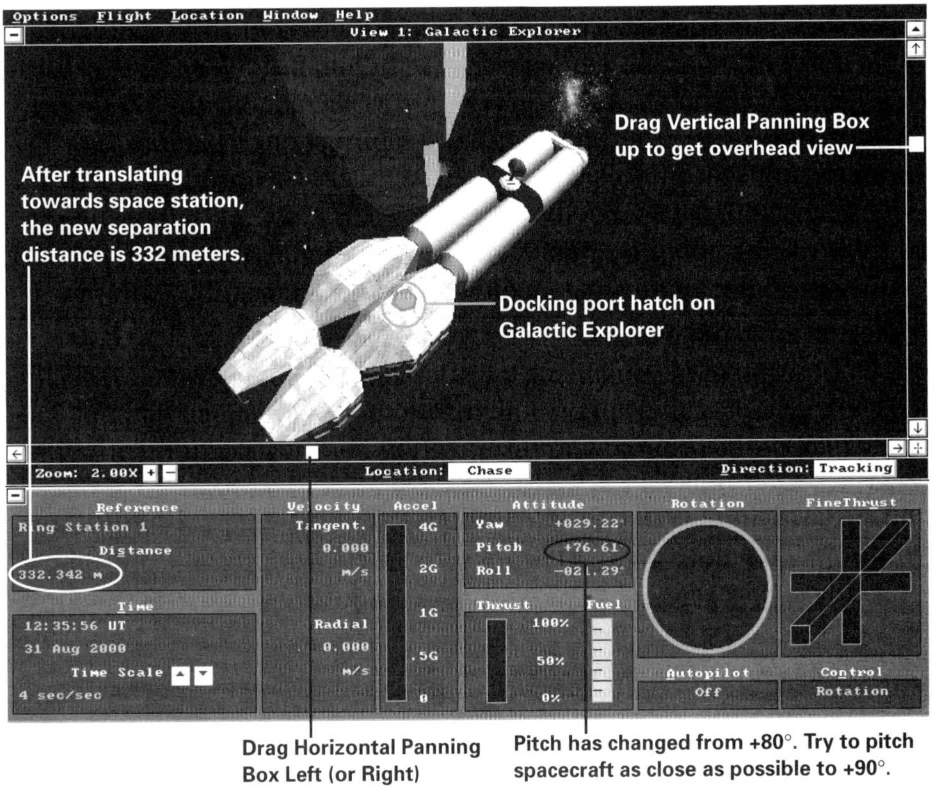

FIGURE 2.3 *Panning your Chase view to see where your docking hatch is in relation to the docking port of the space station*

5 When both docking ports look like they are pretty much lined up (it doesn't have to be very close at the Practice Skill Level), again pitch the spacecraft up (Keypad 2) or down (Keypad 8) as needed until your pitch readout is as close to +90° as you can get it. Press Keypad 5 to stop the pitch rotation.

6 Drag the Vertical Panning Box all the way down to the bottom of the Vertical Panning Bar. This way you'll be able to watch your spacecraft dock from below the space station. Center the Horizontal Panning Bar, if necessary, by clicking the blue Center button in the middle of the bar.

NOTE

Each time you dock your spacecraft at a space station, your fuel tanks are filled. Also, you can take over the flight controls of the space station or spacecraft you're docked with. To transfer command, choose Vehicle Transfer from the Flight menu. To transfer command back to your original ship, again select the Vehicle Transfer command and then select Undock from the Flight menu if you want to leave the space station or docked spacecraft.

7 If you're a perfectionist, you can yaw the spacecraft left (Keypad 4) to match the rotation of the space station. (In Space Simulator, this step is not necessary for a successful docking maneuver, but if you were really piloting a spacecraft in space, you would need to do this.)

8 Translate towards the space station for the final docking maneuver. Press Keypad 3 until your velocity reaches slightly less than 1 m/sec (2.23 miles per hour), then press Keypad 7 to cut all thrust. At velocities greater than or equal to 1 m/sec your spacecraft might crash.

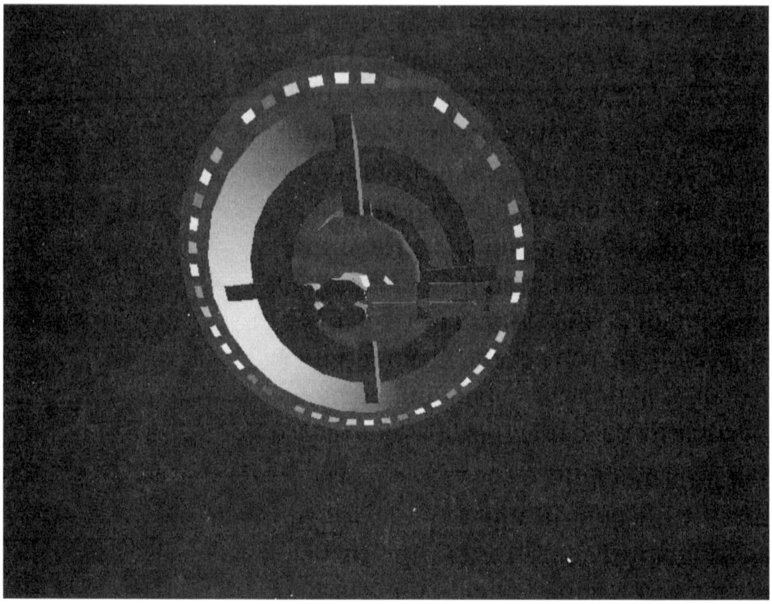

9 At 294 meters from the space station, your spacecraft will dock and assume the rotational speed of the space station.

If you want more of a challenge, you can set the Skill Level of Space Simulator in the Preferences dialog box to Advanced or Intermediate. At these more difficult levels, Space Simulator will be less forgiving of docking mishaps or misalignments.

CLOSE ENCOUNTER WITH THE EARTH

This section instructs you how to pilot your spacecraft into a 1000 km close encounter with the Earth's surface before returning to your current position. We will assume that you have completed the docking maneuver in the last section, but if you haven't, don't worry. As long as you start up the **Flight** situation and are in a circular Earth orbit of approximately 31,696 km radius, you'll be fine.

If you have docked your spacecraft with the space station, you must undock. To do this, select the Flight menu and choose the Undock menu command, or press Shift U. Your spacecraft will be impelled at a velocity of 0.995 m/sec away from the space station, but it will still be yawing with the same rotational speed as the space station.

Preparing for the Earth Encounter

There are some preparations you need to make before your spacecraft changes its orbit around the Earth:

1. To stop the yawing rotation that you acquired from the docked space station, press Keypad 5. If you aren't rotating, proceed to step 2.
2. Click the Reference box to open the Reference Object dialog box. Select the Earth as your new reference.
3. Press the S key twice to bring up the Cockpit view, or click twice on the Location button in the View 1 window.
4. Click the Direction button on the View 1 window until it displays Tracking. Your view will shift and show the Ring 1 Space Station rotating.
5. Press T to call up the Tracking dialog box. Select the Earth as your new tracking object, and return to the simulation. In the View 1 window, you'll see the Earth being tracked.

Executing the Orbital Change

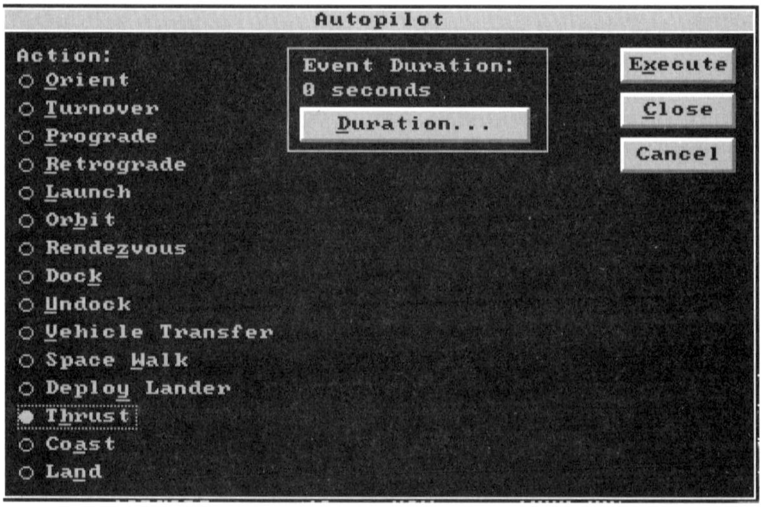

For the next leg of the mission, we will orient the spacecraft in a direction known as *retrograde,* meaning that the spacecraft faces the *reverse* direction from the one it is currently traveling in. Next we will fire our thrusters to bring the spacecraft into an Earth-bound trajectory. Since the amount of thrust applied needs to be very precise, we will use the Autopilot to time the duration of the rocket burn. You could apply the thrust yourself, but if your cutoff timing were off by even 2 seconds, you could bring the spacecraft into a collision course with Earth!

Follow these steps to initiate the new orbit:

1. From the Flight menu, select Autopilot.
2. Click the Retrograde button, then click Execute to return to the simulation. You won't see the movement unless your view window is in Panning mode, but your spacecraft will retrograde so that its rear faces your current velocity vector.
3. Again open the Autopilot dialog box (Alt A).
4. Click Thrust and a Duration button will appear.
5. Click the Duration button. Then click Seconds and type **34.** You are instructing the Autopilot to fire your main thrusters for exactly 34 seconds at an acceleration of four gravities. This will reduce your tangential velocity to approximately 2.184 km/sec, and cause your spacecraft to be nudged into a new orbit.
6. Accelerate time to 17.1 minutes/second. The Earth will loom ever larger in your view screen.

7 Watch your Distance readout until it shows about 10,000 km altitude above the Earth's surface (make sure your Distance display shows *Altitude* and *Radius*; if it doesn't, click the Distance display to toggle on these two readouts). Reduce the time rate to 1.1 minutes/second.

8 Check your Distance readout as you come within perigee distance of 1000 km to the Earth's surface (your perigee distance may vary slightly due to inaccuracies in Space Simulator). You will be passing by the dark side of the Earth at the time of closest approach.

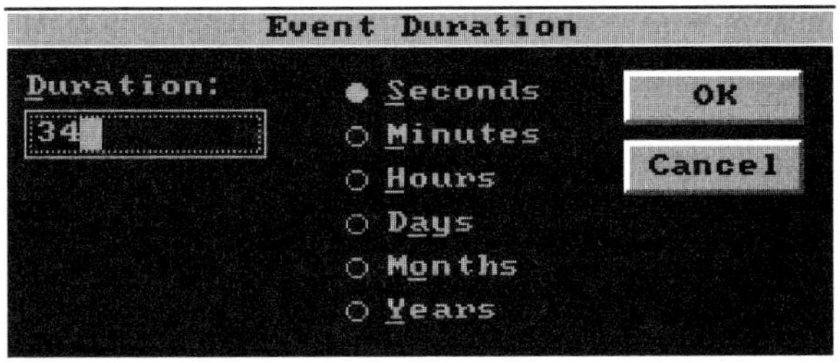

Notice that your tangential speed has increased to a phenomenal 9322 m/sec (your velocity may vary slightly due to inaccuracies in Space Simulator). This demonstrates a physical principal of all orbits; that is—whenever your spacecraft reaches perigee, its velocity will be highest and whenever it reaches apogee, its velocity will be lowest.

As the Earth recedes from view, you can accelerate the time rate to 17.1 minutes/second until you reach an apogee of 25,317 km altitude from the surface (or 31,696 km from the center of the Earth).

RETURNING TO CIRCULAR ORBIT

You can easily return to the circular orbit that you started out with in the **Flight** situation. You'll need to prograde your spacecraft at an apogee of 31,696 km (25,317 km altitude from the surface), and then fire your thrusters at maximum for 34 seconds. In essence, you will be performing the reverse of the procedure for creating the close encounter orbit.

Here are the steps to follow:

1 When you reach an apogee of 25,317 km altitude (31,696 km from the center of the Earth), reduce the time scale to 1 second/second. Your apogee doesn't have to be exactly 31,696 km radius, but the closer you are, the closer your orbit will be to circular rather than elliptical.

ACCELERATION AND ITS EFFECT ON VELOCITY

A gravity, or ***g*** is based on the acceleration of gravity at the Earth's surface, which is 9.8 m/sec^2. Since the Galactic Explorer can accelerate at up to four gravities, or 39.2 m/sec^2, you can figure out the velocity change in a given amount of time by multiplying 39.2 times the duration of thrust measured in seconds. Thus, if you fire your thrusters for 34 seconds, you will have changed your velocity by 1332 m/sec, because 39.2 m/sec^2 × 34 seconds = 1332 m/sec or 1.332 km/sec. So if you fire your thrusters for 34 seconds in a direction *opposite* (*retrograde*) to your initial velocity vector of 3544 m/sec (i.e., 3.544 km/sec), your new velocity will be 3.544 – 1.332 = 2.212 km/sec or 2212 m/sec. On the other hand, if you fire your thrusters for 34 seconds in the same direction (*prograde*) as your initial velocity vector of 3544 m/sec, you will increase your velocity to 4876 m/sec, since 3.544 + 1.332 = 4.876 km/sec.

Because of inaccuracies in the Space Simulator model, your exact velocity can vary by several tens of meters per second when using the Autopilot to precisely meter thrust timings. In the example given in this chapter, firing your thrusters for 34 seconds is *supposed* to change your velocity by 1332 meters, but in fact it can vary by as much as ±30 m/sec or more.

2 Open the Autopilot dialog box (press Alt A). Click Prograde and then click Execute to return to the simulation.

3 Again open the Autopilot dialog box. Click the Thrust button, then the Duration button. In the Duration dialog box, type **34**, then click OK and finally click Execute. Your thrusters will fire for exactly 34 seconds and will bring your tangential speed back up to 3.544 km/sec (3544 m/sec). You will now be in the same circular orbit that you started out with before you began the close encounter orbit.

This chapter has guided you through several high precision orbital maneuvers. In later chapters, you'll learn how to create new and even more interesting orbits. For now, however, it's important to gain some further understanding of your spacecraft's controls and instrumentation, as well as to learn about some other important features of the program. These will be the topics of the next three chapters.

Exploring the Cockpit

THREE

Space Simulator uses the same cockpit display and instrumentation for all types of spacecraft. Each spacecraft differs in fuel capacity and in thrust/acceleration capabilities, but otherwise the controls and readouts are the same. This chapter discusses the cockpit instrumentation and how it is used.

THE INSTRUMENT CONTROL PANEL

Inside the Instrument Control Panel, shown in Figure 3.1, you'll find all the controls and displays you need to fly your spacecraft. The Instrument Control Panel cannot be resized like the map and view windows, but you can close it by clicking the Close button at the upper left corner of the panel. To reactivate the panel, press the I key, or use the Window/Show Instrument Panel menu commands.

The Instrument Control Panel is divided into 11 sections that each have controls or display readouts. The first section on the upper left corner is called Reference, and the section below it is labeled Time. If you click the Time label, a dialog box opens which allows you to change the current time and date, as well as the time scale. If you click the Reference label, a dialog box opens which allows you to change the current reference point for your spacecraft. If you are close to a planet or other smaller object and you click in the Velocity section, the screen display switches between the total velocity/speed of light gauge and radial/tangential velocity readouts.

At the lower right of the Instrument Panel is the Autopilot and Control Indicator. When you click the Autopilot you can switch the Autopilot on or off, and when you click the Control Indicator, you toggle the mouse or joystick's control between Rotation, Thrust, and Panning modes.

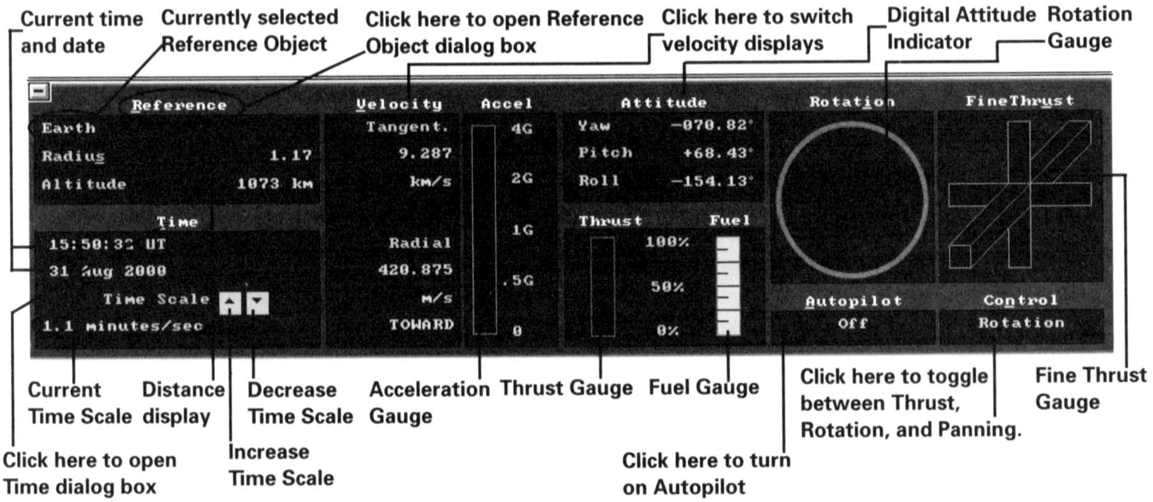

FIGURE 3.1 *The Instrument Control Panel*

Time and Date Display

Time is displayed in 24-hour Greenwich Mean Time (GMT), also called Universal Time or UT. Greenwich Mean Time is based on the mean solar time that occurs at the Greenwich, England meridian, longitude 0°. GMT is used around the world for navigational purposes and serves as an international standard for measuring celestial events and other astronomical phenomena. The world is divided into 24 time zones, with each time zone corresponding to a number of hours before or after UT, so that local noon in each time zone roughly approximates the appearance of the Sun at noon.

Changing the Time

To change the time, follow these steps:

1. Click the Time label on the Instrument Panel.
2. In the Time dialog box, click the Time text entry box and type the time in 24-hour format. Use a colon to separate the hours from the minutes, and the minutes from the seconds.

3. Click OK.

FINDING THE LOCAL MEAN SOLAR TIME

Space Simulator provides a built-in means of determining the time difference between UT and local time in any time zone in the world. You can also find out the latitude and longitude of most major cities around the world, which is useful for figuring out orbital positions and trajectories. Here's how to find this information:

1. Select the Location menu.
2. Choose the Surface menu option.
3. Choose a city nearest the time zone you are interested in. For example, if you choose Bombay, the time zone difference will be displayed at the bottom of the dialog box as *UT −5 Hours 30 Minutes,* meaning you subtract 5 hours and 30 minutes from UT to get the local mean solar time in Bombay. The latitude and longitude of Bombay are displayed at the top of the dialog box.

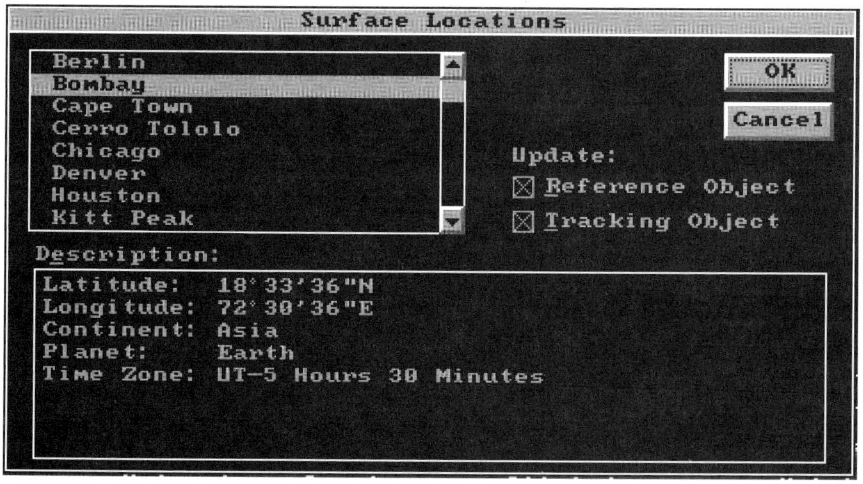

NOTE

Changing the time does not affect your spacecraft's position in space, but it does change the position of planets and other astronomical bodies. For example, if you change the time to 12 hours in the future, your spacecraft will not change its present orbital location, but the planet you are orbiting will move through space (taking you along with it), and the planet surface will rotate to a new position.

Changing Space Simulator's Startup Time

In the Time dialog box, you can decide whether Space Simulator starts up with the time that is stored in your situation files or with your computer's current system time. Here's how to do this:

1. Click the Time label in the Instrument Panel.
2. Under the section of the Time dialog box titled *When Situation Starts,* click Use Situation Time if you want Space Simulator to start up with the time stored in the situation file, or click Use System Time if you want the start-up time to be initialized to your computer's clock.
3. Click OK.

Space Simulator's Time Machine

Yes, time travel is possible in Space Simulator! You can specify the date for any year between 999,999 BC and AD 5,000,000. Thus, you can see what the stars and planets looked like to Ptolemy in Ancient Egypt, or what Halley's comet looked like when it last visited in 1986. If you like, you can turn back the clock to 1758 and re-experience the thrill that Edmund Halley must have felt when he made his famous prediction that the comet would return because it had an orbital period of 76 years. In the Time dialog box, you can change the date displayed on your Instrument Panel. To do this:

1. Click the Time label in the Instrument Panel.
2. In the Date text entry box, type the day of the month, the first three characters of the name of the month, and then the year. If the year is BC, add a **BC** after the year as in **1000BC** for the year 1000 BC. You don't need to add AD for years; Space Simulator assumes that the year is AD unless BC is specified.
3. Click OK.

Viewing Halley's Comet in 1758 Let's see how Halley's comet must have looked to eighteenth-century astronomers:

1. Open the Time dialog box and set the date to **01 Jan 1757**. Halley's comet appeared in 1758, but you'll want to set the date a year earlier to see the comet long before it approaches perihelion. Don't worry about changing the time of day.
2. Under the Window menu, select View Controls.
3. Click the Map View button.
4. You'll see a column of Show on Map checkboxes on the right side of the View Controls dialog box. Click the Comets checkbox to have comets labeled in the map window.
5. If the Map Origin is not set to the Sun for a heliocentric view of the solar system, click the Map Origin button, and set the Sun as the central reference point. Click OK to return to the View Controls dialog box.
6. Click OK to return to the simulation.
7. Press M to open the map window. It will appear with all the planets clearly labeled.
8. Click the View button on the map window until it displays the Top view. You'll be looking down from the North Pole of the Sun as the planets orbit counterclockwise.
9. With the Map window selected, click the – key or + key on the main keyboard, or click the Zoom buttons on the map until you can see Halley's comet.
10. Accelerate time to 6.1 days/second by pressing F1 repeatedly to increase the time scale. You can also click the time scale Up arrow in the Time portion of the Instrument Panel.

NOTE

Changing the date does not affect your spacecraft's position in space relative to the planet or star you are orbiting, but it does change the position of planets and other astronomical bodies. For example, if you are orbiting the Earth, and you change the date so that it is 5 years and 6 months in the future, your spacecraft will not change its present orbital location in relation to the Earth, but the Earth will move to the opposite side of the Sun, and the other planets will move to new positions.

11 As the comet makes its closest approach to the Sun and the Earth, zoom the map window in so that you can see more detail.

12 In the View 1 window, set your Tracking view to Halley's comet, so that you can watch from your spacecraft as it approaches. Select the View 1 window, click the Location button to Cockpit mode, then click the Direction button to Tracking mode. Next, press T to open the Tracking dialog box, click the Comet button and choose Halley's comet. Click OK to return to the simulation, and you'll see Halley's comet in your View 1 screen. Zoom in or out as needed.

NOTE

Space Simulator does not have the accuracy to depict the exact dates and time of cometary positions in the solar system. The date used in this example will work for Space Simulator, but the comet's position and closest approach to the Earth will not accurately match the actual tabulated positions that were observed in the eighteenth century.

TIP

When accelerating the time, be sure to choose Maximum Precision (in the Preferences dialog box under Options/Preferences). This will force Space Simulator to do a better job of plotting your orbital trajectory.

The orbital period for Halley's comet is between 76 and 77 years (it changes slightly due to perturbations by the planets). After its 1758 appearance, it reappeared in 1835, 1910, and 1986. It will return in the year 2062.

Accelerating Time By clicking the Up arrow button in the Time portion of the Instrument Panel, you can accelerate the time scale. By clicking the Down arrow button, you can slow it down. From the keyboard you can press F1 or F2 to increase or decrease the passage of time. The time scale can be slowed down to as much as 0.001 second/second or accelerated to as much as 8710.5 years/second. If you prefer, you can also adjust the time scale in the Time dialog box; just click the Halve button to *decrease* the time rate, or click the Double button to *increase* the time rate. The higher the time acceleration, the greater the error in your plotted orbital trajectory.

CONTROL INDICATOR (PANNING, THRUST, AND ROTATION)

> **WARNING**
>
> **When you accelerate time to more than a few hours/second, Space Simulator cannot accurately plot your orbit and will introduce errors. This will prevent you from flying realistic missions to the planets.**

When you click the right mouse button, your mouse cursor disappears and you enter Panning or Yoke mode. These two modes allow you to use the mouse to control rotation and Fine Thrust of the spacecraft as well as panning of the view windows. The Control Indicator on your Instrument Panel tells you which mode your mouse is in; it displays either *Rotation* or *Thrust* if you are in Yoke mode, or *Panning* if you are in Panning mode. To switch modes, just click the Control Indicator using your mouse.

In Rotation mode, moving your mouse will cause your spacecraft to rotate in space by firing its rotational thrusters. In Thrust mode, moving your mouse will cause the spacecraft to fire its Fine Thrusters and translate down, left, right or up (but not forward or backward—for that you'll have to use the keyboard). In Panning mode, your mouse controls the pan angle of the currently active view window.

REFERENCE

The Reference module on your Instrument Panel displays the distance to the current reference object that is selected in the Select Reference Object dialog box. By clicking Reference, you can open the Select Reference Object dialog box and choose a new reference object, such as another planet, moon, spacecraft, space station, star, asteroid, comet, or surface city.

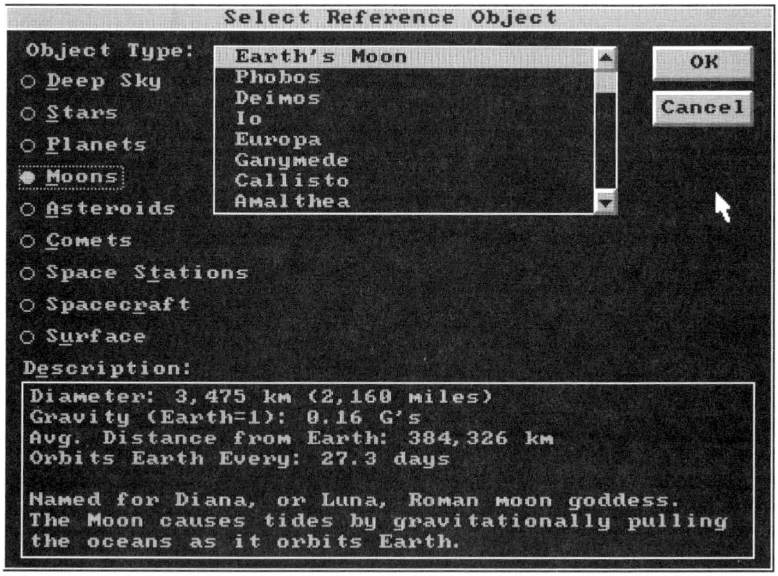

In addition to distance information, the current velocity that is displayed on the velocity readout refers to your spacecraft's velocity *relative* to the current reference object. So, for example, if you've chosen the Earth as your reference object, the distance from and the velocity relative to the Earth will be displayed on your Instrument Panel. If you change the reference object to the Sun, however, your displayed distance will change to show your spacecraft's distance from the Sun, and your velocity readout will change to display the spacecraft's speed relative to the Sun, not the Earth.

Changing Distance and Velocity Readouts

When you select a new reference object, your distance and velocity readouts will display new information relative to the new object. Let's say you are in orbit around the Earth, but you would like to see your spacecraft's distance and speed relative to the Moon. Here's how to do this:

1. Click Reference on the Instrument Panel to open the Select Reference Object dialog box.
2. Click the Moons button.
3. In the Moons list box, highlight Earth's Moon.
4. Click OK. The distance and velocity readouts on the Instrument Panel will show your spacecraft's distance and speed relative to the Moon.

TIP

When you move your spacecraft to a new star system using the Location menu, you'll see a variety of new planets, moons, and other objects. These new planetary objects will also appear in the Select Reference dialog box, as well as in all the other dialog boxes.

Selecting Between Distance and Radius/Altitude

If you are within the *gravitational sphere of influence* of a moon, planet, spacecraft, space station, asteroid, or comet, but not a star or deep space object, your Distance display can show Altitude and Radius data. The gravitational *sphere of influence,* or SOI, is a spherical region of space that surrounds each object in Space Simulator that has mass. If your spacecraft is in a gravitational SOI (also called a *gravitational well*), the force of gravity will attract your spacecraft toward the center of mass of the body which is exerting the gravity. The SOI range depends on the mass of the body, so that the more massive a planet, moon, or star, the larger the sphere of influence. If you are outside the gravitational SOI of a nearby planet, your spacecraft will not experience any gravitational attraction toward the planet but will again be under the influence of the Sun. In other words, it will have returned to the gravitational SOI of the Sun.

Stars and other galactic deep space objects have their distances displayed in units of km, astronomical units (AU), or light years depending on how far they are from you. An astronomical unit, or 1 AU, is the mean distance of the Earth from the Sun (1.496×10^8 km or 92,957,130 miles). A light year represents the distance light travels in one year, and is on the order of 9.46×10^{12} km (5.87 trillion miles). To appreciate these distances, consider the fact that the Earth is about 92 million miles from the Sun and that light takes approximately 498 seconds, or 8.31 minutes, to reach us from the Sun. After traveling another 63,238.7 times the distance between the Earth and the Sun (63,238.7 AU), the light wave that left the Sun will have traveled one light year. To travel to the center of our Milky Way Galaxy, that same light wave would have to travel another 30,000 years!

While in the SOI of a planet, moon, asteroid, or other smaller object, you can switch between either Distance and Altitude/Radius readouts by clicking on the Distance display, or by pressing Alt S. If you've entered the atmosphere of a planet or moon, or have come within 1.01 radii of a planet or moon, and you have selected a surface city as your reference point, the Distance display will show ground distance along with altitude information. Figure 3.2 shows the distance readouts, while Figure 3.3 illustrates the difference between Distance, Radius, and Altitude.

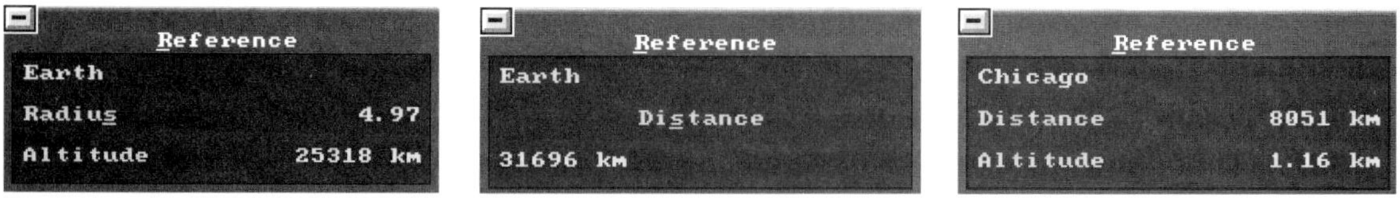

FIGURE 3.2 *Altitude/Radius display gives radius units from planet center and altitude above planet's surface (left). Distance readout (center) shows total distance to center of reference object. Altitude/Ground Distance display (right) appears only when Surface Reference Object is selected and spacecraft is within the planet's atmosphere or very close to the surface.*

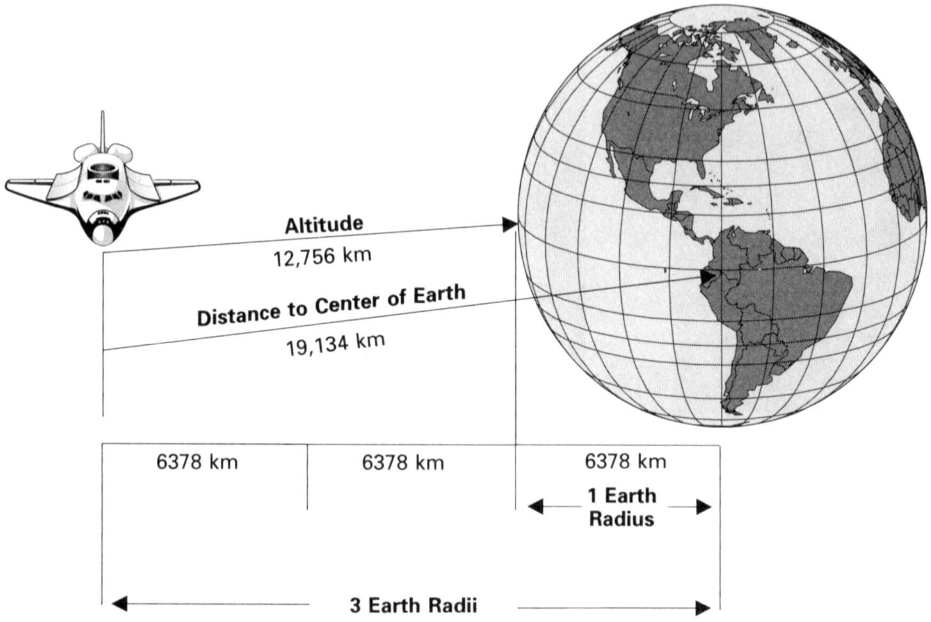

FIGURE 3.3 *Distance, radius, and altitude*

The Radius distance refers to the number of radii you are from the planet, sun, moon, or other object. The radius used for each distance measurement is based on the radius of the selected reference object. For example, if you are orbiting the Earth at 2.00 Radius units and your selected reference object is the Earth, your spacecraft's distance from the center of the Earth is 2 × Radius of the Earth, or 12,756 km (the radius of the Earth is 6378 km).

VELOCITY INDICATOR

The Velocity readout to the right of the reference gauge shows two velocity numbers, one for tangential velocity, the other for radial velocity. If you click anywhere on the Velocity labels or readouts, you'll switch to a second display panel which shows the total velocity and a speed of

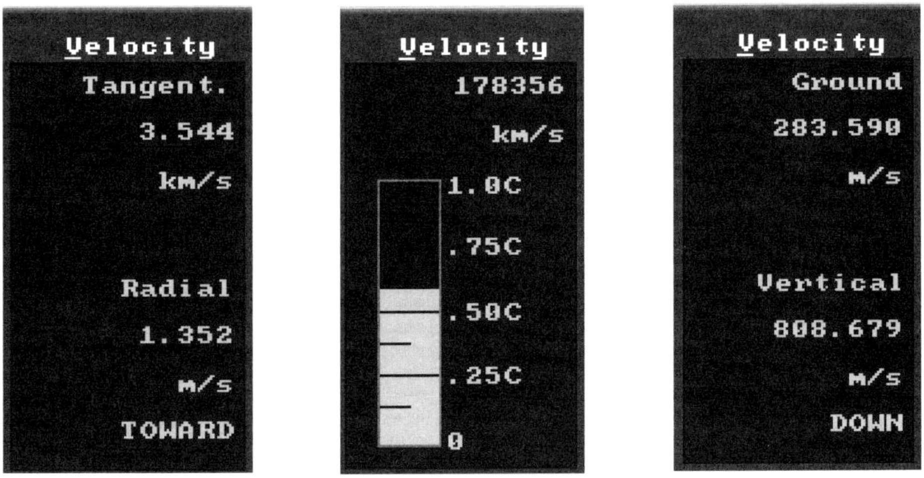

FIGURE 3.4 *Radial/Tangential Velocity display (left), Total Velocity display (center), and Ground/Vertical Velocity display (right). The display on the right appears only when a surface reference object is selected and the spacecraft is within the planet's atmosphere.*

light bar graph. To return to the first velocity panel, just click again in the same region. Figure 3.4 shows the velocity readouts that are available.

Tangential, Radial and Total Velocity

The Tangential Velocity readout shows the velocity of your spacecraft in the direction that is tangential to your orbit. If you were to draw your orbit as a circle, ellipse, parabola, or hyperbola, the tangential velocity direction would be the straight line that tangentially intersects the orbital curve at one point, as illustrated in Figure 3.5.

Radial velocity is the speed your spacecraft is traveling toward or away from the planet, sun, moon, or other reference object. The direction of the radial velocity *vector* is always a straight line directed from your spacecraft to the planet, sun, moon, or other reference object, as shown in Figure 3.5.

Space Simulator doesn't label the velocity displayed in your Velocity/Light Speed readout as Total Velocity, but this velocity is really a vector combination of Tangential and Radial Velocities shown on the other velocity display. It is your spacecraft's absolute speed relative to the planet, sun, moon, or other currently selected reference object.

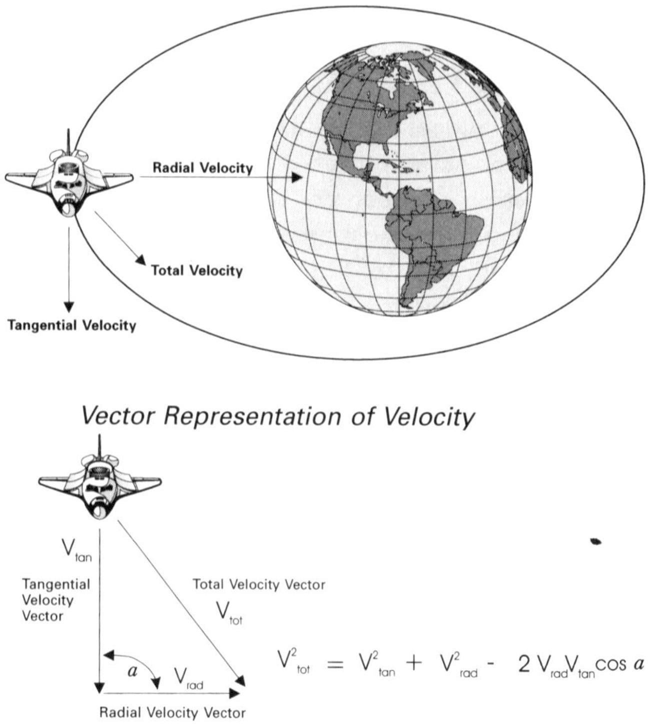

FIGURE 3.5 *Tangential, radial, and total velocity*

Speed of Light Gauge

The bar graph shows the percentage of the speed of light *(c)* at which your spacecraft is traveling. If the bar graph is at 0.25c, you are traveling at 25 percent of the speed of light, or 75,000,000 m/sec. If you are traveling at the speed of light, or 1.0c (100 percent), your spacecraft's velocity is approximately 300,000,000 m/sec (this is equivalent to 300,000 km/sec or 186,000 miles/sec). At speeds below 5000 km/sec, the graph does not register any velocity. This display is useful for interstellar or intergalactic travel, since traveling at near light speed is not practical inside a planetary system. Note that according to Einstein's Special Theory of Relativity, no spacecraft can travel faster than the speed of light.

> **TIP**
>
> **You cannot travel faster than the speed of light in Space Simulator. If you want to travel quickly between distant points, increase your velocity to *c* and accelerate time. Once you reach the speed of light switch off your engines to save fuel.**

VELOCITIES AND VECTORS

A *vector* is a mathematical tool used to describe positions, velocities, and acceleration of objects in three-dimensional space. The *velocity vector* tells you in which direction and at what magnitude your spacecraft is traveling, using a three-dimensional X Y Z Cartesian coordinate system. The coordinate axes of the X, Y, and Z axes for vectors are often labeled I, J, and K, and the velocity vector is broken into components that match the speeds in each of these axes' directions. To find the magnitude of any vector, you square each component, add them and then take the square root:

$$V_{Mag} = \sqrt{V_x^2 + V_y^2 + V_z^2}$$

So, for example, if your spacecraft is traveling at 1.2 km/sec V_x, 0.5 km/sec V_y, 3 km/sec V_z (in vector notation, this would be written <1.2, 0.5, 3>), the total magnitude of your velocity would be 3.269 km/sec, since

$$V_{Mag} = \sqrt{(1.2\ \text{Km/sec})^2 + (0.5\ \text{Km/sec})^2 + (3\ \text{Km/sec})^2} = 3.269\ \text{Km/sec}$$

In the case of the tangential and radial velocity vectors on your Velocity readouts, you only have two vector components $V_{tangential}$ and V_{radial}. Therefore, the magnitude of the total velocity is equal to:

$$V_{Mag} = \sqrt{(3{,}544\ \text{m/sec})^2 + (200\ \text{m/sec})^2} = 3{,}550\ \text{m/sec.}$$

If your spacecraft is traveling at 3.544 km/sec tangential velocity and 200 m/sec radial velocity, your total velocity as seen on the Velocity/Light Speed display, will be 3.550 km/sec, since

$$V_{Mag} = \sqrt{V_{tangential}^2 + V_{radial}^2}$$

Note that the total velocity is rounded off, so all you'll see is 3.550 km/sec.

Ground Velocity

When you enter the atmosphere of a planet, or get within 1.01 radius units of a planet, your velocity display will change to show ground velocity and vertical speed. Ground velocity is simply the speed of your spacecraft measured as if you were traveling on the ground.

Vertical Speed

The Vertical Speed display appears only when your spacecraft has entered the atmosphere of a planet, or when your spacecraft gets within 1.01 radius units of a planet or moon, as measured on your Distance readouts. This speed is a measure of how fast you are gaining or losing altitude. For most landing purposes you want to keep your vertical speed to less than 10 m/sec (22 mph).

ACCELERATION GAUGE

The Acceleration Gauge displays the amount of acceleration your spacecraft is undergoing in units of *g's*. A single *g* is equivalent to 9.8 m/sec^2 and is the same as the gravitational acceleration you feel at the Earth's surface at the equator. At 4 *g*'s your acceleration is 39.2 m/sec^2.

THRUST GAUGE

The Thrust Gauge tells you roughly how much Main Thrust you are applying. It warns you that the engines are on and thrusting, but it doesn't give as accurate an indication of thrust output as the Acceleration Gauge. Due to relativistic effects (see page 95), your acceleration will fall off as you approach the speed of light, even though the Thrust Gauge shows maximum thrust.

FINE THRUST GAUGE

The Fine Thrust Gauge tells you the amount of Fine Thrust you are applying when translating short distances. Keep in mind that when you apply Down Fine Thrust, as it appears on the gauge, your thrusters will actually be firing upwards to push your spacecraft downwards. Likewise, when you apply Right Fine Thrust, the display will light up on the right bar, to indicate movement towards the right—but your thrusters are really firing in the opposite direction. Similarly, when applying Forward Fine Thrust, the forward indicator bar will light up, but your thrusters are really firing from the rear of the spacecraft to push it forward.

FUEL INDICATOR

Fuel level is displayed on the Fuel Indicator. Each of the spacecraft has a different size fuel tank and rate of fuel consumption, so duration of thrust differs. Rather than thinking about actual fuel capacity, it is much more useful to think about velocity change. Fuel capacity is roughly equivalent to the amount of velocity change a spacecraft is able to muster.

The symbol ΔV, called *Delta V*, is often used to describe change in velocity. Table 3.1 shows the maximum velocity changes for each of the spacecraft in Space Simulator. Notice the correlation between fuel capacity, measured in duration of burn time, and ΔV.

The huge ΔV change you see for some of the spacecraft does *not* mean that it can travel faster than the speed of light! It means that the spacecraft can accelerate or decelerate x number of km/sec before all the fuel is exhausted. Thus, if you have a fully fueled Galactic Explorer, your maximum ΔV is 392 million km/sec. This means that if you were to accelerate the spacecraft to light speed ($\Delta V = +300{,}000$ km/sec) and decelerate the spacecraft to a dead stop ($\Delta V = -300{,}000$ km/sec), your total ΔV for the trip would be 600,000 km/sec. But since the Galactic Explorer has a ΔV of 392 million km/sec, you can actually make about 653 round trips at light speed to destinations around the galaxy before refueling, no matter how far away they are (392,000,000 km/sec ÷ 600,000 km/sec = 653 trips). The actual number of trips will be less than this due to relativistic thrust acceleration inefficiencies.

A fuel duration of 317 years is not very long when you consider that getting to light speed at maximum thrust acceleration of 4 *g*'s takes at least 135 days, with another 135 days required to slow down. Note that the Bussard Ram-Jet collects its fuel along the way by scooping up interstellar hydrogen. As such, it has no fuel or ΔV limitations, but it cannot accelerate faster than 2 *g*'s.

TABLE 3.1: *Maximum Velocity Change and Fuel Duration at Maximum Acceleration for Space Simulator Spacecraft*

Spacecraft	Maximum Acceleration	Fuel Duration	Maximum Velocity Change (DV)
Galactic Explorer	4 *g*'s	317 years	392 million km/sec
Bussard Ram-Jet	2 *g*'s	Unlimited	Unlimited
Callisto	4 *g*'s	3000 years	3.711 million km/sec
F-79 Galactic Fighter	8 *g*'s	30 years	74 million km/sec
Zander Freighter	2 *g*'s	634 years	392 million km/sec
All Terrain Lander	3 *g*'s	45 minutes	79.380 km/sec
Space Shuttle	3 *g*'s	8 minutes	14,112 m/sec
Apollo Service Module	2 *g*'s	3 minutes	3528 m/sec
Lunar Excursion Module	1 *g*	5 minutes	2940 m/sec
Manned Maneuvering Unit	0.1 *g*	30 minutes	180 m/sec

ROTATION GAUGE

As is shown in Figure 3.6, the Rotation Gauge tells you in which direction your spacecraft is rotating. The length of the curve or line on the display indicates how fast the spacecraft is rotating.

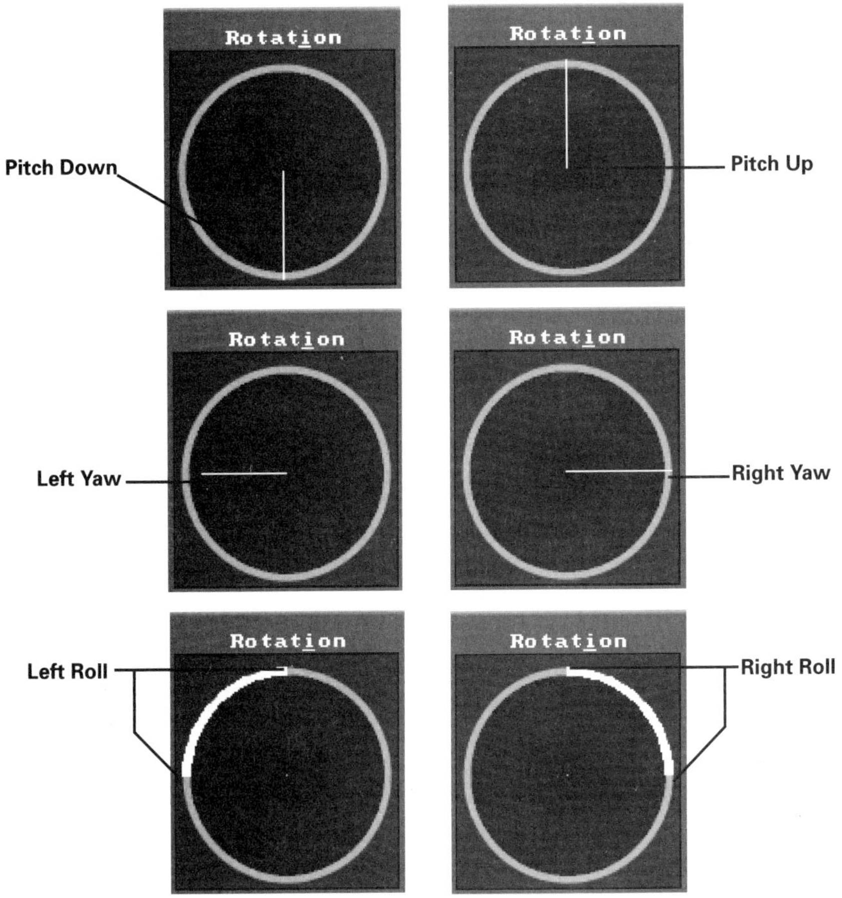

FIGURE 3.6 *Rotation Gauge directions*

ATTITUDE GAUGE

The Attitude Display gives a numerical readout of the current yaw, pitch, and roll of the spacecraft in relation to the selected reference object. This readout replicates the information that appears on your cockpit view screen when you have activated the Head Up Display. You use the attitude information to help you with rotation movements of your spacecraft, especially when you are trying to orient the spacecraft in a particular direction.

Yaw, Pitch, and Roll

Yaw ranges from 0° to +180°, and from 0° to –180°. Yaw refers to the rotation about the spacecraft's vertical axis. If your spacecraft were flat on the ground, when you turned it right or left, you would be yawing.

Pitch ranges from 0° to +90°, and from 0° to –90°. Pitch refers to the rotation about the spacecraft's lateral axis. If the spacecraft were horizontal in midair, and you raised or lowered the nose only, you would be pitching the spacecraft.

Roll ranges from 0° to +180°, and from 0° to –180°. Roll refers to the rotation about the spacecraft's longitudinal axis. When the spacecraft rotates clockwise or counterclockwise this is considered a roll.

HEAD UP DISPLAY

The Head Up Display (HUD) is a navigational system built into your View 1 screen that graphically projects onto the cockpit display your spacecraft's yaw, pitch and roll in relation to the selected reference planet or object. To display the HUD, press the H key. To shut it off, again press the H key.

LANDING GEAR

To extend the landing gear when landing, press the G key. To retract it, again press the G key. Only the Space Shuttle Orbiter, the F-79 Fighter, and the All Terrain Lander have landing gear that can be extended and retracted. You can see the landing gear deploy in Chase view.

AUTOPILOT

The Autopilot Indicator not only tells you whether the Autopilot is on, it is also a switch for turning the Autopilot on. Simply click on the indicator with the mouse, and the display will toggle between *On* and *Off*.

If you want issue a command to the Autopilot, you must open the Autopilot dialog box. To do this: Press Alt A or select the Flight menu and then choose Autopilot. Next, click one of the Autopilot command buttons. Click OK to return to the simulation, and the Autopilot will begin executing the command. To interrupt or shut off the Autopilot, click the Autopilot Indicator until it reads *Off*.

This chapter has dealt briefly with the cockpit instrumentation, and you should now have a clear idea what each control and instrument does. In the next chapter, we will delve more into the actual use of these instruments while flying the spacecraft.

Mastering Spacecraft Thrust and Attitude Controls

FOUR

F O U R

In this chapter, you'll learn how to maneuver and rotate your spacecraft. You'll also learn more about the Head Up Display (HUD) and the Digital Display. These two displays are your only means of orienting your spacecraft in space, so mastering the conceptual information they present is essential. After reading this section, you'll understand why your spacecraft's rotation, as it appears in Cockpit and Chase views, often does not match the rotation that is shown on your Digital Attitude Display and HUD. After the rotation controls are explained, you'll learn how and when to use your Fine Thrusters and Main Thrusters. The chapter concludes with a tutorial on how to use the Autopilot and how to spacewalk in the Manned Maneuvering Unit (MMU).

NOTE

Wherever you encounter the term *light speed* or the character *c* in this chapter, it refers to the speed of light (299,792,458 meters per second). When reference is made to traveling at light speed, you should realize that it is not possible to travel at exactly the speed of light, due to relativistic effects. You can get pretty close to *c*, but your spacecraft's velocity can never equal *c*.

SETTING YOUR SPACECRAFT'S ATTITUDE (ROTATION)

Your spacecraft has three axes of rotation: lateral, longitudinal, and vertical, as shown in Figure 4.1. Rotation of the spacecraft about the lateral axis is known as pitch, while rotation around the vertical axis is known as yaw. Rotation around the longitudinal axis produces roll motion. All three rotation movements have no effect on your position in space; they only change the direction your spacecraft points.

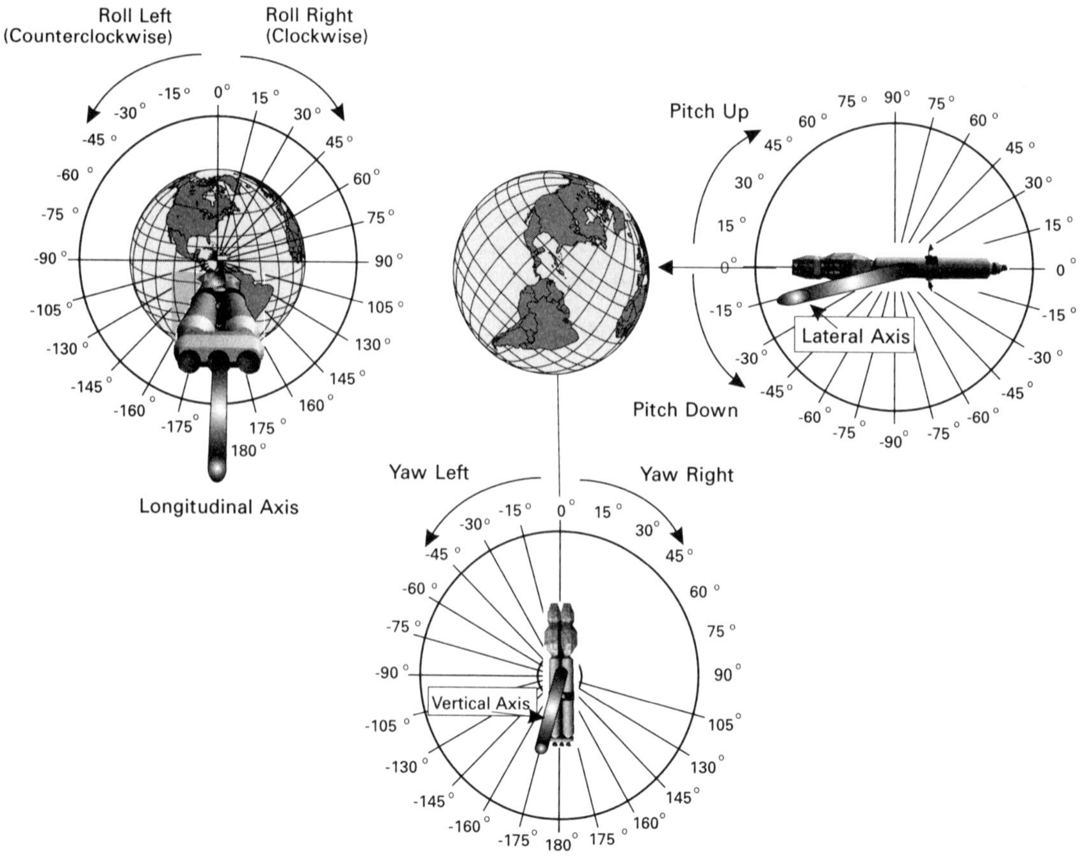

FIGURE 4.1 *Yaw, Pitch and Roll rotational axes and angles*

Each rotational axis of revolution has 360° of arc, meaning that the spacecraft can revolve around each axis in a complete 360° circle. When the spacecraft is pointed directly at the center of the planet or star it is orbiting, it has a pitch and yaw angle of 0°. When you yaw left or right ±90° or when you pitch ±90° up or down, the spacecraft points parallel to the surface of the planet or star. Pointing the spacecraft directly away from the planet or star gives it a yaw angle of 180°.

Before proceeding, it is important to define a few spherical coordinate terms. The terrestrial coordinate system or, for that matter, any other planet's or moon's coordinate system, is based on the equator and the prime meridian. A *great circle* is formed on the surface of a sphere by the intersection of a plane that passes through the center of the sphere. The *equator* is defined as that great circle, encompassing 360° of arc on the sphere's surface, that is formed by passing a plane perpendicular to the sphere's axis midway between the poles. A *meridian* is any great circle on the sphere's surface formed by passing a plane containing the sphere's polar axis so that it is perpendicular to the sphere's equator. Figure 4.2 illustrates these terms in greater detail.

How Roll Angles are Figured

The spacecraft's Digital Roll Attitude and HUD display are both based on the reference object that is currently selected. Roll is always measured from the angle which your spacecraft's longitudinal axis makes with the reference object's meridian, when the spacecraft is pointed directly at the meridian. The

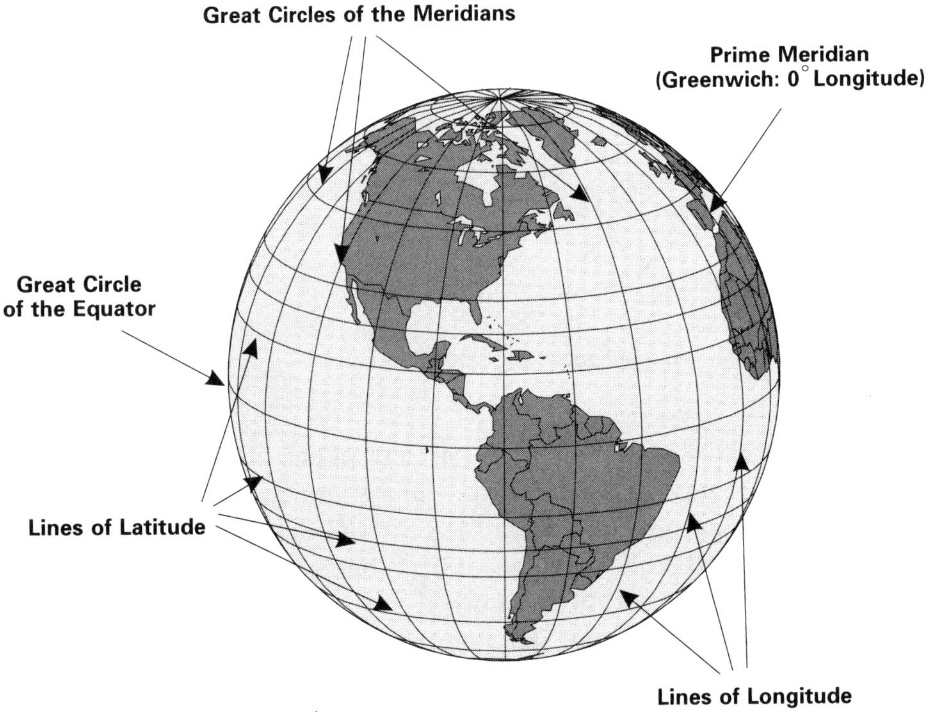

FIGURE 4.2 *The planetary or spherical coordinate system, showing the great circles of the equator and meridians, as well as lines of latitude and longitude.*

meridian used for roll measurements changes constantly as the spacecraft orbits the planet. The current meridian used for roll measurements is the meridian that intersects the direct line of sight between the spacecraft and the center of the planet.

Positive roll is measured clockwise from the meridian when your spacecraft is pointed directly at the meridian and is rolling right. Negative roll is measured counterclockwise from the meridian, when your spacecraft is rolling left. As you orbit the Earth, you cross different meridians, and your roll angle will change, even though your spacecraft's roll attitude does not change in relation to the fixed stars. Figure 4.3 illustrates different roll angles as the spacecraft faces the Earth.

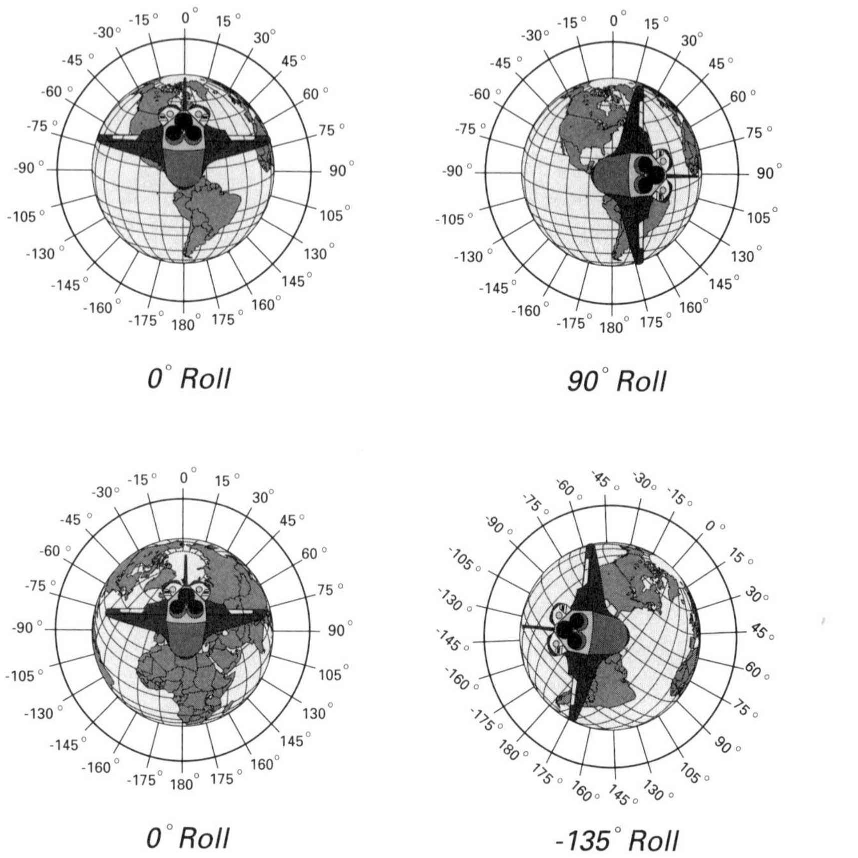

FIGURE 4.3 *Spacecraft attitude when digital attitude shows roll at 0° (for two separate latitudes), 90°, -135°.*

Keyboard and Mouse Roll Controls To roll your spacecraft so that it is rotating clockwise (right) on its longitudinal axis, press the Keypad * key. To roll counterclockwise (left), press the Keypad / key. To stop the roll, press Keypad 5. If you tap the roll control keys several times, or if you hold the keys down, the roll rate will increase, as indicated by the length of the curved line on the Rotation Gauge. To use the mouse rotation controls, you must first click the Control Indicator until it displays Rotation, then click the right mouse button to enter Yoke mode. To roll right, you would then hold down the Ctrl key and roll the mouse right. To roll left, hold down the Ctrl key and roll the mouse left. To stop rolling and exit Yoke mode, click the left mouse button.

Why the Digital Attitude Display Shows Contradictory Rotation Data Many Space Simulator pilots become puzzled about why the Digital Attitude Display doesn't show roll angles as increasing or decreasing when they are rolling the spacecraft. This happens, for example, when the spacecraft is initially oriented so that it is at a yaw angle –90°, pitch angle of 0°, and a roll angle of 0°. When you roll the spacecraft from this orientation, the pitch angle on the Digital Attitude Display starts increasing while the roll angle and yaw angle remain constant!

To see why this is so, you must understand that your spacecraft's yaw, roll and pitch angles are based on the currently selected reference planet or object. When you roll the spacecraft from the orientation described above, the spacecraft's pitch angle changes. Space Simulator shifts the spacecraft's internal yaw-pitch frame of reference so that yaw becomes pitch and pitch becomes yaw. Eventually, if you can continue the roll used in this example, you'll reach a pitch angle of 90° and your new roll angle will be –90°, while the new yaw angle will fluctuate around 0°. Perform these steps and watch from Chase view to see what happens.

1. Reduce the Time scale to .001 second/second. This allows you time to execute the roll.
2. Orient your spacecraft so that it is facing the Earth at 0° roll, 0° yaw, and 0° pitch. Yaw, pitch, and roll your spacecraft as necessary.

3. Select the Chase view of your spacecraft.
4. Press B to set your Chase view to Absolute. This will prevent your Chase view from rotating with the spacecraft.
5. Pan your Chase view until the spacecraft is centered against the Earth as a backdrop.
6. Yaw the spacecraft left (press Keypad 4) until you reach approximately –90° yaw. Press Keypad 5 to stop the rotation.
7. Roll the spacecraft counterclockwise, or left, by pressing Keypad / until your pitch changes to approximately 90°. Don't worry if you can't get it to exactly 90°; the closer the better, though. Notice that initially pitch, *not* roll, is changing even though you are rolling the spacecraft! Press Keypad 5 to stop the rotation.
8. Note your new attitude on the Digital Attitude Display. It should show approximately 90° pitch, –90° roll, and 0° yaw. Try to get the pitch as close as possible to –90° using roll commands; this will get yaw readouts closer to 0°.

Your spacescraft should be orientated as in Figure 4.4 (your roll and yaw might be a few degrees off from this example due to orbital motion displacement). If you were to pitch the spacecraft down to 0°, you would again be pointed at the Earth, but your roll angle would be –90 from the meridian.

How Pitch Angles Are Figured

Space Simulator uses a frame of reference that measures yaw and pitch differently than roll. Like roll, the spacecraft's pitch attitude is based on the reference planet or object that is currently selected. But when your spacecraft is pointed directly at the planet, pitch is measured as the angle up or down that your spacecraft's nose makes as it rotates along its lateral axis. No matter where you are in space or what your rotation angle is, as long as your spacecraft is initially pointed at the center of the selected reference planet or object, when you start raising the nose, pitch will start at 0°,

NOTE

The Microsoft manual incorrectly states that pitch angles are dependent on the equatorial plane of the selected reference planet. In fact, pitch angles are solely dependent on the angle between your spacecraft's nose and the local surface horizon plane.

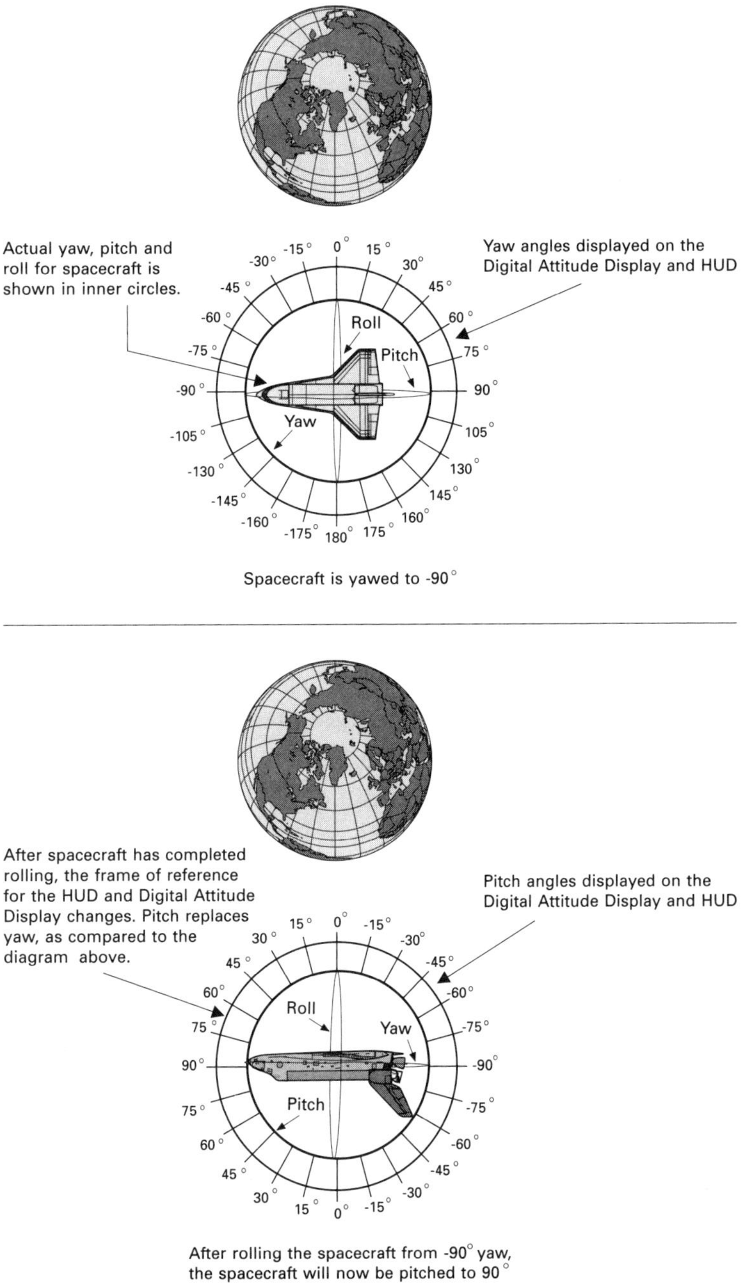

FIGURE 4.4 *Spacecraft orientation is potentially confusing, as demonstrated in this example, where rolling the spacecraft causes the digital attitude display to show your pitch to be changing, not your roll.*

and increase to 90°. Conversely, pitch will decrease and become negative if you lower the nose from 0° to -90°. Unlike yaw and roll, pitch angles are only measured from 0° to ±90°. Despite this, 360° of arc on a complete circle is possible for pitch, as is shown in the Figure 4.5.

FIGURE 4.5 *Pitch at 0°, 90°, –90, and ±180°*

Keyboard and Mouse Pitch Controls To pitch your spacecraft so that the nose rotates up around the spacecraft's lateral axis, press Keypad 2. To pitch the nose down, press Keypad 8. To stop the pitching rotation, press Keypad 5. If you tap the pitch control keys several times, or if you hold the keys down, the pitch rate will increase, as indicated by the length of the vertical line on the Rotation Gauge. To use the mouse rotation controls, you must first click the Control Indicator until it displays *Rotation*, then click the right mouse button to enter Yoke mode. You can then pitch up by rolling the mouse back towards you, and pitch down by rolling the mouse away from you. To stop rolling and to exit Yoke mode, click the left mouse button.

How Yaw Angles Are Figured

Like pitch angles, the spacecraft's yaw attitude is based on the reference planet or object that is currently selected. When your spacecraft is pointed directly at the planet, though, yaw is measured as the angle left or right that your spacecraft's nose makes as it rotates along its vertical axis. When you start turning left, yaw will start at 0°, and decrease to –90°. Conversely, if you start at 0° and turn right, yaw will increase to +90°. When yawing left, yaw readings range from 0° to +180°, and when yawing right, from 0° to –180°. Thus, the two 180° semicircles form a complete 360° yaw circle. Figure 4.6 illustrates several yaw angles to clarify how yaw is calculated for the Digital Attitude Indicator and HUD.

Keyboard and Mouse Yaw Controls To yaw your spacecraft so that it rotates left on its vertical axis, press the Keypad 4 key. To yaw right, press Keypad 6. To stop the yaw, press Keypad 5. If you tap the yaw control keys several times, or if you hold them down, the yaw rate will increase, as indicated by the length of the horizontal line on the Rotation Gauge. To use the mouse rotation controls, you must first click the Control Indicator until it displays *Rotation*, then click the right mouse button to enter Yoke mode. To yaw right, you would then roll the mouse right. To roll left, roll the mouse left. To stop rolling and to exit Yoke mode, click the left mouse button.

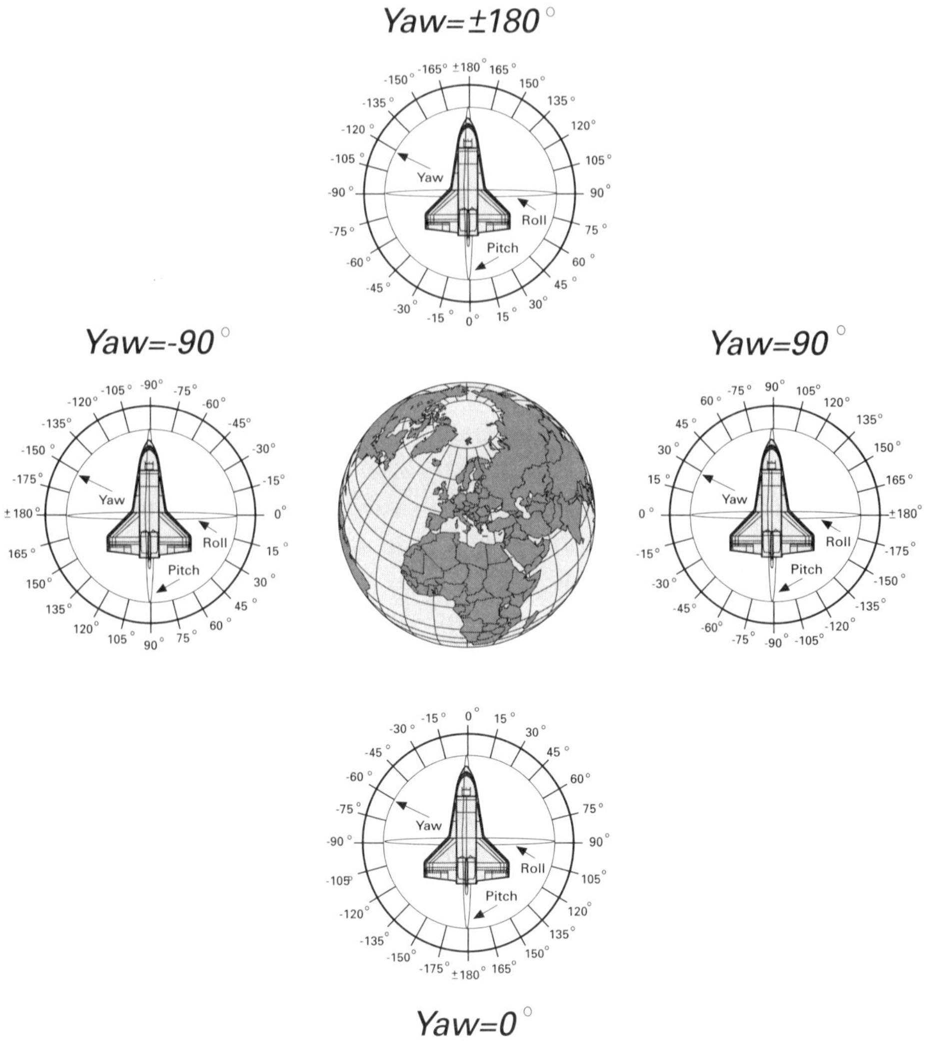

FIGURE 4.6 *Yaw at 0°, 90°, –90, and ±180°*

HOW THE HEAD UP DISPLAY/ATTITUDE WORKS

The Head Up (HUD) display is a navigational system built into your View 1 screen that graphically projects onto the cockpit display your spacecraft's yaw, pitch, and roll. Although the same information is available in numerical form on the Digital Attitude Indicator, the HUD is useful for precisely docking or positioning your spacecraft's orientation in space without taking your eyes off the cockpit view window. You can only view the HUD in your View 1 window, and your view must be centered straight ahead. No panning of your window is allowed, or the HUD will simply disappear. To turn on the HUD, press the H key. To switch it off, press the H key once again.

To visualize how the HUD works, imagine your spacecraft is hovering over a fixed location on the Earth, as shown in Figure 4.7. Now surround the spacecraft with a sphere that has latitude and longitude circles on it and which accompanies the spacecraft where ever it may go. Both 0° latitude and 0° longitude on this imaginary sphere are permanently oriented towards the Earth. The spacecraft's yaw angle corresponds to an angle of longitude on the sphere, while the spacecraft's pitch angle corresponds to an angle of latitude. Thus, if the spacecraft is initially pointed at the center of the Earth, it is pointing at the 0° latitude and 0° longitude point on the imaginary sphere. Then if you were to pitch the spacecraft up, it would point at higher and higher degrees of latitude on the sphere until it finally reached the north pole on the sphere.

While the HUD is activated, the green numbers at the top of the display delineate yaw angles in 10° increments. The HUD also displays pitch; each blue and red pitch ladder line has a pitch angle that is displayed on the top. Roll angles are determined by the degree of slant of the green and red lines from the horizontal. When the pitch ladders of the HUD are horizontal, your spacecraft is at 0° roll or 180° roll. The yellow line in the center of the HUD is your spacecraft's current longitudinal axis indicator, so when it crosses a particular pitch angle line, this is the spacecraft's current pitch angle. Note that the axis indicator merely tells you where your nose is pointed, it does not tell you the direction you are currently traveling.

The dotted green line crossing the planet or selected reference object indicates a plane which is parallel to the equatorial plane of the planet.

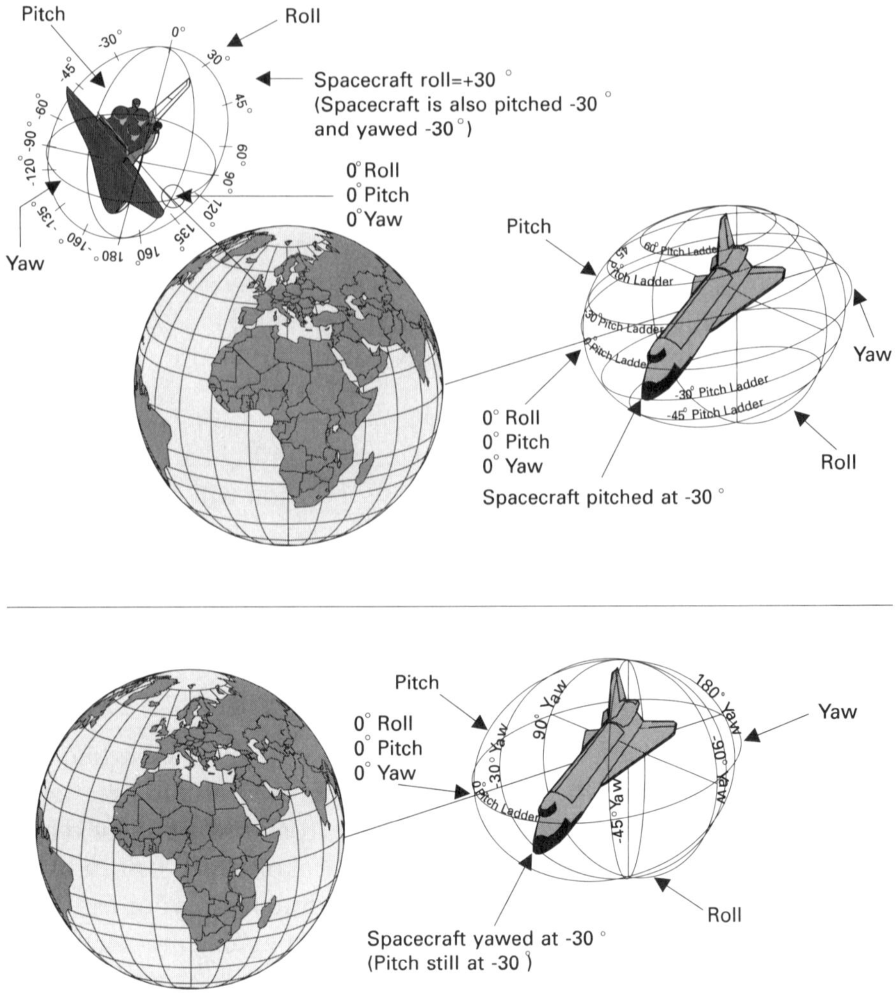

FIGURE 4.7 *The imaginary sphere represents your HUD.*

It is used to describe the reference object's rotational movement (the reference object or planet will always rotate from left to right along this green line if it is horizontal and your pitch angles are displayed right side up). This green line also defines the invisible plane that cuts through your spacecraft to define your roll angle. If the line is horizontal, your spacecraft is aligned so it is at a 0° or 180° roll; if it is vertical, your spacecraft is at a +90° or –90° roll.

You can easily tell which direction your spacecraft is traveling on the HUD; simply prograde your spacecraft using the Autopilot. After executing the autopilot prograde maneuver, your spacecraft will be pointing in the current orbital velocity vector. Note that this is the *only* way to determine which direction you are traveling in space.

Keeping the Head Up Display On Screen

In order to keep the HUD on screen:

1. Click Location to display Cockpit view mode.
2. Click Direction to display Panning mode.
3. Center both the Vertical and Horizontal Panning Bars. Any panning movement away from the center position will cause the HUD to switch off automatically.

After performing the above steps, if you press H the HUD display should appear, as in Figure 4.8.

How to Use the Head Up Display

For many orbital changes, you'll want to fire your thrusters when the spacecraft is yawed or pitched to nearly ±90°, because in this direction you can most efficiently add or subtract speed from your velocity vector. This does not apply, however, for highly elliptical orbits or for orbits which are parabolic or hyperbolic. Note that before firing your thrusters, you should prograde or retrograde your ship via the Autopilot so that you are properly oriented. You can't just yaw or pitch your spacecraft to ±90° and expect that you'll be headed the same direction as your orbit. As an experiment, you should examine your pitch and yaw angles for various parts of the orbit. Make sure you prograde the ship before you take each pitch and yaw reading. Chances are, if your orbit is nearly circular, pitch or yaw will always be very close to ±90°.

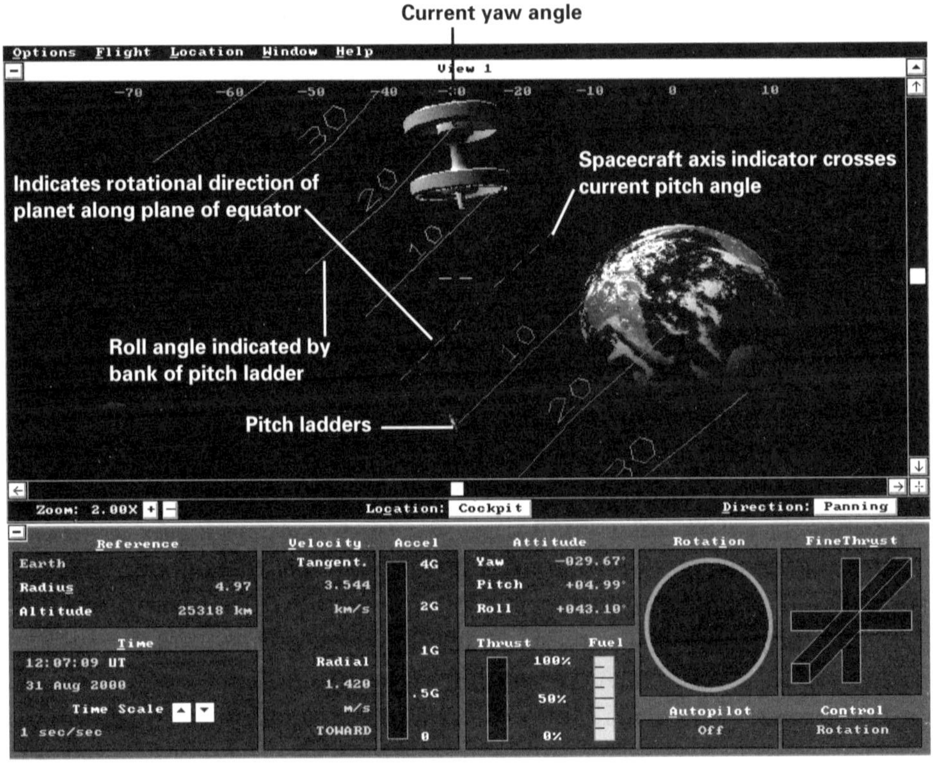

FIGURE 4.8 *The Head Up Display*

Rotating the Spacecraft Using the HUD To get a better handle on the HUD, try rotating the spacecraft by 360° in each of the three axes of motion: roll, yaw, and pitch. This exercise shows you how to do this:

1. Start the **Flight** situation.
2. If the Earth is not the current reference object, click the Reference label on the Instrument Panel. Select the Earth as your new reference, and click OK to return to the simulation.
3. Make sure that the Location button on the View 1 screen displays Cockpit, and that the Direction button displays Panning.

4. Center both the Vertical and Horizontal Panning Bars.
5. Press H to turn on the HUD.
6. Roll the spacecraft until the red and blue attitude lines are horizontal.
7. Yaw the spacecraft until you see the green number 0° at the top of the HUD's yaw readout.
8. Next, pitch the spacecraft until the yellow axis indicator is on the green line. Your spacecraft is now directly oriented at the Earth, just as if you had used the Autopilot's Orient command.
9. Now, yaw the spacecraft right 360°, until you return to your present position facing the Earth. Notice that your yaw angles will increase from 0° to 180°, and then will suddenly jump to –179° and start increasing back to 0°.
10. When you have returned to 0° yaw, and the Earth is centered on your Cockpit view window, pitch the spacecraft up. Your pitch angle will increase steadily to 90°, then decrease back to 0° as you flip over. As you continue the somersault, the pitch will become negative as it passes 0°, where you are pointed directly away from the Earth, and will decrease to –90°. Then at –90, the pitch will start increasing to 0°. At 90° and –90°, the spacecraft is parallel to the planet's surface below.
11. After returning to 0° pitch, try rolling the spacecraft 360°. You won't see any roll indications on the HUD, other than the fact that the blue and red attitude lines are rotating. The actual roll is displayed in numerical form on the Digital Attitude readouts.

Repeat the above exercise from a Chase view perspective. Be sure to press the B key before initiating rotational movements; this will lock your Chase view so that it doesn't rotate with the spacecraft.

Using the HUD to Fly To Mars To use your HUD to aim your spacecraft at Mars, or any other selected reference object, follow these steps:

1. Follow the first 8 steps from the previous example, but make sure you select Mars (or the reference object you want to fly to) as the current reference object.
2. If you want to keep your spacecraft on course for Mars (or the selected reference object), you'll have to constantly fire your Main Thrusters and rotate your spacecraft to keep the yaw and pitch to 0° on the HUD. Since Mars (or your selected reference object) is in motion itself, your interception of the planet requires that you constantly trim your yaw and pitch to 0° as your Main Thrusters continue to fire.

Using the above technique with the HUD, you can fly to any location in the universe. But you'll also need to turn around at the halfway mark to slow the spacecraft down. However, you should realize that this is a terribly inefficient method of navigation, because it is very wasteful of fuel. Most interplanetary flights are planned to minimize fuel requirements and the spacecraft that fly these missions use their rockets only sparingly at the very beginning of the trajectory.

Using the HUD to Establish a New Orbit The HUD is an essential aid in establishing your own orbits around stars, planets, moons, and other celestial objects. Using the orbital velocity information that is available under the Help/Basic Skills menu, you can manually create your own circular orbits around almost any planet or moon in the solar system. To get the velocity information and perform the orbit insertion maneuver, follow these steps:

1. Select the Help menu and choose Basic Skills.
2. Click the Spaceflight Skills Button.
3. Click the Orbital Velocity Table radio button.
4. Click the Moons or Planets button depending on which orbital velocities you want.

5 Find the row in the table which corresponds to the moon or planet you wish to orbit. Write down the orbital velocities that appear for 2, 3, and 5 Radii. The velocities shown are measured in km/sec, and represent the tangential velocity your spacecraft must have at the specified distance from the planet or moon's center.

6 Exit all the Help dialog boxes and return to the simulation.

7 Change the current reference object to the planet or moon you wish to orbit.

8 Select Cockpit view, and Panning mode. Then center your Panning Bars.

9 Press H to turn on the HUD.

10 Pitch and yaw the spacecraft until you are at an attitude of 0° pitch and 0° yaw on the HUD. This will orient you towards the planet or moon.

11 If you can't see the planet or moon on your screen, you are too far away and you'll need to apply your Main Thrusters until you are close enough to establish the orbit.

12 Once you are in sight of the planet or moon, click the Distance display until it shows Radius/Altitude information.

13 Move the spacecraft to either 2, 3, or 5 Radii from the planet or moon.

14 Yaw or pitch the spacecraft to ±90° at one of the three distances.

15 Press F4 to cancel all previous velocity.

16 Fire your Main Thrusters until your tangential velocity is equivalent to the corresponding orbital velocity for the radii distance you chose. Once you've reached orbital velocity, cut all thrust by pressing Keypad 7. You are now in a circular orbit around the planet or moon.

TRANSLATION OF YOUR SPACECRAFT IN THREE DIMENSIONS

To move or translate your spacecraft, you must fire your Fine Thrusters or your Main Thrusters. Once you fire your thrusters and gain momentum, you will continue to move unimpeded until you fire your thrusters in the opposite direction to cancel out the original motion. The great eighteenth-century physicist, Sir Isaac Newton, first formulated this law of inertia, by stating that objects in motion tend to stay in motion, and that objects at rest tend to stay at rest, unless acted upon by forces.

> **TIP**
>
> **Once you thrust your spacecraft, it will continue to move even if you disengage thrust. To cancel the spacecraft's velocity, you'll have to apply reverse thrust.**

If you don't like to fly with realistic momentum and inertia effects, you can move the spacecraft in a special non-flight Slew mode, which allows you to stop and start the spacecraft whenever you take your foot off the "gas pedal" thrust controls. Simply press the Y key to toggle on or off Slew mode.

Why Spacecraft Don't Travel in Straight Lines in Space

One source of frustration and confusion for novice space pilots is the difficulty of rendezvousing with other space vehicles in Space Simulator. Spacecraft that are coasting don't travel in straight lines in space; instead they travel in curved paths called conic sections. In fact, the family of curves called conic sections, represent the only possible paths for an orbiting object in a two-body system. Unless you are firing your thrusters all the time, it simply isn't possible to travel in a straight line in space.

Another rendezvous difficulty occurs because spacecraft that are to link up must travel in the same orbital plane around a planet, and they must have similar orbital speeds and similar orbits at the time of rendezvous. The two spacecraft must be traveling so that one is not too far ahead of the other in the same orbit. Even if you can spot your rendezvous target, unless you match all its orbital parameters, you'll never be able to catch up to it.

FORCE, ACCELERATION, INERTIA, MASS, AND WEIGHT

Force is an everyday phenomena that we all encounter. When you push or pull an object, you exert a force on it. The object moves and we say that it was *accelerated* to some velocity. Forces do not always cause an object to move. For example, the force of gravity acts on you as you sit at your desk, yet you remain stationary. When the velocity of an object changes with time, the object is said to be under *acceleration*. For example, if you increase your car's speed, it is said to be accelerating. If you step on the brakes and slow down, the car is decelerating. In Space Simulator, the units of acceleration are measured in meters per second per second (m/sec^2). Average acceleration and instantaneous acceleration are defined by the following equations:

$$a_{avg} = \frac{v_{final} - v_{initial}}{t_{final} - t_{initial}} = \frac{\Delta v}{\Delta t}$$

$$a_{instant} = \lim_{\Delta t \to 0} \frac{\Delta v}{\Delta t} = \frac{dv}{dt}$$

where $a_{instant}$ is the instantaneous acceleration. The mathematical symbol *lim* to the right of the = sign means it is a limit. The entire term is defined accordingly: as the limit of the time interval Δt approaches zero, the instantaneous acceleration is equal to the change in velocity divided by the change in time. Thus, when you are under an instantaneous acceleration of 9.8 m/sec^2, your velocity will change by 9.8 meters for each second of elapsed time. After 2 seconds, it will change by 19.6 m/sec; after 10 seconds, it will change by 98 m/sec, and so on.

When an object has a uniform velocity that does not change, no net forces are acting upon it. This does not mean that no forces are acting upon it, it means that no force is required to maintain motion. Only an application of force can cause a change in velocity of the object. When the velocity of an object is constant, or if it is at rest, it is said to be at *equilibrium* and the net force is zero. In a circular orbit, even though your velocity is constant, your direction is changing and therefore you are not at equilibrium. Thus, there is a net accelerative force acting on your spacecraft which causes the velocity direction (but not speed) to change.

Newton had earlier defined force to be proportional to acceleration for a given mass ($F = ma$). In his First Law of Motion, Newton also defined the concept of inertia as that property of matter which resists a change in motion. For instance, it takes more effort to roll a bowling ball than a basketball due to the greater inertia of the bowling ball.

To measure inertia, the term *mass* is used. The greater the mass of a body, the less it will accelerate under an applied force. For example, if a given force acting on a 1 kg mass produces an acceleration of 10 m/sec^2, the same force when applied to a 2 kg mass will produce an acceleration of 5 m/sec^2 ($F = 1 \text{ kg} \times 10 \text{ m/sec}^2 = 2 \text{ kg} \times 5 \text{ m/sec}^2$). In other words, the 1 kg mass has less than half the inertia of the 2 kg mass, and it can therefore be accelerated twice as much.

Mass and weight are two different quantities. Weight is the force of gravity acting on a mass, and can change depending on how far the mass is from the gravitational source of attraction. Weight is measured in SI units, called Newtons, or in pounds (lbs.). Weight will differ depending on which planet or moon you are on. For example, if you weigh 180 lbs. on the Earth, you'll weigh only 30 lbs. on the Moon. Mass, on the other hand, is invariant and is the same everywhere. An object having a mass of 10 kg on the Earth's surface will have the same mass of 10 kg in orbit, or 10 kg on Jupiter.

If you are a little too far ahead or too far behind in the orbit of your target spacecraft, you may be tempted to increase or decrease your speed to close the remaining distance. This attempt to rendezvous will actually have the *opposite* effect! Due to the laws of celestial dynamics, when you increase your orbital speed you'll actually climb to a slightly higher orbit and slow down, thereby dropping farther and farther away from the destination spacecraft.

What's more, if you're slightly ahead of your rendezvous target, and you decide to slow down to allow the other spacecraft to gain on you, you'll actually speed up your orbit while descending to a slightly lower orbit. Meanwhile the other spacecraft will draw away from you as it slows down relative to your spacecraft! These two orbital paradoxes are illustrated in Figure 4.9.

So, if you want to catch up to a spacecraft that is ahead of you in the same orbital plane, you slow down slightly. This will depress your orbit's altitude slightly, but you'll gain tangential velocity in the process. And, if you want to slow down to allow a spacecraft that is behind you in the same orbital plane to catch up to you, you speed up slightly. This will increase your orbit's altitude slightly and you'll lose some tangential velocity.

TIP

All spacecraft motion in space is curved due to gravity force fields which cause the spacecraft to be attracted towards the source of the gravity field.

The next section describes the two types of thrusters that are available in Space Simulator: Main Thrusters and Fine Thrusters.

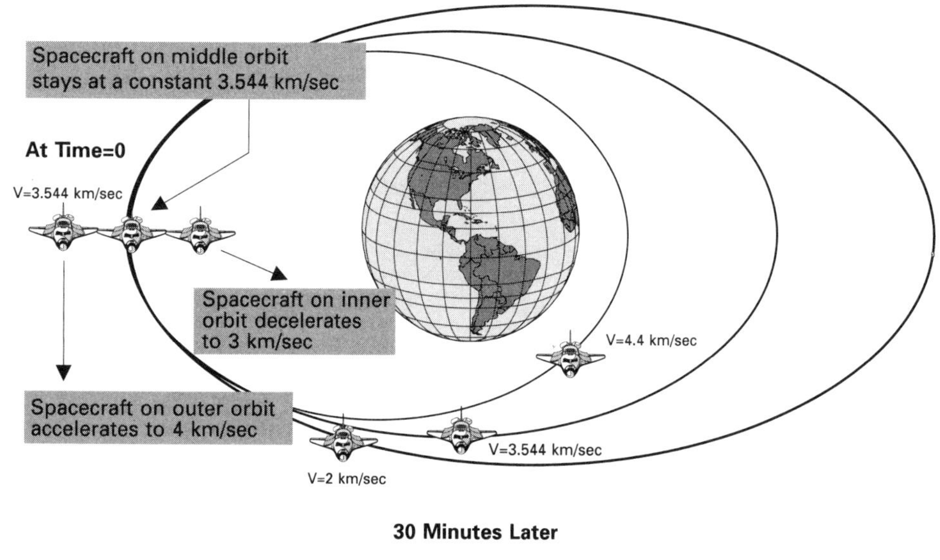

FIGURE 4.9 *The orbital paradox: Speeding up will cause you to slow down, and slowing down will cause you to speed up*

Fine Thrust

There are six individual Fine Thrust reaction engines, each of which points in a different direction to give you six degrees of motion. You can translate up, down, left (sideways), right (sideways), forward, or backward.

The Fine Thrusters have a very low thrust output, so you can only use them to make very small changes in your spacecraft's velocity. These tiny thrusters are primarily used for rendezvousing and docking with a spacecraft or space station that is within sight of your spacecraft. For all other high velocity maneuvers, such as changing orbits, landings and takeoffs, you should use the Main Thrusters. If you plan on rendezvousing and docking with another spacecraft, make sure that you select the spacecraft or space station as your current reference object *before* using your Fine Thrusters. If you carelessly use the F4 key to zero your velocity while maneuvering, you will not only zero your spacecraft's velocity relative to the intended rendezvous target, but you'll also lose *all your orbital velocity!* (This will only happen if you are outside the gravitational sphere of influence for the space station or spacecraft you intend to dock with.)

Keyboard and Mouse Fine Thrust Controls In addition to the keypad thrust controls, you can use the mouse to apply up, down, left, and right Fine Thrust, but not forward or backward Fine Thrust (forward and backward Fine *Thrust* controls are only accessible via the numerical keypad). Before you can use the mouse, you must click on the Control Indicator so that it displays *Thrust*, then click the right mouse button to enter Yoke mode. To thrust up, roll the mouse towards you; to thrust down, roll the mouse away from you. For right Fine Thrust, roll the mouse right, and for left Fine Thrust, roll the mouse left. To stop thrust and exit Yoke mode, click the left mouse button. Your Fine Thrust controls and the translational directions are shown in Figure 4.10.

Whenever you fire your Fine Thrusters, you'll see the direction and thrust output displayed on the Fine Thrust Gauge. Once you apply Fine Thrust, the thrusters will continue to fire until you reduce thrust by tapping the opposite direction's Fine Thrust control, or until you press Keypad 7 to cut all thrust (or click the left mouse button while in Yoke mode). Remember that you must apply translational thrust in the opposite direction to slow the spacecraft down again.

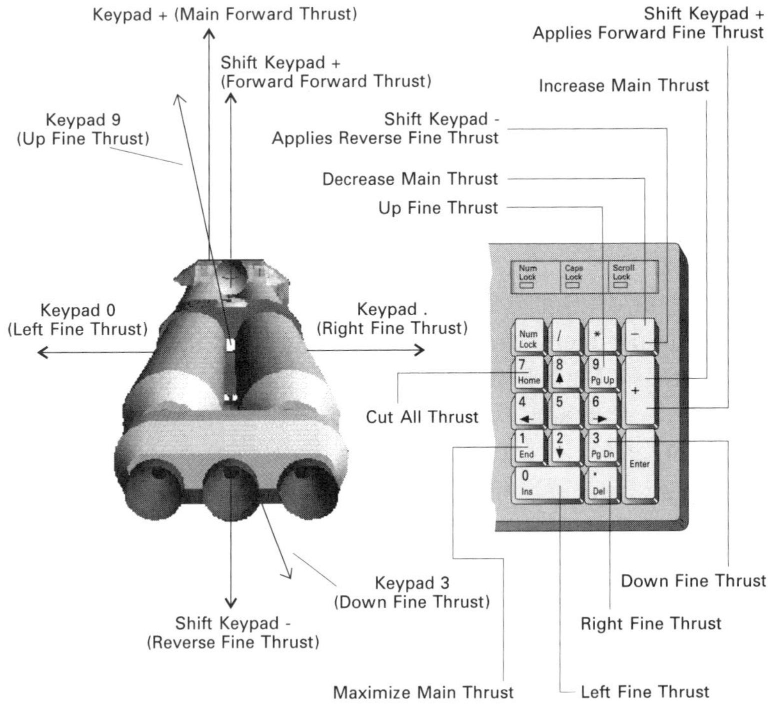

FIGURE 4.10 *Translation directions and thrust controls on the numeric keypad (for both Fine and Main Thrusters)*

Cutting All Velocity You can also use the F4 key to zero your velocity relative to the currently selected reference object. Be very careful using F4: if you lose your orbital velocity, this will cause your spacecraft to plummet into the surface of the planet, since you no longer have any tangential velocity to keep it in orbit. To avoid this fate, make sure the nearby target spacecraft or space station is selected as your reference object before using the F4 command.

TIP

Use Keypad 7 to cut all Fine Thrust, and F4 to zero all velocity relative to the currently selected reference object. Note that, even though you may have selected the Earth as your reference object, if you are very close to a space station, pressing F4 will not cancel your velocity relative to the Earth.

If you have inadvertantly pressed F4 and lost all tangential velocity, in order to regain orbit you'll have to select the nearby planet, moon, or star as your reference object, then manually yaw or pitch the spacecraft to ±90° before firing your thrusters to gain enough tangential velocity to regain orbit. Note that once you've lost all orbital velocity, you cannot use the Autopilot's Prograde command to regain proper orbital orientation. This is because the Autopilot no longer remembers where your previous orbital velocity vector was. If you use the Prograde command after pressing F4, most likely the Autopilot will turn the spacecraft nose first towards the planet's surface. Why does this happen? Because as you pick up radial velocity towards the planet due to the force of gravity, the Autopilot will sense this new velocity as your current orbital direction.

Main Thrusters

The Main Thrusters are your spacecraft's main engines and are to be used where high velocity changes are needed, such as when changing orbits or when landing and taking off. Don't use the Main Thrusters for close up docking maneuvers because they are much too powerful; you can easily lose control of the spacecraft by gaining too much momentum.

The Main Thrusters can only thrust in one direction: out the rear of the spacecraft. In order to change thrust directions, you have to maneuver the spacecraft into an orientation to effect the velocity change you want. For example, if you fire the Main Thrusters for 5 seconds at maximum, your spacecraft will start traveling forward. If you then want to decelerate to a stop, you first have to yaw or pitch your spacecraft 180° so that the engine faces forward in the direction you are traveling. You must fire the Main Thrusters for another 5 seconds to cancel the velocity you previously acquired. Figure 4.11 illustrates this concept.

For maneuvers such as the acceleration and deceleration maneuver described in Figure 4.11, you can use the Autopilot's Turnover command to flip your ship 180° so that it has reversed its former direction.

Now that you understand a little about spacecraft inertia and momentum, you can appreciate the difficulty of controlling your velocity. It's not easy to stop your ship once you fire your thrusters. Velocity and direction are everything in Space Simulator. Therefore, you must *never* fire your thrusters indiscriminantly.

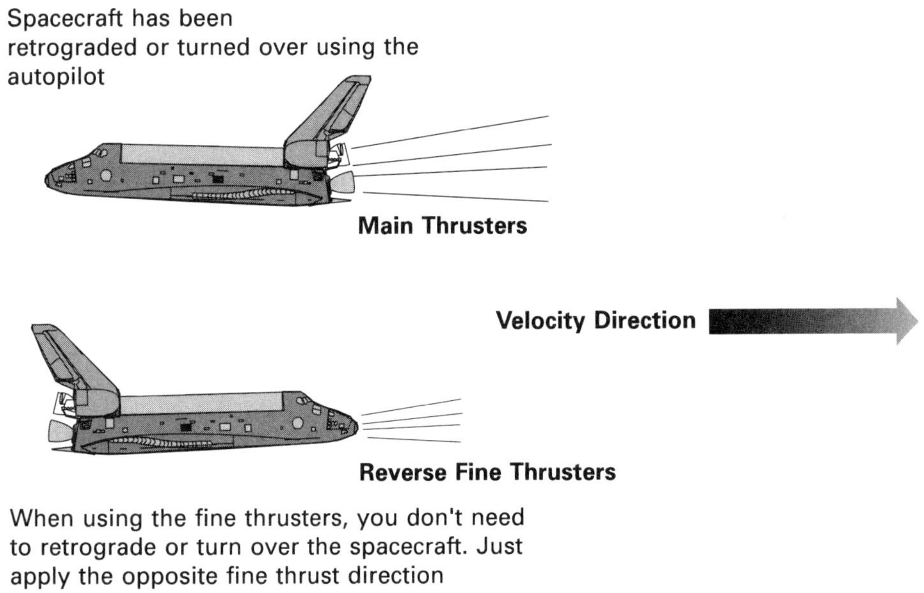

FIGURE 4.11 *To slow the spacecraft, apply reverse thrusters to the velocity direction*

The Autopilot has two commands which help you manually change your orbit: prograde and retrograde. These two commands rotate your spacecraft; they do not change its position in space. Prograding the spacecraft causes it to point in the current orbital velocity direction, while retrograding it causes it to point in the direction opposite of its current orbital velocity, as shown in Figure 4.12. When your ship is retrograded, the main engines in the tail are facing forward in your orbit's velocity direction, and firing them will decrease orbital velocity. When your spacecraft is prograded, the main engines are facing backward, and when fired will increase orbital velocity.

Keyboard Controls for Your Main Thrusters

To gradually increase thrust from your Main Thrusters, press Keypad +. To gradually decrease thrust, press Keypad –. You can quickly apply maximum thrust by pressing Keypad 1 and cut all thrust by pressing Keypad 7. As mentioned before, you can use the F4 key to zero all velocity relative to the selected reference planet or object.

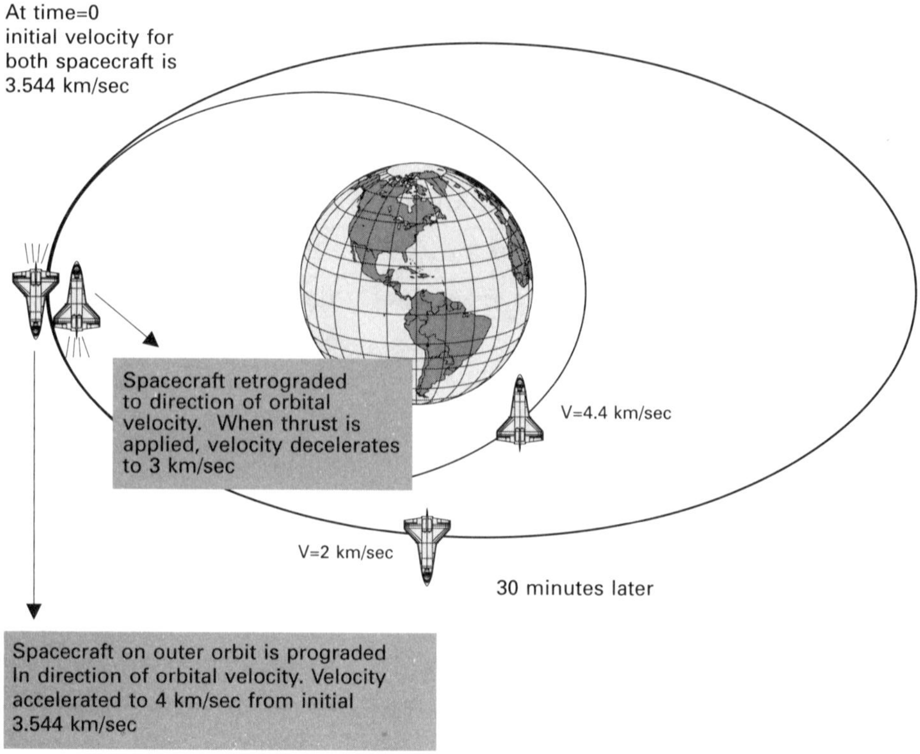

FIGURE 4.12 *Prograding and retrograding the spacecraft to change your orbit*

Thrust Levels Thrust is measured in acceleration units of *g* based on the acceleration of gravity at the Earth's surface (1 *g* = 9.8 meters/sec^2). Table 4.1 shows what your spacecraft's final velocity would be after undergoing various accelerations of a specified duration.

Due to relativistic effects, when you reach velocities close to the speed of light *c*, acceleration drops off and the length of time to increase velocity is not linear, as is shown in Table 4.1.

Taking relativistic effects into consideration, at maximum thrust of 4 *g*'s for the Galactic Explorer, reaching near light speed will take over 135 days. If relativistic effects were not considered, reaching near light speed would take only 88 days. The F-79 Galactic Fighter, with its higher thrust acceleration of 8 *g*'s, will take only 67.5 days to reach near light

TABLE 4.1: *Acceleration, Velocity, and Time*

Time	Velocity at 1 *g*	Velocity at 2 *g's*	Velocity at 3 *g's*	Velocity at 4 *g's*
1 second	9.8 m/sec	19.6 m/sec	29.4 m/sec	39.2 m/sec
2 seconds	19.6 m/sec	39.2 m/sec	58.8 m/sec	78.4 m/sec
1 minute	588 m/sec	1.17 km/sec	1.76 km/sec	2.35 km/sec
1 hour	35.280 km/sec	70.5 km/sec	105.8 km/sec	141.1 km/sec
1 day	846 km/sec	1,693 km/sec	2,540 km/sec	3,386 km/sec
1 month	26,248 km/sec	52,496 km/sec	78,744 km/sec	104,993 km/sec
2 months	52,496 km/sec	104,992 km/sec	157,488 km/sec	209,984 km/sec

speed. In llight of the length of time needed to reach *c*, you must use the Time acceleration controls.

Slowing down from light speed takes equally as long. In the Galactic Explorer, it will take you 135 days to accelerate to near light speed and another 135 days to decelerate from light speed, for a combined total of 270 days for just one light speed trip (actual results may vary slightly by a few days due to internal errors in the program).

WARNING

When decelerating your spacecraft from light speed at 4 *g's*, start your deceleration at least 0.235 light years away from your destination! If you don't start the deceleration at this point, you won't be able to stop your spacecraft in time before reaching your target.

ACCELERATION DROPS TO ZERO WHEN APPROACHING LIGHT SPEED

Due to limitations on velocity imposed by the Universe, your spacecraft cannot travel faster than light speed. As you approach light speed, you'll note that the Acceleration Gauge will drop off to zero. This is a manifestation of Einstein's Theory of Relativity which states that the mass of an object increases with speed according to the relation:

$$\text{Relativistic Mass of Moving Spacecraft} = \frac{\text{Mass of Non Moving Spacecraft}}{\sqrt{1-\frac{v^2}{c^2}}}$$

where *v* is the spacecraft's velocity in meters per second or kilometers per second, and *c* is the speed of light, or very nearly 300,000,000 m/sec (*c* is actually equal to 299,792,458 m/sec, but you can round it off to 300,000,000 to simplify things). If you examine the equation, at speeds of 42 million m/sec (42,000 km/sec), your spacecraft's mass will increase by an insignificant 1 percent. At a speed of 124 million m/sec (124,000 km/sec), your spacecraft's mass will increase by 10 percent. As you approach the speed of light at 299,000,000 m/sec (299,000 km/sec or 99.7 percent of *c*), your spacecraft's mass will increase to 13 times its original rest mass. The closer you get to *c*, the relativistic mass will increase exponentially. At 299,762,478 m/sec (99.99% of *c*), your spacecraft's relativistic mass is 70 times its original rest mass.

Since your engines can only apply a fixed amount of thrust force when you are accelerating, as the mass of the spacecraft increases, the acceleration drops according to the relation $F = m \times a$ With a fixed amount of force *F* from your engines, when the mass *m* increases without bound as you approach light speed, your acceleration *a* will decrease.

Using the Autopilot to Precisely Meter Thrust

Using the Autopilot's Thrust command, you can time engine burns with great precision. When using this command, however, the spacecraft's thrusters always fire at maximum thrust, thereby causing the spacecraft to accelerate at its maximum rate. If you are using this command to increase or decrease your orbital velocity, you should either prograde or retrograde your spacecraft so that it is facing the right way before the burn begins. For some maneuvers, such as changing your orbit's inclination angle, or interplanetary transfer orbits, you'll manually calculate your flight path angle, so you won't bother with prograding or retrograding the spacecraft.

To meter thrust precisely, follow these steps:

1. Press Alt A (or select the Flight/Autopilot menu command) to open the Autopilot dialog box.
2. Click the Thrust button.
3. Click the Duration button.
4. Select the time unit for the burn. For simple maneuvers around the solar system, you can click Seconds.
5. Type the duration of the burn in the Duration text entry box.
6. Click Execute.

The spacecraft's Autopilot will take over and your main engines will fire for the length of time you specified. If you get bored waiting for the burn to finish, you can speed up the time scale to a few seconds or minutes per second. For best precision, however, don't accelerate time, since this introduces errors to your burn rate, and this will in turn cause your actual velocity change to differ from the expected.

Calculating Thrust Timings for Specific Velocity Changes You may need to change your velocity by a certain amount to change to a particular orbit. You could manually fire your thrusters until you achieve the desired speed, but this is tricky. It is better to figure out exactly how long the thrusters need to be on, and then use the Autopilot to time the burn. Using the following equation, you can figure out to the millisecond how much time the velocity change will take for various acceleration levels.

$$\mathit{Time\ in\ Seconds} = \frac{\mathit{Velocity}}{(\mathit{Acceleration\ in}\ \mathrm{Gs}) \times 9.8 \frac{\mathrm{m}}{\mathrm{sec}^2}}$$

For example, say you need to increase your velocity by 5 km/sec in order to leave the Earth's gravitational field while your spacecraft is in high Earth orbit. Since you are using the Galactic Explorer, applying maximum thrust will produce an acceleration of 4 *g*'s. Using the equation, plug in 5000 m/sec (be sure to change km/sec to m/sec in the above equation by multiplying by km/sec by 1000) and plug in the acceleration factor of 4 *g*'s. Solving for *Time in Seconds*, we get 127.5 seconds (because Time in Seconds = 5000 m/sec ÷ (4 *g*'s × 9.8m/sec) = 127.5 seconds). Thus, if you wanted to increase your velocity by 5 km/sec, you would first prograde your spacecraft so that it is oriented correctly, then fire your thrusters at maximum for 127.5 seconds. For greater accuracy, you should use the Autopilot's Thrust Duration timer. You would use the same procedure to decrease velocity, but instead of prograding your ship, you should retrograde it before firing.

NOTE

Due to inaccuracies in Space Simulator, your calculated change in velocity due to carefully timed thrust accelerations will not be the same as what you see on your velocity readouts. The magnitude of the error isn't too bad; in most cases it is only in the tens of meters per second. But this small error can cause big problems when you are trying to calculate precise orbits.

Chapter 2 provides a useful example of how to change your orbit using the Autopilot's Thrust command.

TAKING A SPACEWALK IN THE MMU

Space Simulator comes equipped with a Manned Maneuvering Unit (MMU) which allows you to take spacewalks. The MMU is really a spacesuit that is attached to a small backpack-sized thrust unit that provides 6 degrees of translational motion, as well as yaw, pitch, and roll rotational motion. The thrust and rotational controls are identical to those found on the Galactic Explorer. In addition, all the instruments and screens display the same type of data and perspectives.

To begin a spacewalk:

1. From the Flight menu, select Space Walk (or press Shift W). Immediately, Space Simulator ejects you from your spacecraft or the space station where you are docked, into the MMU. The MMU will be thrust away at a velocity of 1 m/sec from the spacecraft or space station.
2. Press S to get a Chase view of you inside the MMU, and pan the screen to get different perspectives.

To finish a spacewalk, select Reboard Craft from the Flight menu (or press Shift W *to reboard the spacecraft). Or you can end a spacewalk by docking with the spacecraft or space station.*

You can also begin a spacewalk with the MMU by using the Autopilot's Space Walk command. This feature is provided so that you can enjoy spacewalking as a part of the flight plan that you create using the flight computer.

Using Space Simulator's Special Features

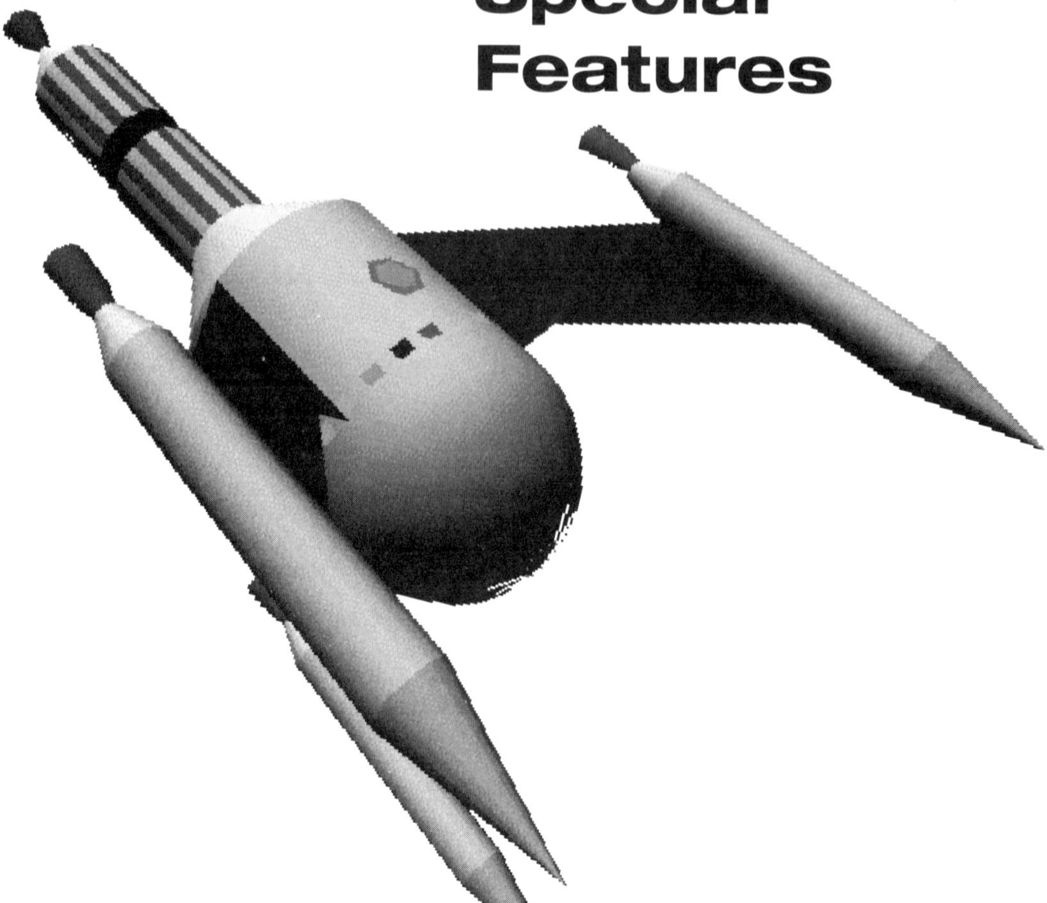

FIVE

F I V E

This chapter introduces you to some of Space Simulator's special features that allow you to customize the simulation. You will learn how to slew the spacecraft, use the Flight Computer to fly your spacecraft, and set your spacecraft's location anywhere in the universe. You will also learn how to customize your view screens, take screen shots and videos of your trips, choose different spacecraft, and dock and transfer spacecraft controls.

SLEWING YOUR SPACECRAFT AROUND THE UNIVERSE

Slewing is a special non-flight mode that allows you to move quickly from point to point in the Space Simulator universe, without worrying about the effects of gravity or momentum. If you cut off the slewing thrusters, rather than continuing to move as you would in the Newtonian world, you come to a complete stop. Furthermore, in slew control, your spacecraft is not gravitationally attracted to nearby planets, moons, stars, asteroids, or other celestial objects. For example, you can float over the surface of Jupiter, surf over the Sun as closely as you like, and hover over a black hole without crashing due to gravity.

While in slew control, you can translate the spacecraft in three dimensions or rotate the spacecraft to any attitude.

Using Slew Control

You enter slew control by pressing the Y key, or by selecting Slew Control from the Flight menu, shown here. When in slew control, you'll see the word *Slew* displayed in the lower right corner of the view window. To exit slew control and return to normal flight mode, press Y again, or pull

down the Flight menu and select the Flight Control menu option.

All your slewing translation and rotation controls are identical to the keyboard controls you use for normal flight mode translation and rotation. There are, however, a few differences between slew mode and flight mode that bear mentioning:

- There is no difference in thrust magnitude between Fine Thrust and Main Thrust in slew control (except for Forward Fine Thrust). In flight control there is a huge difference in thrust magnitude between Fine Thrust and Main Thrust.
- In slew control mode, except for Forward Fine Thrust, each press of a thrust control key doubles your velocity (up to the speed of light), while in flight control mode, each key press of a thrust control results in only an incremental velocity increase.
- In slew control mode, you can reverse slew thrust by pressing Shift Keypad – and slow down your velocity as much as you like; in flight control mode, pressing Shift Keypad – applies your Reverse Fine Thrusters, and these rockets can only slow your spacecraft by a very small amount.

Tables 5.1 and 5.2 list all of the slew commands and their keyboard equivalents.

TABLE 5.1: *Slewing Translation Using the Keyboard*

Slewing Translation	Key (With NumLock Off)
Up	Keypad 9
Down	Keypad 3
Left	Keypad 0
Right	Keypad .

TABLE 5.1: *Slewing Translation Using the Keyboard (cont.)*

Slewing Translation	Key (With NumLock Off)
Forward	Keypad +
Backward/Reverse	Keypad –
Cut Slew Thrust	Keypad 7

TABLE 5.2: *Slewing Rotation Using the Keyboard*

Slewing Rotation	Key (With NumLock Off)
Roll Left	Keypad /
Roll Right	Keypad *
Yaw Left	Keypad 4
Yaw Right	Keypad 6
Pitch Up	Keypad 2
Pitch Down	Keypad 8
Stop Pitch	Keypad 5

To cut all translational velocity while in slew control, shut off your thrusters by pressing Keypad 7. To stop rotation, press Keypad 5. (This only works if the NumLock key is off).

Slewing Via the Mouse You can also use your mouse or joystick to control slew motions. Before you can do this, click the Control Indicator on the Instrument Panel until it displays *Rotation* or *Thrust* depending on which slew motion you want. Then click the right mouse button to enter Yoke mode. To exit mouse Yoke mode, click the left mouse button. Figure 5.1 illustrates the mouse control directions.

> **TIP**
>
> **While in mouse Yoke or Panning mode, you can switch between Thrusting, Rotation, and Panning mode by pressing Alt N.**

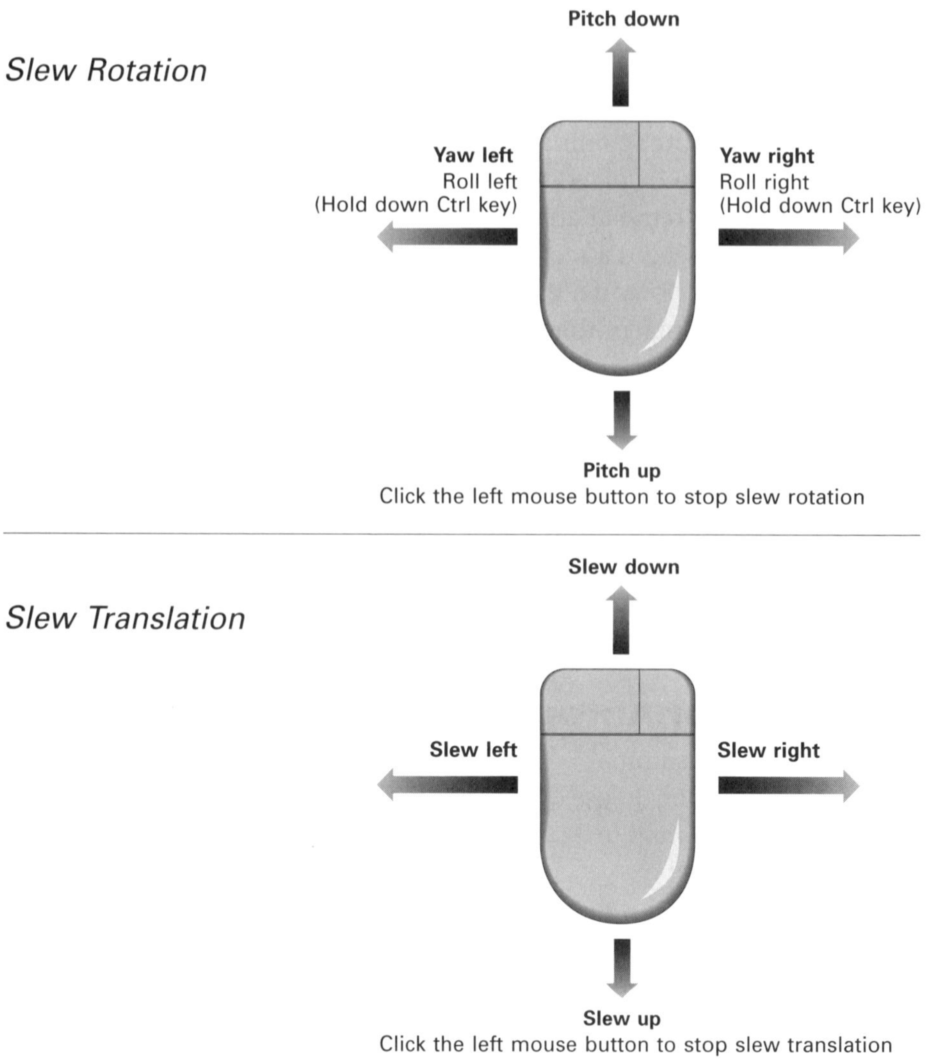

FIGURE 5.1 *Mouse slewing controls for rotation and translation*

USING THE FLIGHT COMPUTER AND AUTOPILOT

Using the Autopilot and Flight Computer, you can issue commands that calculate orbits and fire your rocket engines for precision rendezvous maneuvers, docking, launches, orbit changes, and landings. You can combine Autopilot commands into a sequence of recorded steps that a special flight computer sequentially executes. These linked computer commands, called a *command macro*, can be saved to disk and recalled instantly for reuse at any time. For example, you can record a series of commands that will fly you on a grand tour of the solar system, or you can record a command macro that will bring you back to the Earth and then place you in an equatorial orbit, no matter where you are in the Universe.

> **NOTE**
>
> **Space Simulator's Autopilot uses a brute force method of solving orbital dynamics problems. Later on, you'll learn how to plot your own more energy-efficient trajectories.**

Before learning how to use the Flight Computer, you'll first need to know what Autopilot instructions are available. The next section lists all the Autopilot commands. Note that you can use the Autopilot by itself, by issuing individual commands one after the other without using the Flight Computer. However, if you want to create a single flight plan that links many Autopilot commands in a step-by-step order, you'll need to use the Flight Computer.

Summary of Autopilot Commands

The next section summarizes and explains how to use all the commands found in the Autopilot dialog box shown here. To open this dialog box, from the Flight menu select Autopilot, or from the keyboard press Alt A.

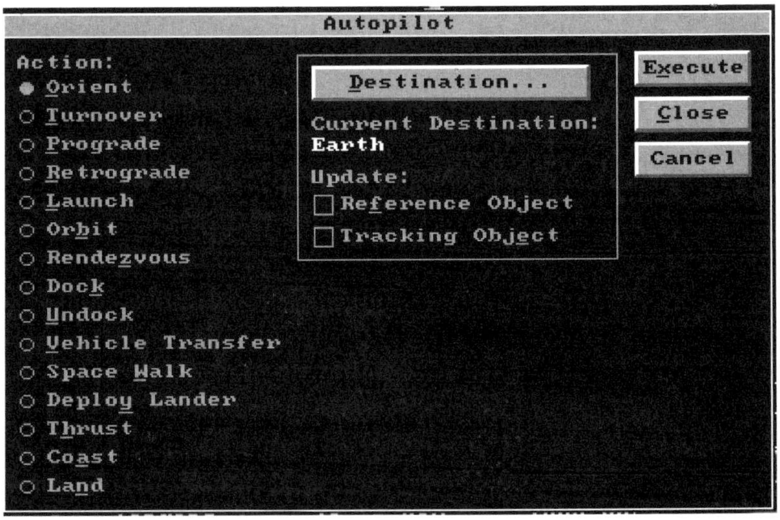

Orient This command orients your spacecraft toward the object you select in the Destination dialog box, which you open by clicking on the adjoining Destination button. Your pitch and yaw are set to 0°, even though your spacecraft roll is not. If you toggle on the Update Reference Object check box your reference object will be changed to the new destination object, and your distance and velocity readouts will be updated to show distance and velocity with respect to the destination. In addition, if you toggle on the Update Tracking Object button, your view window will be set to track the destination object.

After selecting your destination object, you can:

- Click the Execute button, and the Autopilot will rotate the spacecraft so that it faces directly at the destination you want.
- Click Close, and you'll return to the simulation without executing the Autopilot command. You can execute the command later when you switch on the Autopilot.

TIP

When you are ready to execute a previously selected Autopilot command, press the Z key, or click the Autopilot Indicator on the Instrument Panel so that it displays *On* or *Off*.

Turnover The Turnover maneuver causes your spacecraft to reverse the direction it is pointing. In other words, you turn around by 180°. But performing the Turnover maneuver does not always mean that you have reversed the direction the spacecraft is currently traveling.

You may be confused by the difference between the Turnover and Retrograde commands, since both commands can be used to rotate the spacecraft so that it is ready to slow down. Retrograding *always reverses the spacecraft so that it is pointing in the direction opposite to its orbital velocity*. Turning over, on the other hand, only *reverses the spacecraft from its previous orientation* by yawing or pitching the spacecraft by 180°, regardless of current orbital velocity.

The Turnover command is an excellent way to reduce unwanted velocity. For example, if you fire your Main Thrusters for 30 seconds and accelerate in a particular direction, then turn over and fire your thrusters again for 30 seconds, you will cancel out the velocity that you acquired in the first thrust.

Prograde Use the Prograde command to orient the spacecraft's nose in the direction it is currently traveling *with respect to its current destination* *object (e.g. body that it is orbiting around).* This is crucial! When you select the Earth as your destination, and you prograde the spacecraft, it will turn to face the direction that it is currently orbiting around the Earth. However, if you had selected the Sun as your current destination, but were still in Earth orbit when you prograded the spacecraft, it would not face the same direction as in the previous instance. Instead, the prograded spacecraft would face the direction that the Earth is traveling in its orbit around the Sun, since this is the general prograded direction for the spacecraft in Solar orbit. Figure 5.2 illustrates this concept.

Prograding your spacecraft is the only way you can determine in which direction your spacecraft is currently traveling. In general, whenever you prograde your spacecraft and fire your thrusters, you increase the energy of your orbit and increase your altitude.

Retrograde Retrograding your spacecraft causes it to face tail first in the direction of its orbit, with respect to *the current destination object (e.g. body that it is orbiting around).* Again, as with prograding, this is very important,

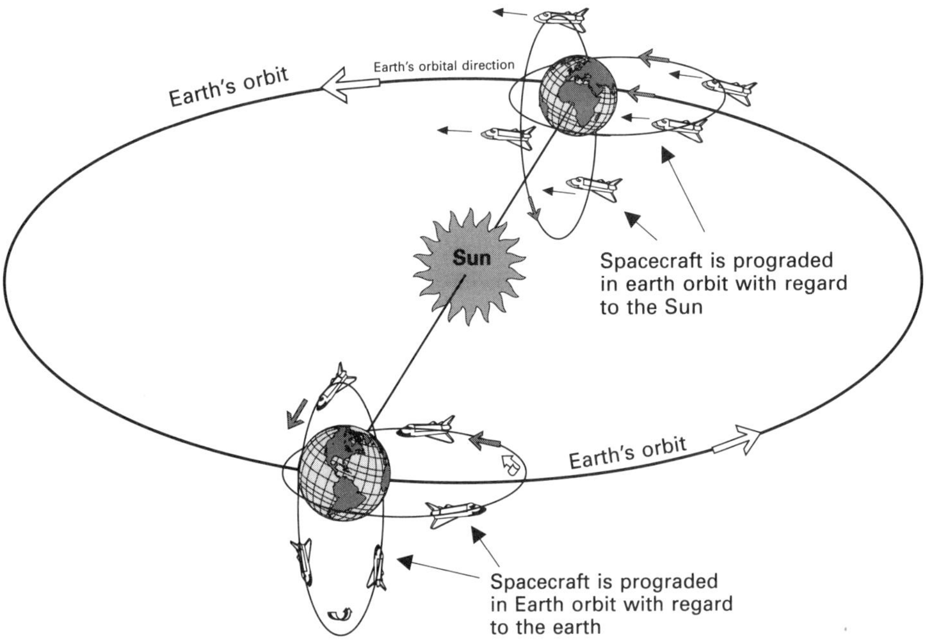

FIGURE 5.2 *Prograded direction for an Earth-orbiting spacecraft changes when the Sun is selected as the destination object.*

since your retrograde orientation will change for each destination object you select, regardless of what entity you are currently orbiting.

Assuming that your selected destination object is the planet, moon, or star you are currently in orbit about, if you fire your thrusters while retrograded, you will decrease the energy of the orbit and the spacecraft will descend to a lower altitude.

Launch The Launch maneuver can only be undertaken if your spacecraft is on the surface of a planet, moon, or other object. You must choose the orbital radius the spacecraft will assume, and the launch azimuth the spacecraft will head toward when taking off. Launch Azimuth is based on the horizon coordinate system, where 0° is due north, +90° is due west, –90° is due east and ±180° is due south.

Assuming that you are taking off from the northern hemisphere of a planet, if you want a direct orbit (one that moves westerly in the same direction as a planet or moon's west-to-east rotation), you should choose a launch azimuth between +1° and +179°. For a polar orbit, choose 0° or ±180°. For a retrograde orbit (one that moves opposite to the planet's rotation), choose a launch azimuth between –1° and –179°.

Because of spherical geometry constraints, *the inclination of any orbit cannot be less than the latitude of the launch site (without a plane change once in orbit).*

Orbit The Orbit command allows you to send your spacecraft into a stable circular orbit around any destination planet, moon, star, or asteroid. Using this command, for example, you can order your spacecraft to leave the Earth and orbit Mars at any altitude and any angle of inclination you specify. Simply choose the destination, by clicking the Destination button, and then choose the orbit altitude/radius and inclination angle by typing in the data.

Rendezvous When you rendezvous with another spacecraft, your spacecraft matches the orbital velocity and position of the selected target. Using this command, you can rendezvous with any space station, or even catch up to Halley's comet to see what it looks like. Simply click the Rendezvous button, then select the destination and, when you are ready to go, click the Execute button.

Dock To dock with any spacecraft or space station, choose the Dock command. All you need to do is specify which object you wish to dock with in the Destination dialog box.

Undock This command simply undocks you from whatever spacecraft or space station you are docked to.

Vehicle Transfer The Autopilot's Vehicle Transfer command is identical to the Vehicle Transfer menu command found under the Flight menu. This command, as well as the Space Walk command and the Deploy Lander command, is provided here so that you can incorporate it into the Flight Computer instructions, for complex command macros.

Space Walk This Autopilot command causes the MMU to be deployed with you in it, and is identical to the Space Walk menu command found under the Flight menu.

Deploy Lander You can deploy the All Terrain Lander (ATL) by using this command.

Thrust This command lets you add precise amounts of thrust for orbital maneuvers. After clicking the Thrust button, a Duration button will appear off to one side in the Autopilot dialog box. When you click the Duration button, a special dialog box opens in which you can choose the time interval to fire your thrusters.

> **NOTE**
>
> **You can only fire the Main Thrusters at maximum thrust when using the Autopilot's Thrust command.**

Coast This command tells your spacecraft to do nothing for a specified period of time. It will just coast in orbit until the measured amount of time elapses. You can coast for as many seconds, minutes, hours, days, months, or years as you want.

Land This command instructs the Autopilot to land at a destination that you specify by clicking on the Destination button.

Choosing Your Landing Location The location your spacecraft is currently overflying, will be the spot where the landing will occur. So in order to land at a particular location on the Earth or other planet, you'll first need to move your spacecraft to the latitude/longitude where the landing will take place. For example, you could wait until your spacecraft's orbit crosses over San Francisco, but that could take a while, so to expedite things use the Set Location command to put the ATL spacecraft over San Francisco. After doing this, you can use the Autopilot's Land command to put down the spacecraft at San Francisco, California.

1. From the Flight menu, select the Spacecraft command and then choose the ATL spacecraft.
2. From the Location menu, choose Set Location.
3. In the Set Location dialog box, make sure the current Base Object is set to the Earth.
4. In the Latitude text box, type **37 21 00** for San Francisco's latitude of 37° 21′ 00″ N.
5. Click the North button, to instruct Space Simulator to use a north latitude measurement.
6. In the Longitude text box, type **122 16 12** for San Francisco's longitude of 122° 16′ 12″ W.
7. Click the West button.
8. For now, ignore the Distance text box, where you would ordinarily enter the altitude or distance to the planet's surface or center. Click the OK button to have the spacecraft instantly relocated above San Francisco.
9. Open the Autopilot and click the Land button, then make sure that the Earth is selected as the current destination. Click Execute to initiate the landing.

10 Deploy the landing gear just before touchdown by pressing G.

> **TIP**
>
> **To see a list of latitudes and longitudes for cities around the world, choose Surface from the Location menu.**

Touring the Solar System Using the Flight Computer

Now that you know how to use the Autopilot commands, let's learn how to create a flight plan for the Flight Computer. We'll design a flight plan that will take your spacecraft on a grand tour of the solar system, where you'll visit each and every planet. The flight path will start at Mercury, and work its way out through the inner planets of Venus, Earth, and Mars. After passing through the asteroid belt, your spacecraft will go on to the outer planets and you'll have a chance to tour the spectacular moon systems of Jupiter and Saturn, before proceeding on to Uranus, Neptune, and Pluto.

But first, let's discuss some of the features of the Flight Computer. From the Flight menu, select Flight Computer and you'll see the Flight Computer dialog box, as shown in Figure 5.3.

First click the Clear button inside the Flight Computer dialog box. This will clear all previous instructions from the Instruction Queue and each new instruction you add will be added in the order you enter it. The instructions will be executed in numerical order when you click the Execute button. To give an existing instruction a particular Autopilot command, first highlight the instruction, then either double-click on it, or click the Edit button. To insert blank new instructions, highlight the point where you wish to insert a new instruction, then click the Insert button. To delete any instruction from the Queue, highlight it, then click the Delete button. If you want to save your flight plan, click the Save button and give it a DOS file name in the dialog box that opens. Be sure to save your flight plans to disk if you want to reuse them. To reopen this flight plan, or any other flight plan, click the Open button and select the flight plan's DOS file name.

The Close button allows you to close the Flight Computer without losing your current instructions. You can later execute these instructions, if you haven't yet exited the program. The Cancel button is used to close the Flight Computer dialog box without saving any instructions.

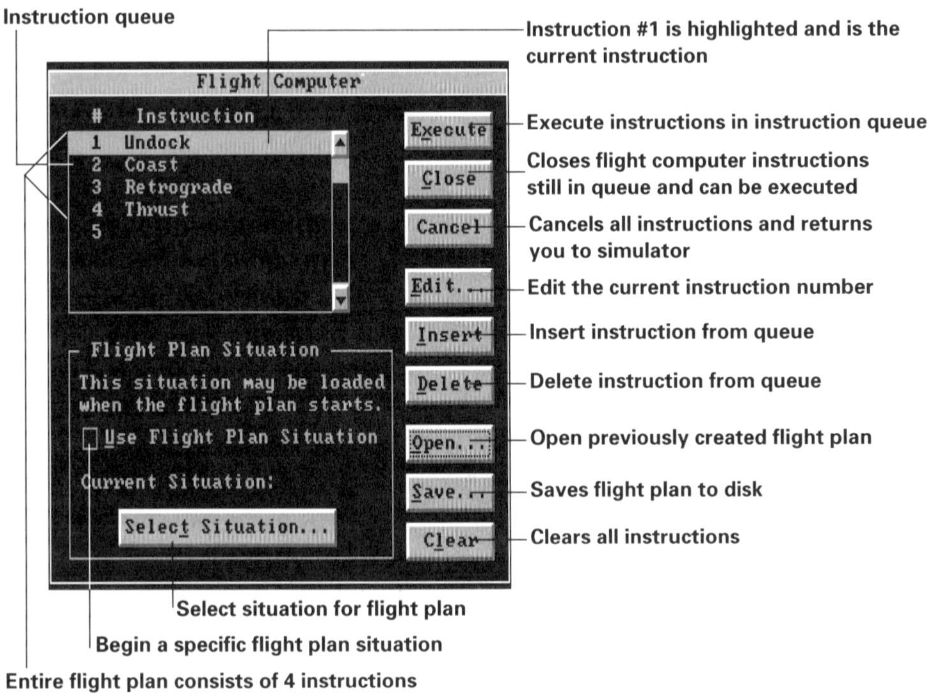

FIGURE 5.3 *The Flight Computer dialog box*

You can also specify a particular situation that your flight plan will use. Click the Use Flight Plan Situation check box, and then click the Select Situation button to choose a situation from your hard disk.

Now let's create the Grand Tour of the Solar System Flight Plan:

1. Select Flight Computer from the Flight menu. The Flight Computer dialog box will open.
2. Click the Clear button to erase all previous instructions in the Queue.
3. Double-click instruction #1 in the Queue to open the Instruction dialog box. The Instruction #1 dialog box resembles the Autopilot dialog box and contains the same commands and sub-dialog boxes. For this instruction, we'll tell the Autopilot to send us into a polar orbit 2000 km above the surface of Mercury. Perform the following steps for the Instruction #1 dialog box.

A Click the Orbit radio button.

B Click the Destination button, and select Mercury as your first destination. Click OK to return to the Instruction dialog box.

C Click the Reference Object and Tracking Object check boxes so that they are switched on, as indicated by an X mark. This will allow the Distance and Velocity displays, as well as your view window to be reset to Mercury.

D Click the Orbital Radius button and, in the dialog box that opens, type 2000 in the text box. While still in this dialog box, click the Kilometers and the Altitude Above Surface radio buttons. Click OK.

E Ignore the Orbital Inclination angle for now; you can leave it at 90°, which will put you in a polar orbit around Mercury. Click the OK button to exit the Instruction dialog box and return to the Flight Computer dialog box.

4 Double-click on Instruction #2. The Instruction #2 dialog box will open. After entering orbit, you'll instruct the Autopilot to coast for 2 days before executing the next instruction in the Queue. Follow these steps:

A Click the Coast radio button.

B Click the Duration button.

C In the Duration dialog box, type **2** then click the Days radio button. Click OK to return to the Instruction dialog box.

D Click OK to return to the Flight Computer dialog box.

5 Repeat steps 3 and 4 for Venus, Earth, Mars, Jupiter, Saturn, Uranus, Neptune, and Pluto. You will add a new Auto pilot instruction for each planet's orbit and coast command. Make sure that you choose the correct planet in step 3; don't keep using Mercury! At the end of this step you will have 18 instructions in the Queue.

6 In the Flight Computer dialog box, click the Save button and then type the name **Tour** to give your flight plan a file name. Then click the OK button to return to the Flight Computer dialog box.

7 Click the Execute button to begin the tour.

When the tour begins, be sure to select Tracking for your View 1 mode. Otherwise the planet you are heading for will not remain in view in the cockpit's window. Also, after your Autopilot puts you into orbit around each planet, you'll want to accelerate time to 17 minutes/second or greater so that you don't have to wait the full 2 days that the coasting maneuver is programmed to last.

Now that you've saved the flight plan to disk, you can bring it up at any time by clicking the Open button in the Flight Computer's dialog box and selecting the Tour file name.

SETTING YOUR SPACECRAFT LOCATION

To facilitate travel around the Space Simulator universe, you can use the commands found under the Location menu to locate your spacecraft anywhere in the Universe. Using this menu, shown here, you can place your spacecraft near any planet, moon, asteroid, comet, star, deep space object, or other space station or spacecraft, and instantly see what that destination looks like. You can also place your spacecraft on the surface of any planet, moon, or asteroid and specify the latitude and longitude of your position.

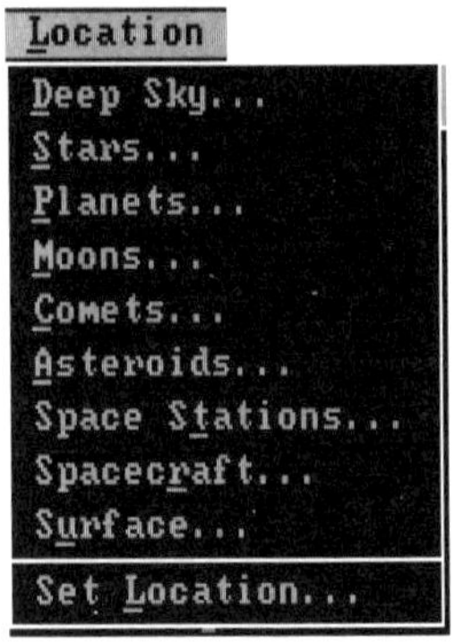

All the Location menu commands cause the Reference object selected on your Instrument Panel to adjust to the new location you've selected. Thus your velocity and distance readouts will automatically show you information relevant to your new location. Also, the Track view will be automatically locked on your new location, so that you can keep the selected object always in view on your cockpit window when you toggle the window to Tracking mode.

Moving Your Spacecraft to a New Location

To locate your spacecraft near any object in the Space Simulator universe, perform the following procedure. Note that using this method will give your spacecraft enough velocity to maintain orbit.

1. From the Location menu, select one of the following menu options: Deep Sky, Stars, Planets, Moons, Comets, Asteroids, Spacecraft, Space Stations, or Surface. Depending on your current situation, some of these options may or may not be available.
2. Choose the particular object near which you want your spacecraft to be located and click the OK button. When you return to the simulation, your spacecraft will assume its new location.

> **TIP**
>
> **When your spacecraft is at a different planet or star system, new locations become available under the Planets, Surfaces, and other Location menu sub-options.**

Using the Set Location Command

The Set Location menu option, under the Location menu, gives you much more precise control over your spacecraft's location than any other method in Space Simulator. You can specify your spacecraft's exact longitude and latitude over the surface of any planet, moon, star, or asteroid, and you can determine the exact separation distance.

> **WARNING**
>
> **If you use the Set Location command under the Location menu to locate your spacecraft near a planet, moon, or star, your craft will initially have zero velocity. This means that it is not in orbit, and that it will come crashing down to the nearest gravitational body, without additional tangential velocity being added. If you want your spacecraft to arrive at the selected celestial body already in orbit, you should instead select the Location menu option for Stars, Planets, Moons, or Asteroids.**

Putting Your Spacecraft 10,000 km Above the Earth's North Pole The Set Location dialog box allows you to specify the distance, and the precise latitude and longitude of your spacecraft in relation to any destination object. If you wanted the spacecraft to be placed over the North Pole of the Earth at a distance of 10,000 km you would perform the following steps:

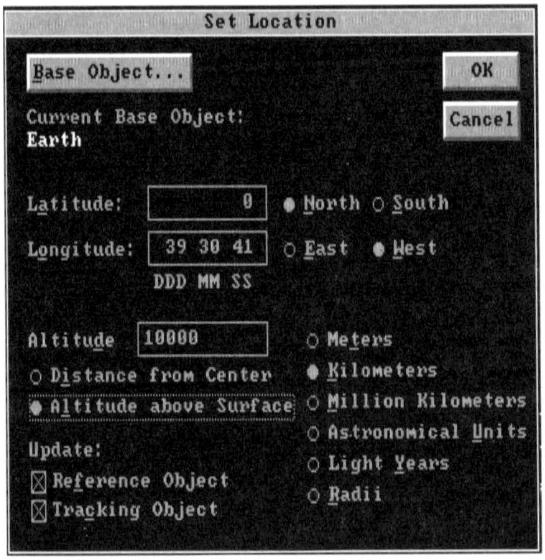

1. From the Location menu, choose the Set Location menu option to open the Set Location dialog box shown here.
2. Click the Base Object button, and in the dialog box that opens, click Planets. Choose the Earth from the list of planets that appears, then click OK to return to the Set Location dialog box.
3. In the Set Location dialog box, click the pointer in the Latitude text box, and type **0**, making sure to first delete any existing numbers.
4. Click the North radio button, since the latitude you want is in the northern hemisphere. (If you clicked on the South radio button, the spacecraft would be placed over the South Pole.)
5. Since longitude is irrelevant at the North Pole, ignore the longitude text box for now.
6. In the Distance text box, type **10000** without a comma.
7. Click the Kilometers radio button, to specify the unit of measurement for the Distance text box.

> **TIP**
>
> **In the Set Location dialog box, you can enter decimal latitude/longitude numbers or you can enter latitude/longitude numbers in degrees-minutes-seconds format. In the latter format, be sure to separate degrees-minutes and minutes-seconds with a space between the numbers. No commas between numbers are allowed.**

8. Click the Altitude Above Surface radio button so that the 10,000 km distance you entered will be measured from the planet's surface.
9. Click the OK button to return to the simulation. Your spacecraft will placed exactly 10,000 km above the North Pole of the Earth with an initial velocity of 0 m/sec.

Finding Your Spacecraft's Current Latitude/Longitude Over a Planet's Surface

While in orbit, there is a clever way to figure out your current latitude and longitude position projected over the surface of a nearby planet, moon, or star. To do this:

1 From the Location menu, choose Set Location.

2 In the Set Location dialog box, you'll see the current latitude and longitude of your spacecraft. North-South latitudes and East-West longitudes are indicated by whether the relevant radio button is on.

For example, when you first start the **Flight** situation, your spacecraft is over the southern tip of South America. To find your exact coordinates, open the Set Location dialog box and you'll find that the latitude is 42° 51′ 09″ South, and the longitude is 39° 42′ 16″ West.

Moving a Space Station with the Location Menu

Here's how to move a space station to a new location in the universe:

1 Dock your spacecraft with the space station. If you have trouble doing it yourself, use the Autopilot Dock command under the Autopilot dialog box.

2 Under the Flight menu, choose Vehicle Transfer. Your spacecraft controls will now be assigned to control the space station.

3 Under the Location menu, select your new destination. The space station and docked spacecraft will instantly be moved to the new location you specified.

After you move the space station, be sure to save the situation to disk, giving it a descriptive file name. By doing this, each time you start Space Simulator, you can reopen the situation and not have to move the space station again.

CUSTOMIZING SPACE SIMULATOR

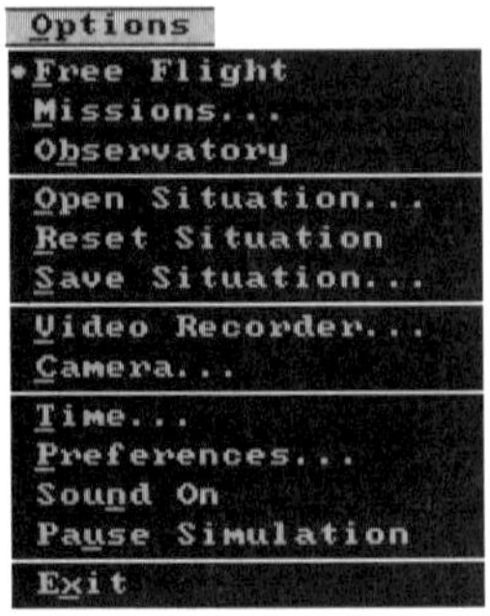

When you select the Preferences menu command under the Options menu, a dialog box, shown here, opens that allows you to customize how Space Simulator runs. Once the Preferences dialog box opens, you can choose skill levels, raise or lower simulator precision, modify keyboard and mouse preferences, activate certain sound features, select the amount of scenery detail that will be displayed, and even have your frame rate displayed.

Scenery

When you click the Scenery radio button, a dialog box opens that allows you to choose the kind of objects displayed. To increase your frame rate, you might want to toggle off some of the more spectacular graphics, such as the blue Milky Way haze. You can also improve your frame rate by lowering the Star Magnitude Scale. The Star Limiting Magnitude refers to the brightness of stars which Space Simulator will display; the higher the magnitude, the fainter the stars and the more stars will be displayed, causing your frame rate to slow.

Rendering

When you click the Rendering button, a dialog box appears that allows you to modify the graphics rendering capabilities of Space Simulator. This allows you to increase your frame rate by toggling off some features. A typical 486DX2 66 Mhz equipped with a fast local bus SVGA video accelerator card, will get about 4–5 frames per second (fps) with maximum detail enabled, and about 13.5 fps with minimum detail.

To increase your frame rate, you can reduce image quality by removing shading and texturing features. Under Shading choose *Solid* for a basic shading that is faster to draw on screen, or *Dithered* for a more realistic image that takes longer to draw. You can also decide to have *Faceted* objects, in which objects are polygonal shaped with sharp corners, or *Smooth* objects, in which objects are rounded.

For faster frame rates, choose *Sparse* detail, in which you'll get less detail on surfaces of moons, planets, and stars. Choose *Complex* if you care more about scenery quality and detail.

Depending on your room's lighting conditions, choose *Normal* or *Bright* Ambient Light .

Labels

When you click the Labels radio button, a dialog box appears that allows you pick the kinds of objects labeled in your View screens (but not your Map window).

> **TIP**
>
> **From the keyboard, you can press L to quickly turn the labels on or off.**

Displaying Labels in Map View Your map view can display moons, asteroids, comets, spacecraft, or any other object only if you specifically turn the label on. To turn on a specific map label:

1. Open the Window menu, and select the View Controls menu option.
2. In the View Controls dialog box, click the Map View radio button. The View Controls for map Window dialog box will open.
3. Click the check boxes for the kinds of objects you want to have displayed in the map window. You can label stars, planets, moons, comets, asteroids, spacecraft, and space stations.
4. Click the OK button to return to the simulation.
5. Press M to bring up the map window, if it is not already open. The labels will now be displayed.

Keyboard

Clicking the Keyboard radio button brings up the Keyboard Preferences dialog box. In this dialog box, you can adjust keyboard sensitivity, or reverse the pitch controls so that Keypad 8 pitches you down, and Keypad 2 pitches you up. This may be more intuitive for you than the existing keyboard pitch, but real spacecraft use the default setting.

Mouse

Clicking the Mouse radio button brings up the Mouse Preferences dialog box. In this dialog box, you can adjust mouse sensitivity by sliding the scale higher, for more sensitivity, and lower for less sensitivity.

Joystick

After you click the Joystick radio button, you'll see the Joystick Preferences dialog box. In this dialog box, you can adjust null-zone sensitivity, or the amount of free-play your joystick has, and you can adjust joystick sensitivity. To make your joystick less sensitive, move the sliding scale to a lower setting; to make your joystick more sensitive, move the sliding scale to a higher setting.

TIP

You can also calibrate your joystick from the keyboard by pressing the J key.

You can also turn off your joystick in this dialog box by clicking the Joystick Off check box. To calibrate the joystick, first center the joystick, then click the Calibrate button.

Skill Level

To pick a skill level, click the Skill Level radio button and, in the Skill Level Preferences dialog box, select one of the following three categories:

- **Practice**: Easiest and most forgiving of your piloting skills. You won't crash when docking or landing.
- **Intermediate**: For more experienced pilots; you'll have to be very precise when docking or landing.
- **Advanced**: For crackerjack space pilots who can stop their spacecraft on a dime.

Precision

The Precision dialog box that allows you to specify the precision by which Space Simulator makes its orbital calculations. At higher precision, the simulation slows down and your frame rate goes down. At lower precision, your frame rate goes up, but your plotted position in space becomes less precise.

I recommend that all Space Simulator pilots with a 486 66 Mhz Local Bus equipped PC or better, select the highest precision possible. Accuracy is much better, and you can enjoy more precise orbits when flying your own manually created trajectories. Unfortunately, due to Space Simulator's time acceleration errors, if you choose a low precision rate, you can't really perform manual orbital maneuvers with any degree of success.

There is a frame rate counter that you can switch on to check the display frame rate on your PC. If you are getting a frame rate greater than 4 fps when you start up the default **Flight** situation that comes with Space Simulator, you are getting acceptable results. Slower than this and your scenery will tend to look choppy, as it takes longer to redraw each frame.

Sound

Space Simulator also comes equipped with different melodies you can choose.

> **TIP**
>
> **Because the music or sound feature on Space Simulator often jams, or freezes on a particular tone, you'll need to turn off the sound to avoid going to the nuthouse. To quickly turn the sound on or off, press Q.**

Customizing your View Windows

You can further customize your view windows by using the menu options found under the Window menu, shown here. You can, for example, decide whether a view window, map window, or Instrument Panel is open, and also choose the arrangement, placement, and appearance on screen of multiple windows.

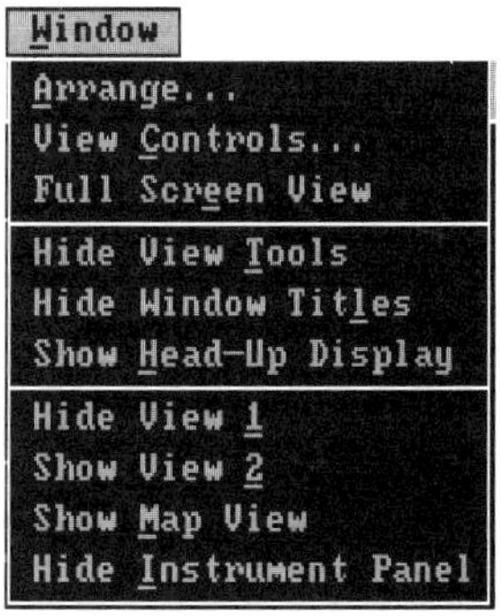

Removing View Tools and Title Bars from Your Windows

Here's how to remove the View Tools and Title Bars from your windows:

1. Open the Window menu.
2. Select Hide View Tools. You'll return to the simulation.

3 Open the Window menu again.
4 Select Hide Window Titles.

Arranging Your Windows

You can also arrange your windows to show a full screen view minus the Instrument Panel, or any combination of windows. To do this:

1 Open the Window menu.
2 Select the Arrange menu option.
3 In the Arrange dialog box, choose one of the following:

- **Full Screen View**: The view window will appear enlarged to full screen and the Instrument Panel, view Tools, Window Titles, and Menu Bar disappear.
- **Menu Bar and Windows**: When you click this check box on, you will have four radio button options that you can toggle on or off in combination with the other radio buttons. You can choose View 1, View 2, Map View, and Instrument Panel. If you wanted to display only the View 1 and View 2 windows, you would click on the View 1 and View 2 radio buttons.

4 After you have made your selections, you'll see a preview of your new window arrangement displayed alongside the radio buttons under Window Preview. Click the OK button to return to the simulation. Your new window arrangement will now be displayed.

How to Use the Assigned View Camera The Assigned View Camera allows you to place a camera at any location in the Space Simulator universe. You can place a camera on a space station and command it to track your approaching or departing spacecraft, or you can place it on a distant moon and watch a planet's surface as the moon orbits the planet.

Using this camera, you can for example, specify Saturn's moon Titan as your vantage point, and then have the view window track Saturn as Titan completes its orbit around Saturn. To experience this view using the Assigned View camera, follow these steps:

1. From the Window menu, select the View Controls menu option. The View Controls dialog box will open, as shown here.
2. Click the View 1 radio button.
3. Under View Location, click Assigned.
4. Click the Assigned View button to select the location for the Assigned View Camera.
5. In the Select Assigned View Location dialog box, select the Moons radio button, then choose Titan.
6. Click OK to return to the View Controls dialog box.
7. Now you must tell the View 1 window to track Saturn. Click the Tracking Object button.
8. In the Tracking Object dialog box, click the Planets radio button, and select Saturn from the list box.
9. Click OK to return to the View Controls dialog box.
10. At the bottom right corner of the View Controls dialog box under *View Direction*, click the Tracking radio button.
11. Click OK to exit the View Controls dialog box and return to the simulation. You should immediately see Saturn and its rings in the center of the view screen.

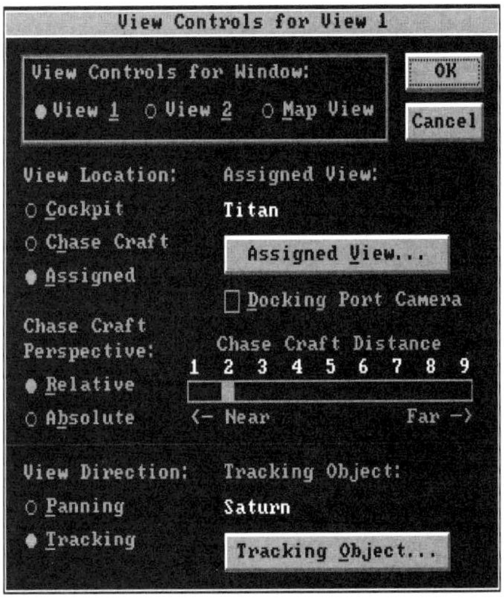

Once Saturn is displayed, you should advance the time scale so that you can see how Titan orbits around the planet. Notice the little black dots that crisscross the disk of Saturn. These are Saturn's other moons.

TIP

Your Assigned View camera has a limited resolving power when it tracks spacecraft. This means that when it is farther away than 5000 km from your spacecraft, it cannot see your spacecraft, even when zoom is set to maximum magnification.

TAKING SCREEN SHOTS WITH THE BUILT-IN CAMERA

Space Simulator allows you to take snapshots of your screens to print later. Here's how:

1. Under the Options menu, choose Camera.
2. In the Camera dialog box, you need to name the file that the screen capture will be saved to. Type in an 8-letter or less DOS file name (with no spaces or illegal DOS file name characters). Don't type a file extension, such as **.pcx** or **.bmp**.
3. Below the file name text box, type in the directory path where you want the screen capture file saved. If you don't care, just leave it alone, and the file will be saved to the directory where Space Simulator was installed.
4. Choose the kind of graphic file format you want the file to be saved under. You can choose between PCX or BMP.
5. Click OK, and the file will be saved to your hard disk.

If you want, you can enlarge your view window to full screen and eliminate the menus so that your screen capture includes only scenery. To do this, select your view window, then press W to enlarge it to full screen. Then repeat the steps outlined above to take the picture.

TIP

Keyboard Shortcut: You can also take a screen shot by pressing the Print Screen button.

HOME VIDEOS OF YOUR TRAVELS

With a built-in video recorder, Space Simulator allows you to record videos of your flights for later playback.

Recording a Video

To record a video, follow these steps:

1. Under the Options menu, choose Video Recorder.
2. In the Video Recorder dialog box, type the file name for the video you wish to save to disk.

3 In the Directory box, type the name of the directory path where you wish the file to be stored.

4 In the Description box, type a description of your video.

5 You'll now need to choose what portion of the screen you want to record. There are three options to choose from in the Under Region To Record check boxes:

- **Active Window**: Records only the active view window. Creates the smallest recording file size, since only the window's scenery is recorded.
- **Full Screen View:** Records a full screen view of your scenery. No menu bars or view tools will be visible on screen.
- **Entire Screen**: Records everything on your screen, including multiple windows, view tools, and the instrument panel. You can change the arrangement of windows during recording.

6 Click the Record button. You'll return to the simulation and Space Simulator will begin recording. At the upper left corner of the view window, Space Simulator displays the frame rate and the current file size of the video. Notice that it grows at a rate of almost 2 Megabytes for each 13 frames of scenery you record. Unless you have gobs of hard disk space, you'll need to keep a close eye on this display so you don't run out of disk space!

7 To end the recording, press the \ key. The video recorder will stop recording, and you can continue with your space flight.

NOTE

Keyboard Shortcuts for Videos: Press R to begin recording a video. To stop recording or to stop playing a video, press the \ key. Press P to play a video, and U to pause and resume recording or playback of a video.

You can edit your recordings using the pause function by pressing the U key. While the video recorder is paused, you can change your spacecraft location, vantage point, or even change situations, before resuming the recording by again pressing the U key.

Playing Back a Video

You can only play back a Space Simulator video that has been recorded at the same display resolution that you've installed Space Simulator to run with. Because there are several different display resolutions for Space Simulator, you need to know whether a video has been recorded in 800x600, 640x400, or 320x400 pixels resolution. If you are playing back your own videos, this shouldn't be a problem since your display will be set to the resolution at which you recorded the video. But, if you have downloaded or have obtained a Space Simulator video from someone else, you should check the video's description to see what display resolution it was recorded at.

To play back a video, follow these steps:

1. Under the Options menu, select Video Recorder. The Video Recorder Dialog box will open.
2. Select the video you want to play from the list that is displayed in the File Name list box.
3. In the Description Box, check to make sure that the video was recorded with the video resolution at which you have installed Space Simulator.
4. Click the Looping Playback check box if you want the video to repeat itself indefinitely.
5. Click the Play button. The video will begin and, when it is over, the simulation will return to normal space flight mode.
6. Press the \ key to end video playback while the video is in progress.

NOTE

To give video recordings a smoother, less choppy look, make sure that your video recording is smaller than your Smartdrv.exe cache size.

CHALLENGING YOURSELF WITH THE BUILT-IN MISSIONS

If you like challenges, there are two built-in missions to test your skills. The first mission, called "Shuttle," scores you on your ability to take off from Cape Canaveral and then rendezvous and dock with the Space Station Freedom before returning to Earth. The second mission, called "Apollo 17," recreates the Lunar Excursion Module's de-orbit and descent to the Moon's surface, where you will be scored on how gentle a landing you can make. Both missions have spectacular photorealistic scenery, and are accessed via the Missions menu option under the Options menu.

If you want to perform the undocking of the LEM from the Command Module yourself, as well as performing the retrograde de-orbit maneuver, after starting the "Apollo 17" mission, reset the simulation by selecting Reset from the Options menu (or just start the **1972** situation). This will prevent Space Simulator from using the Autopilot.

CHOOSING YOUR SPACECRAFT

You also have a choice of different spacecraft to fly, from the Apollo Command Module and Lunar Excursion Module, to the advanced Callisto and Galactic Explorer starships. In addition, there are four space stations that you can dock with and even fly to new destinations. To see your currently selected spacecraft, you must select Chase view, but you can also check to see which spacecraft you are flying by selecting the Spacecraft menu option under the Flight menu and then checking the Current Spacecraft box.

Only the following spacecraft can be used to land on the surface of a planet, moon, or asteroid.

- F-79 Galactic Fighter
- All Terrain Lander (ATL)
- Space Shuttle
- Apollo Service Module
- Lunar Excursion Module (LEM)

Just before landing, make sure you deploy the landing gear by pressing the G key. After taking off, raise the gear by again pressing G. In Chase view, you'll be able to see the landing gear deploy and retract, with the exception of the Apollo Service Module and the LEM. The F-79's wings will fold up when you extend the landing gear.

When flying the other interstellar spacecraft, if you want to land on a planet, moon, or asteroid, you should use the built-in All Terrain Lander (ATL), which you deploy by selecting Deploy Lander from the Flight menu. From there on, you take control of the ATL, while your interstellar mother ship remains in orbit. To return to the mother ship and regain control of it, you have two choices:

- Select Retract Lander from the Flight menu, and your lander will instantly return to the mother ship. This is not very realistic, since you don't need to rendezvous or dock with the mother ship.
- For more realism, rendezvous and dock the ATL with the mother ship; then use the Transfer Control menu command from the Flight menu to regain control of the mother ship.

Spacecraft

To choose a spacecraft, select the Flight menu and choose Spacecraft. After choosing the spacecraft in the dialog box that opens, click the OK button to return to the simulation.

The following section describes the spacecraft and space stations that are available in Space Simulator.

Galactic Explorer The Galactic Explorer is a nuclear fusion-powered starship that is capable of traveling vast distances throughout the galaxy. It can accelerate at 4 *g*'s for up to 317 years before exhausting the hydrogen slush in its twin fuel tanks. Table 5.3 lists the specifications for the Galaxy Explorer, as well as the performance and operating specifications for all the other Space Simulator spacecraft.

In the Spacecraft Specification table the last column, titled "Total Velocity Change Possible," tells you the amount of velocity the spacecraft can change before it needs to be refueled. For the Galactic Explorer, this amounts to a ΔV of 392 million km/sec. This does *not* mean that the

TABLE 5.3: *Spacecraft and Space Station Specifications*

Spacecraft and Space Station Specifications

Spacecraft	Mass (Metric Tons)	Length (Meters)	Propulsion System	Maximum Acceleration (In *g*'s)	Fuel Duration at Maximum Acceleration	Total Velocity Change Possible
Galactic Explorer	10,000	200	Nuclear Fusion	4	317 years	3.921×10^8 km/sec
Bussard RamJet	10,000	400	Nuclear Fusion	2	Unlimited	Unlimited
Callisto	1000	132	Gravity Synthesis	4	3000 years	3.711×10^9 km/sec
F-79 Galactic Fighter	100	40	Antimatter	8	30 years	7.422×10^7 km/sec
Zander Freighter	100,000	1100	Nuclear Fusion	2	634 years	3.921×10^8 km/sec
All Terrain Lander	100	50	Chemical	3	45 minutes	79.380 km/sec
Space Shuttle	100	66	Chemical	3	8 minutes	14.112 km/sec
Apollo Service Module	10	26	Chemical	2	3 minutes	3.528 km/sec
Lunar Excursion Module (LEM)	5	20	Chemical	1	5 minutes	2.940 km/sec
Manned Maneuvering Unit (MMU)	200 kg	2	Compressed Nitrogen	0.1	30 minutes	180 m/sec
Space Station	**Mass (Metric Tons)**	**Length (Meters)**	**Propulsion System**	**Maximum Acceleration (In *g*'s)**	**Fuel Duration at Maximum Acceleration**	**Total Velocity Change Possible**
Space Station Freedom	200	122.768	Chemical	0.1	Unlimited	Unlimited
Ring Station 1	500,000	1200	Chemical	0.1	Unlimited	Unlimited
Lunar Orbiter	200	400	Chemical	0.1	Unlimited	Unlimited
Mars Orbiter	300,000	1220	Chemical	0.1	Unlimited	Unlimited

Galactic Explorer can travel faster than the speed of light at 300,000,000 m/sec. It only means that while accelerating and decelerating, you'll run out of fuel once you've used up a total ΔV of 392 million km/sec.

The ΔV measurement is used here because it is a more convenient yardstick of range and fuel capacity in Space Simulator than actual fuel capacity or fuel duration. In space, you are primarily concerned with, "Do I have enough ΔV to get there?" Knowing how much fuel you have or how long it can last is not really relevant to this question, since each spacecraft has different thrust and mass specifications. But if you know your total ΔV, you can instantly compare the performance of each spacecraft to one another. Thus, looking at the table, the most powerful spacecraft with the longest range is the one with the highest ΔV, which is the Callisto. But you'll also note that the Galactic Explorer has the same ΔV as the Zander Freighter, which means that it has the same range as the Zander Freighter, even though the Zander Freighter takes longer to accelerate and decelerate.

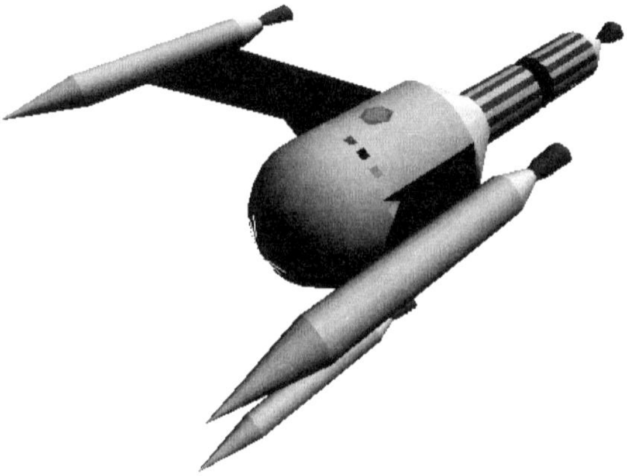

Callisto The Callisto spacecraft is really an alien craft that was discovered in orbit around Jupiter's moon, Callisto. It is propelled by three artificial gravity drives that create gravity fields in front of the spacecraft that pull it forward. The propulsion system is not understood by Earth's scientists, but it is so efficient that its fuel can last for over 3000 years! This spacecraft has the greatest ΔV of any of the Space Simulator spacecraft and, as such, has the longest range before needing refueling.

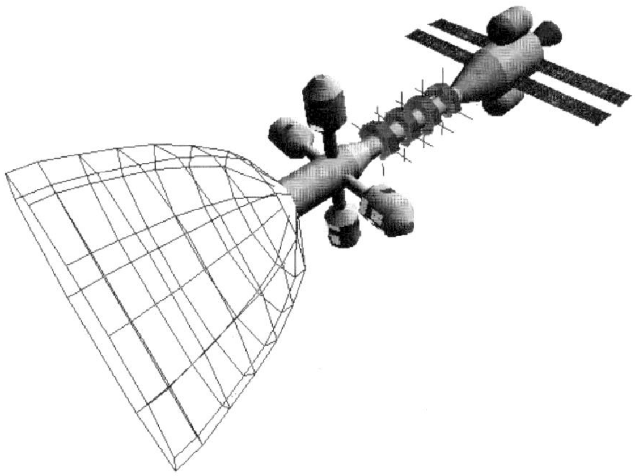

Bussard RamJet Named after the American physicist Robert Bussard, the Bussard RamJet uses gigantic magnetic funnels to gather interstellar hydrogen to fuel its fusion engines. However, the Bussard RamJet can only collect the hydrogen when its magnetic funnel is pointed in the direction of travel. This means that while decelerating the spacecraft, the funnels are retrograded to the velocity direction, and no fuel is collected. Thus, if you miscalculate while decelerating and run out of fuel, you will never be able to stop the spacecraft! You can also refuel the Bussard RamJet whenever it is docked at a space station.

Zander Freighter The Zander Freighter is the largest spacecraft, with a length of over 1100 meters and a mass of 100,000 metric tons. The orange cargo pallets are dropped off at space stations, surface colonies, and asteroid mining sites.

F-79 Galactic Fighter The F-79 Galactic Fighter is the only spacecraft capable of attaining 8 *g*'s of acceleration. This means that the spacecraft can achieve light speed in almost half the time that the Galactic Explorer, or any other 4-*g* spacecraft, takes. The F-79 is so versatile that it is the only spacecraft capable of both interstellar flight and atmospheric entry and landing.

All Terrain Lander (ATL) The ATL is used for landing on planets, moons, or asteroid surfaces. This spacecraft is carried in the belly of each interstellar spacecraft, and is deployed automatically when you select the Deploy Lander command from the Flight menu.

Space Shuttle The venerable 1970's vintage Space Shuttle comes in several guises in Space Simulator:

- **Lander**: The Space Shuttle Orbiter's cargo bay doors are shut and the craft is ready for atmospheric re-entry and landing.
- **Launch**: The Space Shuttle Orbiter is attached to the two SRBs (Solid Rocket Boosters) and the gigantic External Fuel Tank. It is ready for ground launch to low Earth orbit.
- **Orbiter**: The Space Shuttle Orbiter's cargo bay doors are open to vent excess heat and retrieve cargo. The Orbiter is prepared for low Earth orbital maneuvers, such as docking with the Space Station Freedom.

The space shuttle is the United States' first reusable spacecraft, capable of delivering 29,545 kilograms (equivalent to 65,000 lbs. at the Earth's surface) of cargo into a low Earth orbit of up to 1100 km altitude (684 miles).

Apollo Service Module The Apollo Service Module was the spacecraft that was used to carry the Apollo astronauts to the moon and back. It was connected to the Lunar Excursion Module (LEM) at the front docking hatch. Upon insertion to a lunar orbit, two astronauts exited the Service Module and entered the LEM through the docking hatch. There, they undocked and descended to the Moon's surface in the LEM.

In Space Simulator, you'll use the "Apollo 17" mission, found under the Options/Mission menu, to practice departing from the Service Module and landing on the moon in the LEM.

Manned Maneuvering Unit (MMU) The Manned Maneuvering Unit, or MMU, is a small self-propelled backpacked-sized unit that allows space-suited astronauts to move around untethered in space. In 1984, the MMU was given its first trial use when astronaut Bruce McCandless left the Space Shuttle and flew around in space.

Lunar Excursion Module (LEM) After undocking from the Apollo Service Module, the LEM is used to descend and land on the Moon's surface. Upon ascent from the moon's surface, the LEM leaves behind a lower-stage rocket, and then makes a rendezvous with the Apollo Service Module. After docking, the astronauts transfer back to the Service Module and the LEM is discarded and left to crash onto the moon's surface.

Space Stations

Space Simulator has four space stations that are all found in the Solar System: the Earth-orbiting Ring Station 1, the low Earth orbit Space Station Freedom, the Lunar Orbiter, and the Mars Orbiter.

> **TIP**
>
> **To refuel any spacecraft, simply dock it to a space station.**

Space Simulator allows you to transfer your flight controls to a space station (or another spacecraft) once you have docked. After taking control of a space station, you can fly it to a different location or orbit by firing its thrusters. You can also transport a space station to a different location by using the Location menu.

Docking to a Space Station Docking your spacecraft is done by linking up the orange docking hatch on your spacecraft with the docking port on the space station or other spacecraft you wish to dock with. When actual contact is made, you have to be careful that your spacecraft is traveling no faster than 1 m/sec, or a crash may occur. By using the MMU, you can transfer aboard a space station or another spacecraft without docking.

Using the Docking Port Camera Space Simulator comes equipped with a special Docking Port Camera which you can use to aid you when docking. You can specify either the View 1 or View 2 window to be assigned to the docking port camera.

To set up this camera, follow these steps:

1. Under the Window menu, select View Controls. The View Controls dialog box will open.
2. Select the View 1 or View 2 radio button.
3. Click the Docking Port Camera check box under the Assigned View button so that it is toggled on.
4. Click the Assigned View button and select the space station or spacecraft where you want to place the docking port camera. Click OK twice to return to the simulation. The Docking Port Camera will now be set up.
5. To see the view through the docking port camera, press S to cycle the Docking Port View window's Location to Assigned view.

Transferring Control to a Space Station When you transfer control to a space station or another spacecraft, all your flight controls and instruments take on the readings and settings of the new craft. Your view windows shift to the vantage point of the space station and, if you fire your thrusters, you will move the space station. Unless you abandon the spacecraft which you first arrived on, it will be remain docked to the space station regardless of where you translate the space station.

> **TIP**
>
> **To see which spacecraft you are currently controlling, select the Flight menu and choose the Spacecraft menu option. Then in the Spacecraft dialog box that opens, check the listed name under Current Spacecraft.**

To transfer control from a spacecraft to a space station follow these steps: simply dock with the space station, then under the Flight menu, choose Vehicle Transfer.

Ring Station The Ring 1 Station is in a geocentric orbit of 31,696 km radius around the Earth, with an orbital period of 15.57 hours. Don't confuse *geocentric* with *geosynchronous*, since the latter is used to describe orbits with periods of 24 sidereal hours.

The Ring 1 Station rotates to create artificial gravity for the comfort of its inhabitants.

Space Station Freedom When it is finished in the late 1990s the Space Station Freedom will be located only 200 km above the Earth's surface in low Earth orbit. It will be an international facility, built by the United States in cooperation with the European Community, Russia, and Japan.

The large, flat, blue solar panels collect light energy from the sun, and convert it to electrical power for use by the station. Unfortunately, because of the large surface area, these panels cause some drag resistance, due to collision with stray molecules from the upper atmosphere. To maintain orbit, the Space Station is equipped with a single rocket engine that must be fired periodically to boost its altitude.

You can't visit the Space Station Freedom, shown in Figure 5.4, using the commands found under the Location menu. The only way to see the station is to open either the **1999** or **SHTDOCK** situations from the Options/Open Situation menu command.

Lunar Orbiter The Lunar Orbiter is built of spent External Fuel Tanks from the Space Shuttle. This facility was originally intended as a way point for construction workers on their way to the moon, but is now being used as a transfer point for the growing lunar colony. The station is in a 6910 km radius circular orbit around the moon.

Mars Orbiter The Mars Orbiter was originally built in Earth orbit before being flown out to Mars and placed in a 6780 km radius *aerocentric* circular orbit. As it rotates, the station exerts a centripetal force of acceleration for the inhabitants inside, thereby giving a sensation of gravity.

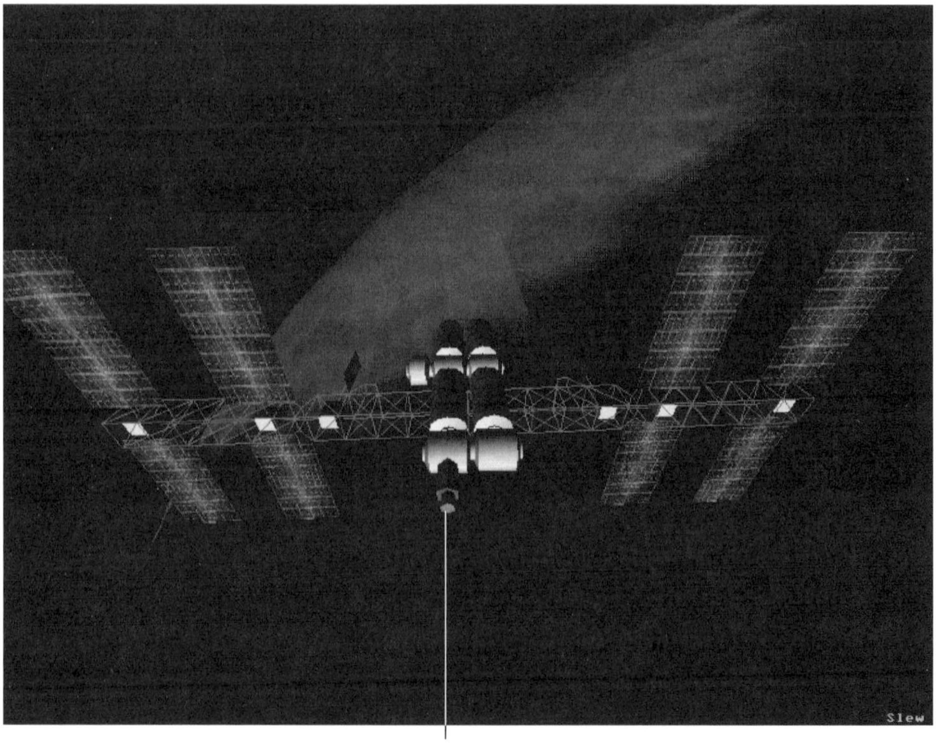

FIGURE 5.4 *The Space Station Freedom*

PART TWO

ASTRODYNAMICS FOR ASTRONAUTS

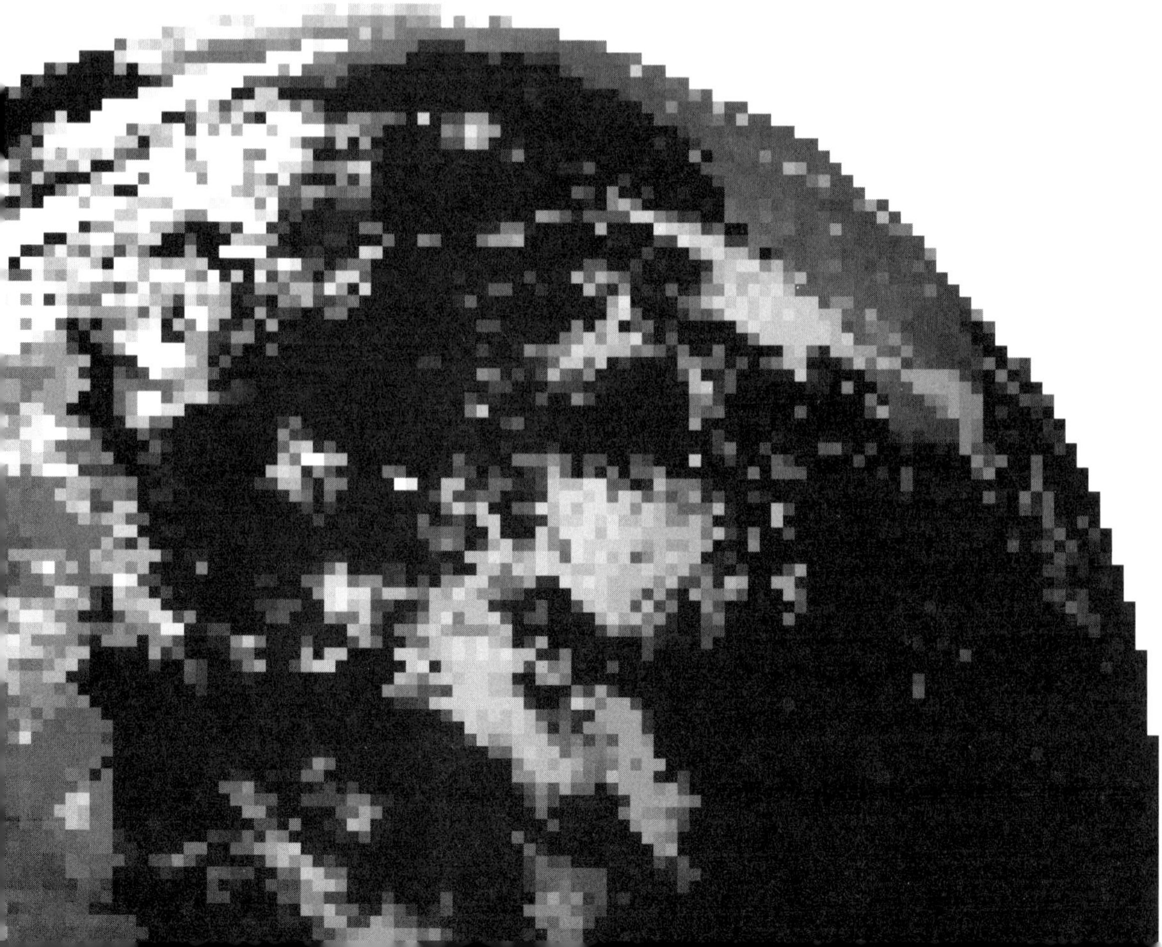

Understanding Two-Body Orbital Mechanics

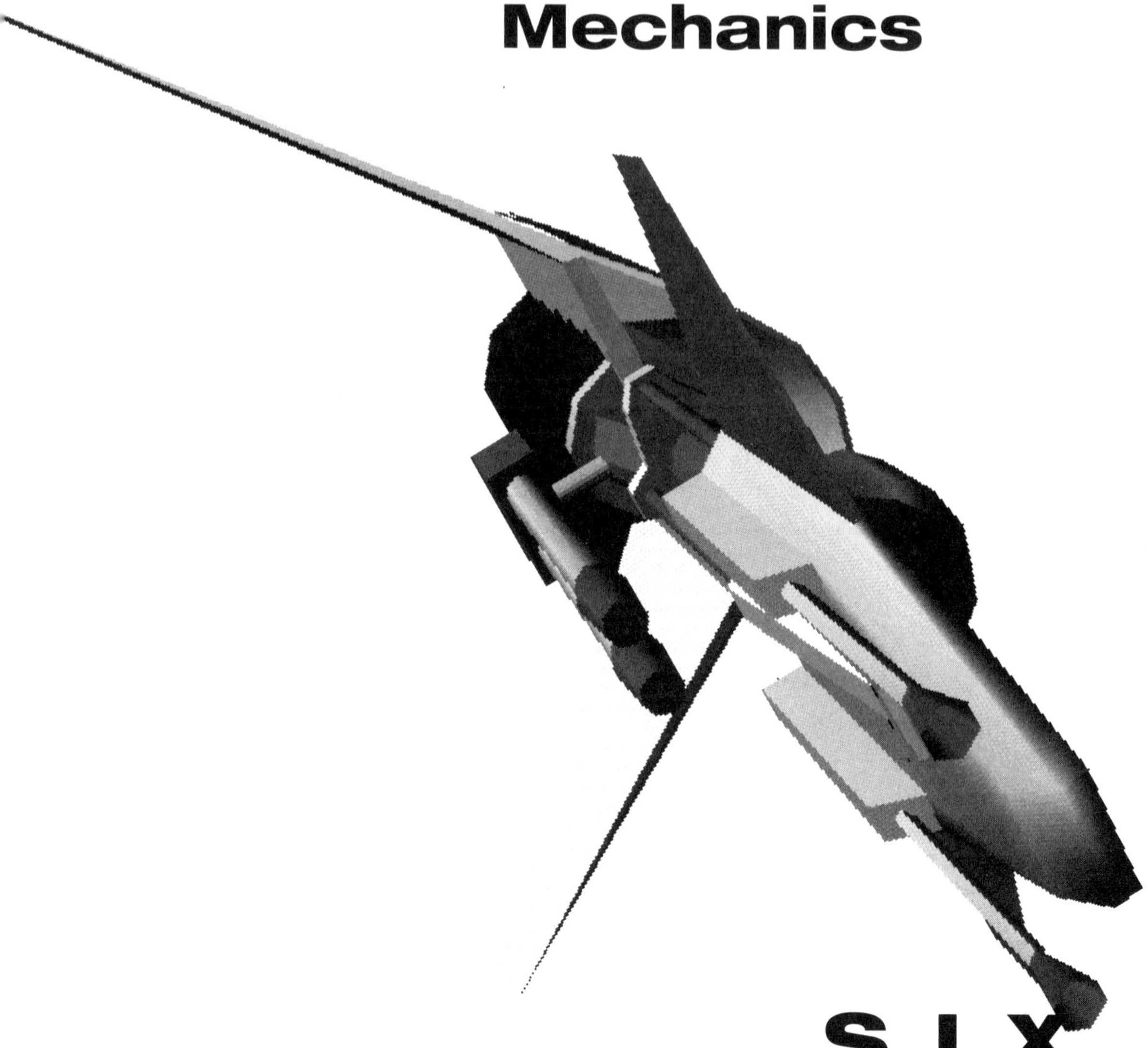

SIX

S I X

This chapter will introduce you to some of the theory behind orbital mechanics. In particular, you will be introduced to the geometry and equations of conic sections, and will learn that all orbits are either circular, elliptical, parabolic, or hyperbolic. Armed with this information, you'll be able to understand your orbits better and then tinker with them in interesting new ways.

THE USE OF VECTORS TO DESCRIBE MOTION

As you may recall from analytic geometry, vectors are used to describe motion and position in three-dimensional space. A vector is a quantity having both magnitude and direction, and can be broken into component parts for each direction. Examples are displacement in position, velocity, force, and acceleration. A bold letter or a letter with a bar above it is used to represent a vector quantity in this chapter.

Using an X-, Y-, and Z-axis Cartesian coordinate system, it is possible to resolve each vector direction in terms of X, Y, and Z directions. Thus, a position vector can be described in terms $\mathbf{R_x}$, $\mathbf{R_y}$, and $\mathbf{R_z}$, and a velocity vector can be described in terms of $\mathbf{V_x}$, $\mathbf{V_y}$, and $\mathbf{V_z}$. When you add two vectors such as $\mathbf{R_1}$ and $\mathbf{R_2}$, you really add only the components for each X, Y, and Z direction. Thus, $\mathbf{R_1} + \mathbf{R_2} = <\mathbf{R_{1x}},\mathbf{R_{1y}},\mathbf{R_{1z}}> + <\mathbf{R_{2x}},\mathbf{R_{2y}},\mathbf{R_{2z}}> = <\mathbf{R_{1x}} + \mathbf{R_{2x}}, \mathbf{R_{1y}} + \mathbf{R_{2y}}, \mathbf{R_{1z}} + \mathbf{R_{2z}}>$. When you multiply a scalar number by a vector, as in $5\mathbf{R_1}$, you multiply each component by the scalar. The vector $5\mathbf{R_1}$ is equivalent to $<5\mathbf{R_{1x}},5\mathbf{R_{1y}},5\mathbf{R_{1z}}>$.

There are other vector operations which are used in astrodynamics, in particular the dot product and the cross product. If you are unfamiliar with these operations, refer to Appendix A for a quick review.

KEPLER'S THREE LAWS

From the time of Ptolemy and Aristotle, astronomers believed that the heavenly bodies moved in perfect circles. The great astronomer Johann Kepler discovered in 1609 that planetary orbits were in fact ellipses. From this epochal discovery, Kepler was able to accurately describe and predict the motions of all the planets. Kepler's three laws of planetary motion are:

First Law: The orbit of each planet is an ellipse, with the sun as a focus (see Figure 6.1).

Second Law: The line joining the planet to the Sun sweeps out equal areas in equal times (see Figure 6.2).

Third Law: The square of the period of a planet is proportional to the cube of its mean distance from the Sun.

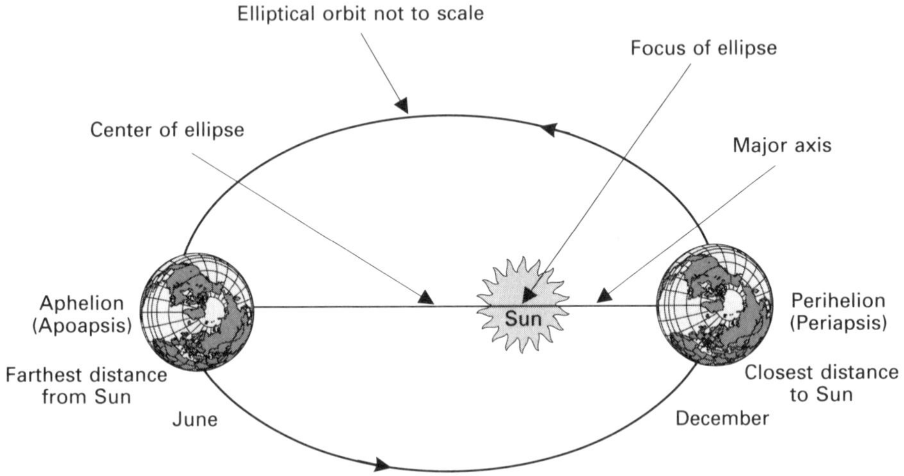

$R_{aphelion}=$ 152,000,000 km	$R_{perihelion}=$ 147,000,000 km
$a_{Semi\text{-}Major\ Axis}=$ 149,500,000 km	$a_{Semi\text{-}Major\ Axis}=$ 149,500,000 km

$$2a = R_{perihelion} + R_{aphelion} = 299{,}000{,}000 \text{ km}$$

FIGURE 6.1 *Kepler's First Law: The orbit of each planet is an ellipse*

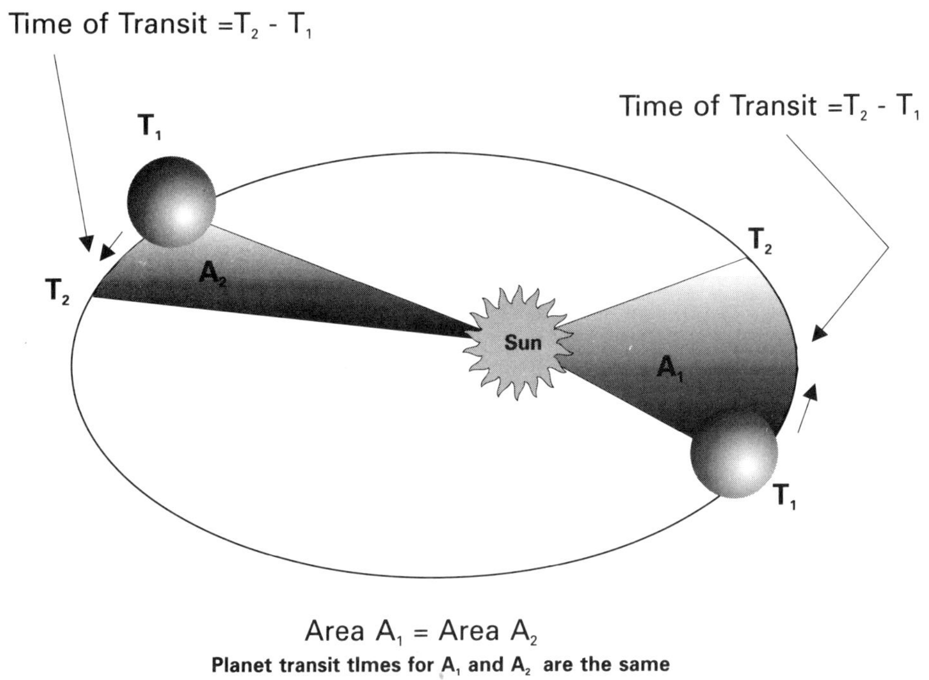

FIGURE 6.2 *Kepler's Law of Equal Areas for Equal Times*

Equation 6.1 shows how Kepler's Third Law works for planets orbiting the Sun. Note that the period, the time for a complete revolution around the Sun, is measured in seconds. To convert the seconds to days, you must divide by 3600 (seconds/hour), then divide the result by 24 (hours/day) to arrive at the number of days for the period.

EQUATION 6.1

$$(Period\ in\ Seconds)^2 \propto a^3$$

$$Period\ in\ Seconds = 2\pi\sqrt{\frac{a^3}{u}}$$

In Equation 6.1, a is the semi-major axis in km (approximately half the diameter of the orbit), and u is the gravitational parameter of the Sun ($u = 1.3272 \times 10^{11}$ km^3/sec^2). Using the Earth's period as an example, one complete revolution around the Sun is equal to 31,556,952 seconds, for the Earth's semi-major axis a = 149,596,781 km. This works out to 365.2422 days/year (31,556,952 × 3600 × 24 = 365.2422 days). To make a solar year fit into our 365-day calendar, the extra 0.2422 days per year mean that we need to add a leap day every 4 years on February 29. If we didn't do this, the Earth's rotation around the Sun would get progressively more out of step with our calendar. After 100 years the discrepancy would be 24 days; after 1500 years the seasons would be reversed so that summer in the northern hemisphere would be in December!

Understanding the Gravitational Parameter *u*

The *gravitational parameter u* is used to simplify many of the equations used in this text. The value of u is different for each star, planet, moon, or asteroid and is dependent on the mass of the body. The next equation shows how u is calculated for the Earth and the Sun. In the equation $u = GM$, G is the *universal gravitational constant* and it has a fixed value of 6.672×10^{-20} $km^3/(kg\ sec^2)$ no matter what object you are orbiting. The values of u for the planets of the solar system are listed in Appendix C.

EQUATION 6.2

$$u = G(M_{Sun/Planet/Moon/orAsteroid} + M_{spacecraft}); \quad but\ since\ M_{Sun/Planet/Moon/orAsteroid} >> M_{spacecraft}$$

$$u \cong GM_{Sun/Planet/Moon/orAsteroid}$$

where

$$G = 6.672 \times 10^{-20} \ \frac{km^3}{kg\ sec^2}$$

$$M_{Sun/Planet/Moon/orAsteroid} = Mass\ of\ Sun,\ Planet,\ Moon,\ or\ Asteroid\ that\ the\ spacecraft\ is\ orbiting$$

<u>*Example*</u>

$$u_{Earth} = GM_{Earth} = \left(6.672 \times 10^{-20} \ \frac{km^3}{kg\ sec^2}\right)\left(5.975 \times 10^{24}\ kg\right) = 3.986 \times 10^5 \ \frac{km^3}{sec^2}$$

$$u_{Sun} = GM_{Sun}\left(6.672 \times 10^{-20} \ \frac{km^3}{kg\ sec^2}\right)\left(1.99 \times 10^{30}\ kg\right) = 1.327 \times 10^{11} \ \frac{km^3}{sec^2}$$

Calculating the Period for Elliptical and Circular Orbits

Kepler's equation for the orbital period can be applied to satellites and spacecraft orbiting planets, such as the Earth. All you need to do is substitute the gravitational parameter *u* for the planet you are orbiting. For example, in the case of the Galactic Explorer orbiting the Earth, the semi-major axis *a* is 31,656 km, and the gravitational parameter *u* for the Earth is 3.986 $\times 10^5$ km^3/sec^2. Using our first equation, we find that the period P is equal to 56,052 seconds. Dividing 56,052 seconds by 3600 seconds/hour gives us the 15.57 hours(15h 34m) for the orbital period (your actual period will vary slightly due to internal Space Simulator errors). Note that regardless of whether an orbit is *circular or elliptical,* if it has *the same semi-major axis a,* the period is the same.

Another interesting use of this equation is to find the distance for synchronous orbits, such as *geosynchronous* orbits around the Earth or *aerosynchronous* orbits around Mars. These orbits, which keep your spacecraft above a fixed position over the planet, are very useful for telecommunications satellites or other relay satellites that need to cover the same area of the Earth from day to day. A spacecraft in an equatorial geosynchronous orbit orbits the Earth, like any other spacecraft, but its period is synchronized with the Earth's daily rotation. Thus, a spacecraft in this orbit appears to hover over a single location over the Earth at all times.

You can use Equation 6.1 to find synchronous orbit radii. For example, to find a geosynchronous orbit around the Earth, you need to know the number of seconds in one sidereal day, and then solve for *a*. The Earth rotates once on its axis every 23 hours 56 minutes in what is known as a sidereal day. Therefore, 23 hours $\times$ 3600 seconds/hour + 56 minutes $\times$ 60 seconds = 86,160 seconds. To find the radius distance your circular orbit needs to be, plug 86,160 seconds into the above equation and solve for *a*. For circular orbits, *a* turns out to be the distance *R* to the center of the planet. You will find that geosynchronous orbits need to be 42,162 km from the Earth.

To help you find synchronous orbits for the planets, there is a listing of the sidereal rotation times for each planet in Appendix C.

NEWTON'S THREE LAWS OF MOTION

In 1665, during an outbreak of plague which closed Cambridge University, student Isaac Newton formulated the basic laws of motion and the law of gravitation. The three laws of motion are summarized as follows:

First Law: Every body continues in its state of rest or of uniform motion in a straight line unless it is compelled to change that state by forces acting upon it.

Second Law: Acceleration is proportional to the force applied. ($\mathbf{F} =-m\mathbf{a}$)

Third Law: For every action there is an equal and opposite reaction. ($\mathbf{F}_{12} = -\mathbf{F}_{21}$)

NEWTON'S LAW OF UNIVERSAL GRAVITATION

Newton's discovery of the Law of Universal Gravitation was brought to the attention of the world by Edmund Halley, discoverer of Halley's comet. Halley was visiting Newton in 1685, and casually posed the question, "If the Sun pulled the planets with a force inversely proportional to the square of their distances, in what paths ought they to go?" To Halley's utter astonishment, Newton replied, "Why, in ellipses of course. I have already calculated it and have the proof among my papers somewhere." Newton was referring to a paper he had casually written some 20 years earlier and tossed away!

The law of universal gravitation can be expressed in vector notation as:

EQUATION 6.3

$$F = \frac{-Gm_1m_2}{R^2}\frac{\mathbf{R}}{R}$$

where F is the gravitational force of attraction between two masses m_1 and m_2, G is the *universal gravitation constant,* R is the distance between m_1 and m_2, and $\mathbf{R}/R$ is the unit vector of magnitude 1 that points from m_1 to m_2.

According to Newton's Second Law, **F** = m_2**a**, where **F** is the force vector, and **a** is the acceleration of the mass m_2. Equating this to the law of gravitation, we find:

EQUATION 6.4

$$F = m_2 a = \frac{-Gm_1 m_2}{R^2}$$

$$a = \frac{-Gm_1}{R^2}$$

This makes clear a very important fact: the acceleration of gravity is equal to $-Gm_1/R^2$ and is independent of the mass of m_2! This means that, in the absence of air resistance, if you drop a feather (m_2) and an iron ball (m_2) from a tower, as Galileo did in his famous experiment, they will both fall to the Earth (m_1) at the same time, since the mass of m_2 is irrelevant to the acceleration of gravity! Another important fact you can learn from Equation 6.4 is that the acceleration of gravity drops off with the inverse square of the distance.

Gravitational Sphere of Influence (SOI)

In the Earth-Moon system, the Earth's gravitational SOI extends out to 637,000 km in Space Simulator (in the real solar system it extends out to 900,000 km). If your spacecraft were farther than this distance from the Earth, you would no longer be attracted to the Earth, but instead would be under the SOI of the Sun. Then, if you came closer than 20,000 km to the Moon, your spacecraft would be under the Moon's SOI, and the Sun or the Earth would no longer exert as much influence. You can see this happen in Space Simulator by setting your Location with the Set Location command, then noting if your radial velocity starts increasing. If it doesn't you are outside the SOI of the planet, moon, or star in question.

Table 6.1 lists the SOI for each of the planets in the solar system. Note that Space Simulator uses its own values for planetary SOIs and not the real solar system values. Therefore, any calculations you make should make use of the second column of numbers, not the third column.

TABLE 6.1: *Radius of Gravitational Sphere of Influence*

Planet/Moon	R_{SOI} in Kilometers (Space Simulator)	R_{SOI} in Kilometers (Real Solar System)
Mercury	243,000	60,710
Venus	605,000	616,300
Earth	637,000	924,415
Earth's Moon	20,000	66,970
Mars	339,000	578,100
Jupiter	7,130,000	48,200,000
Saturn	6,200,000	56,270,000
Uranus	2,500,000	51,172,000
Neptune	86,600,000	86,640,000
Pluto	150,000	33,320,000

The R_{SOI} is governed by the following relationship in Equation 6.5:

EQUATION 6.5

$$R_{SOI} = R\left(\frac{m_2}{m_1}\right)^{0.4}$$

where R is the semi-major axis distance between the two masses.

Using the Earth-Sun system as an example,

EQUATION 6.6

Example

$$R_{SOI\ of\ Earth} = R_{semi-major\ axis}\left(\frac{m_{Earth}}{m_{Sun}}\right)^{0.4} = 1.4957\times10^{8}\ Km\left(\frac{5.979\times10^{24}\ kg}{1.991\times10^{30}\ kg}\right)^{0.4} = 924{,}415\ Km$$

THE TWO-BODY EQUATION OF MOTION AND CONIC SECTIONS

From Newton's Law of Gravitation, one can develop the two-body equation of motion that governs all orbits.

EQUATION 6.7

$$\ddot{\mathbf{R}} = \frac{-G(M_{Sun/Planet/Moon/orAsteroid} + M_{spacecraft})}{R^3}\mathbf{R}$$

$$\ddot{\mathbf{R}} + \frac{u}{R^3}\mathbf{R} = 0$$

where $\ddot{\mathbf{R}}$ *is the acceleration vector between the spacecraft and the star, planet, moon, or asteroid, and* $\mathbf{R}$ *is the position vector between them* (R^3 *is magnitude of* $\mathbf{R}$ *cubed*)

In the equation above, the constant u is the gravitational parameter for the star, planet, moon, or asteroid that forms the gravity well.

Constants of Motion

The constants of orbital motion include the specific mechanical energy E, and the angular momentum h. These two constants remain the same no matter where a spacecraft is in its orbit. Due to space limitations, we will not perform a derivation of the constants of motion from Equation 6.7. However, the proofs are simple, and can be found in many textbooks on astrodynamics.

Conservation of Specific Mechanical Energy

Simply stated, the specific mechanical energy of a spacecraft equals the sum of the spacecraft's total potential and kinetic energy. Potential energy refers to the energy that a spacecraft gains the farther away it is from the Earth. Kinetic energy refers to the spacecraft's velocity energy. Equation 6.8, which is sometimes called the *vis-viva energy equation*, summarizes the different relationships.

EQUATION 6.8

$$E_{Total\ Energy} = Kinetic\ Energy + Potential\ Energy$$

$$Potential\ Energy = \frac{-u\ m_{Spacecraft}}{R}$$

$$Kinetic\ Energy = \frac{m_{Spacecraft} V^2}{2}$$

$$E_{Total\ Energy} = \frac{m_{Spacecraft} V^2}{2} - \frac{u\ m_{Spacecraft}}{R}$$

Simplifying by dividing out $m_{spacecraft}$:

$$E = \frac{V^2}{2} - \frac{u}{R}$$

Notice that potential energy has a negative sign in front of it. When the spacecraft's distance *R* is at an infinite distance, potential energy will approach zero, but will still be negative. When *R* approaches the Earth's surface, the potential energy becomes even more negative, meaning that there is less gravitational potential energy than was the case when *R* was infinite.

Using Equation 6.8, if you plug in your velocity *V* and distance *R* relative to the star, planet, or moon your spacecraft is orbiting, you can figure out your specific mechanical energy constant *E*. Just make sure you use the correct gravitational parameter *u* for the star, planet, or moon your spacecraft is orbiting. For example, using the Galactic Explorer in the **Flight** situation, the specific mechanical energy will always be -6.295 km^2/sec^2 when $R = 31{,}696$ km, $V = 3.544$ km/sec and u for the Earth is 3.986×10^5.

From the sign of E, you then determine your orbit's shape! Since E is negative in the above example, this means that the Galactic Explorer's orbit is either an ellipse or a circle and will always be bound to the Earth. If E were 0, your orbit would be parabolic, and if E were positive, your orbit would be hyperbolic. In both these cases, your orbit would no longer be bound by the Earth, and you would escape from the Earth's gravity well.

TIP

You can always calculate your orbit's energy *E* from your velocity and distance readouts on the Instrument Panel. If you know whether your energy *E* is negative or positive, you can figure out your orbit shape!

Table 6.2 summarizes the different Energy-Orbit shape possibilities.

TABLE 6.2: *The Relationship Between Energy and Orbit Shape*

Energy E	Orbit Shape	Bound to Planet/Moon/Star
$E < 0$	Ellipse or Circle	Yes
$E = 0$	Parabola	No
$E > 0$	Hyperbola	No

Conservation of Angular Momentum Spacecraft motion in any orbit is always confined to a single plane that is fixed in space (except for low altidude orbits which are perturbed by the equatorial bulge of the Earth). The angular momentum defines both a vector direction and a magnitude that is constant for a particular orbit. The direction of the angular momentum vector **h** is always perpendicular to the plane of the orbit and can be calculated from the vector cross product of **R** and **V**. Figure 6.3 shows how the **R** and **V** vectors form the **h** vector.

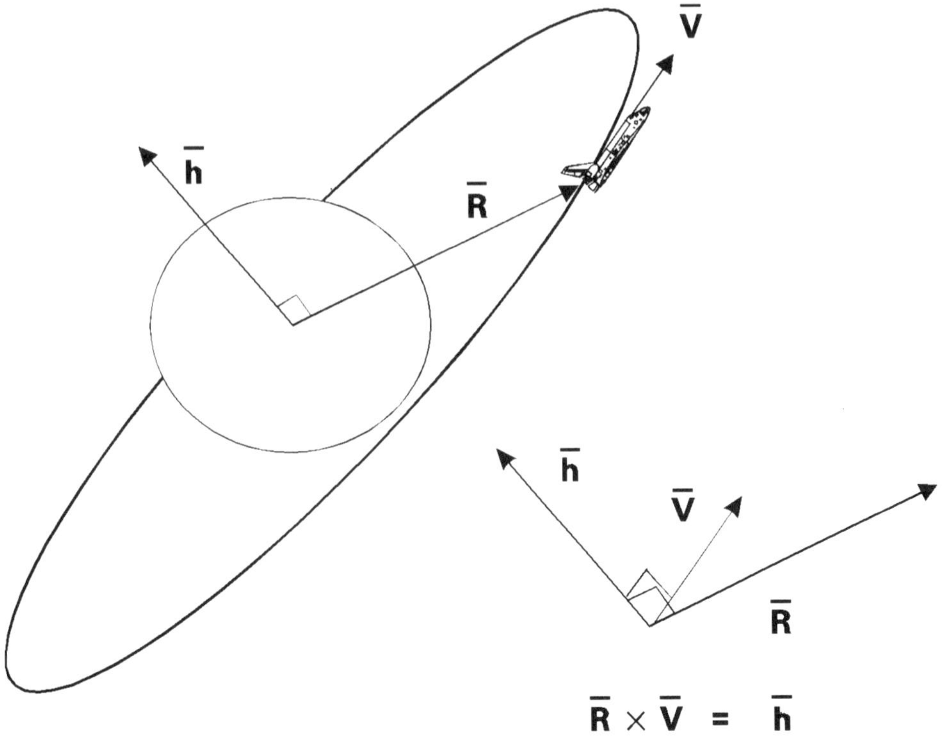

FIGURE 6.3 *Angular momentum vector*

Notice that in Equation 6.9, no matter where your spacecraft is in its orbit, **R** × **V** always equals **h** and that *h* is always the same! (Note that **R** × **V** is not a multiplication product, but a vector cross product.) This has important ramifications, as we shall see later in this chapter.

EQUATION 6.9

$$\mathbf{h} = \mathbf{R} \times \mathbf{V}$$

The Polar Equation of a Conic Section (Circle, Ellipse, Parabola, Hyperbola)

The family of curves called *conic sections* (circle, ellipse, parabola, hyperbola) represent the *only possible paths* for orbiting objects in the two-body equation of motion.

Through various manipulations of the two-body equation of motion, in Equation 6.7, it is possible to derive the polar equation of a conic section, shown in Equation 6.10. This equation describes any orbit in polar coordinates. To plot an orbit, you simply plug in the orbital constants of the eccentricity e, and the semi-latus rectum p, then vary the angle v around the conic section to find different distances R, as shown in Figure 6.4.

EQUATION 6.10

$$R = \frac{p}{1 + e\cos v}$$

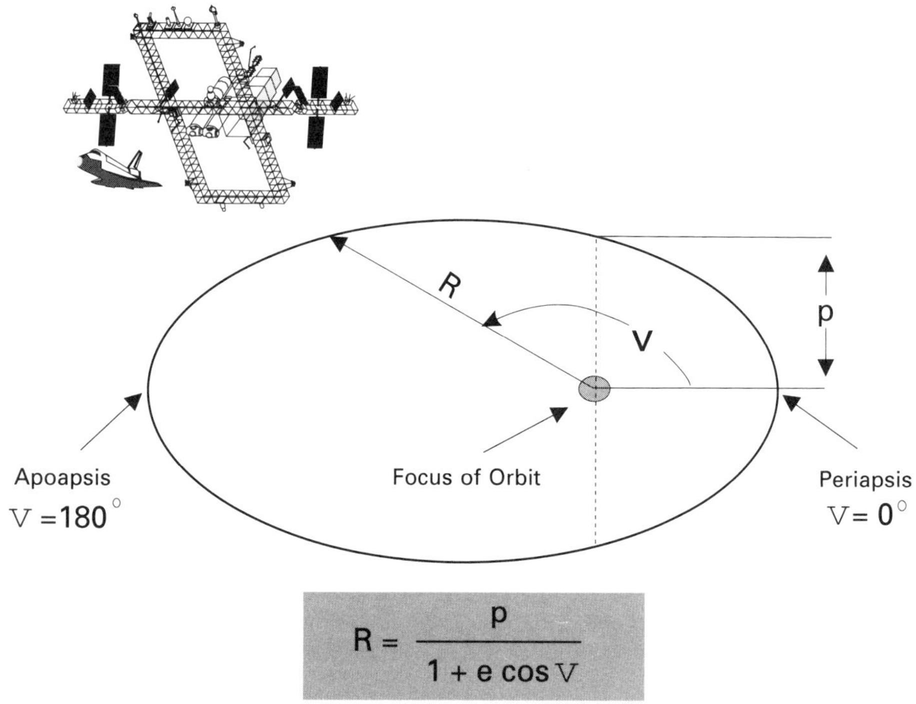

FIGURE 6.4 *Plotting orbits using the polar equation of a conic section*

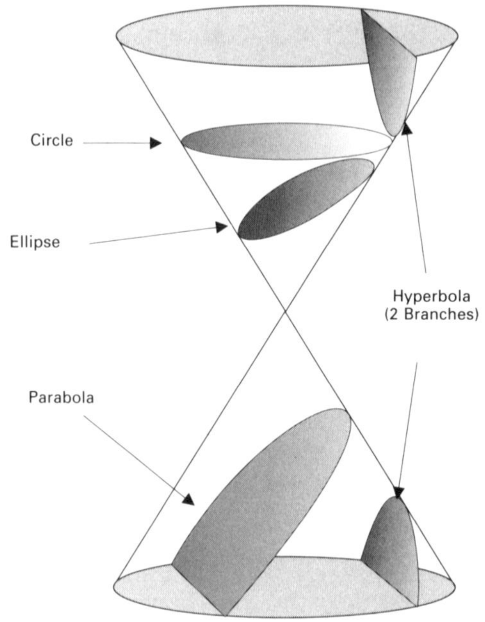

FIGURE 6.5 *The conic sections*

Geometric Properties of All Conic Sections

When a plane intersects a cone, the intersection with the cone creates a *conic section*. Figure 6.5 shows the circle, ellipse, parabola, and hyperbola intersections of various planes with a cone.

Radius If you know the true anomaly v, the eccentricity e and the semi-latus rectum p, you can calculate the radius R using the polar equation of a conic section (Equation 6.10). Of course, to find out what R is immediately, simply look at your Distance readout on the Instrument Panel.

Semi-major Axis *a* Referring to Figure 6.6, *a* is the semi-major axis, *b* is the semi-minor axis, and they are all related to *c* by the equation:

EQUATION 6.11

$$a^2 = b^2 + c^2$$

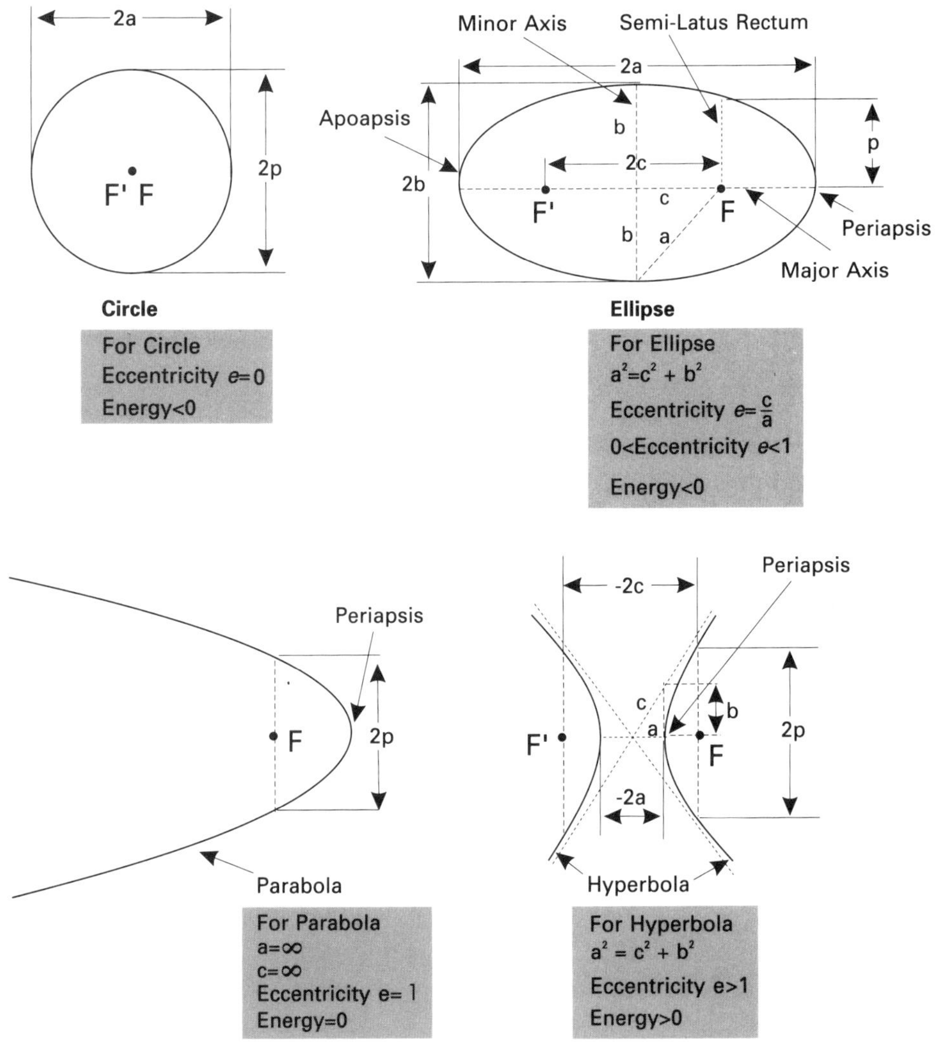

FIGURE 6.6 *Geometrical dimensions common to all conic sections*

The extreme end-points of the semi-major axis a are referred to as *apses*. The apses nearest the planet or sun focal point, is called *periapsis,* while the point farthest from the focal point is called *apoapsis* (see Figure 6.1). If the Earth is the primary focal point, then the terms *perigee* and *apogee* are used in place of apses. Other terms used are *perihelion* and *aphelion* for Sun-based orbits, and *periselenium* and *aposelenium* for Moon-based orbits.

When your spacecraft is at periapsis, it is as close as it will ever get to the star, planet, moon, or asteroid it is orbiting. When your spacecraft is at apoapsis, it is at the farthest distance in its orbit from the star, planet, moon, or asteroid it is orbiting.

To calculate the semi-major axis value a, use one of the following equations:

EQUATION 6.12

$$a = \frac{R_{apoapsis} + R_{periapsis}}{2}$$

$$a = \frac{-u}{2E}$$

For example, the Galactic Explorer in the **Flight** situation has a semi-major axis a = 31,656 km, when R_{apoapsis} = 31,724 km and $R_{\text{periapsis}}$ = 31,588 km.

Eccentricity *e* The eccentricity e determines the shape and type of conic section. Table 6.3 summarizes the relationship between e and orbit shape.

To calculate the eccentricity's value, use one of the following equations:

EQUATION 6.13

$$e = \frac{c}{a}$$

$$e = \sqrt{1 + \frac{2Eh^2}{u^2}} = \frac{R_{apoapsis} - R_{periapsis}}{R_{apoapsis} + R_{periapsis}}$$

TABLE 6.3: *The Relationship between Eccentricity e and Orbit Shape*

Eccentricity e	Orbit Shape	Bound to Planet/Moon/Star
$e = 0$	Circle	Yes
$0 < e < 1$	Ellipse	Yes
$e = 1$	Parabola	No
$e > 1$	Hyperbola	No

For example, when calculating the Galactic Explorer's eccentricity in the **Flight** situation, it was found that $e = 0.002$, when $R_{apoapsis} = 31{,}724$ km and $R_{periapsis} = 31{,}588$ km. This means that the orbit is very nearly circular, since e is close to zero. For comparison's sake, the Earth's orbit around the Sun has an eccentricity of .0167, which makes it eight times more elliptical than the Galactic Explorer's orbit.

Semi-Latus Rectum *p* The width of each curve, as shown in Figure 6.6, is known as the semi-latus rectum p. To find its value, use one of the equations below:

EQUATION 6.14

$$p = a(1 - e^2) = \frac{h^2}{u}$$

For example, in the **Flight** situation, the Galactic Explorer's semi-latus rectum $p = 31{,}656$ km, when $a = 31{,}656$ km, and $e = 0.002$.

True Anomaly *v* The true anomaly v is the angle measured from R to periapsis in the orbital plane. To find its value, use the equation below:

EQUATION 6.15

$$v = \cos^{-1}\left[\frac{1}{e}\left(\frac{p}{R} - 1\right)\right]$$

For example, in the **Flight** situation, the Galactic Explorer's true anomaly v when you first start is approximately 234°, when $R = 31{,}696$ km. Because of incorrect quadrant resolution, your calculator will show $v = 134°$. To correct for this, subtract 360° – 134° = 234°. The actual true anomaly is 242°, but this is close enough for Space Simulator's accuracy.

How to Find Periapsis/Apoapsis Distances

The two methods described below allow you to find periapsis and apoapsis for certain orbits. Note that circular orbits don't have a periapsis or apoapsis, since the distance to the planet is always the same. Also, there is no apoapsis for parabolic or hyperbolic orbits, since the trajectory is not bound to the planet and the spacecraft can travel to infinity.

To find periapsis while in any orbit, perform these steps:

1. Accelerate time to 1 minute/second or greater.
2. On your Instrument Panel, click the Velocity Indicator until you see the Radial Velocity displayed.
3. Watch the TOWARD flag. When it changes to AWAY you have reached periapsis. At this exact instant, your radial velocity will be zero.
4. Read the distance on your Distance readout. This is your $\mathrm{R}_{\mathrm{periapsis}}$.

If you use this method in the **Flight** situation, you will find that the Galactic Explorer's $R_{\mathrm{periapsis}} = 31{,}588$ km. Note that the above method will work for parabolic and hyperbolic orbits only if you are heading towards the planet.

To find apoapsis while in an elliptical orbit, repeat the steps above but watch as the AWAY flag changes to TOWARD. Read the distance on the distance display as before, but it will now be your R_{apoapsis} distance (your radial velocity will again be zero).

Using Equation 6.16, you can also calculate $R_{\mathrm{periapsis}}$ or R_{apoapsis} if you know p and e. Thus, using the Galactic Explorer in the **Flight** situation as an example, you can see that $R_{\mathrm{apoapsis}} = 31{,}719$ km, as is shown in Equation 6.16. Note that because the Galactic Explorer's orbit is very near circular ($e = 0.002$), the values of $R_{\mathrm{periapsis}}$ and R_{apoapsis} are only accurate to 3 significant digits, but for orbits with greater eccentricity, you'll get better accuracy.

EQUATION 6.16

$$R_{apoapsis} = R_{\max} = \frac{p}{1-e} = \frac{31{,}656}{1-0.002} = 31{,}719\ Km$$

$$R_{periapsis} = R_{\min} = \frac{p}{1+e} = \frac{31{,}656}{1+0.002} = 31{,}592\ Km$$

If you know the semi-major axis a and either the eccentricity e, or one of the values of $R_{periapsis}$ and $R_{apoapsis}$, you can figure out the periapsis or apoapsis using Equation 6.16a

EQUATION 6.16a

$$R_{apoapsis} + R_{periapsis} = 2a$$

$$R_{apoapsis} = R_{\max} = 2a - R_{periapsis} = a(1+e)$$

$$R_{periapsis} = R_{\min} = 2a - R_{apoapsis} = a(1-e)$$

Finding Your Orbit's Maximum and Minimum Velocity You can also figure out the maximum velocity in your orbit, which always occurs at periapsis, with the following equation:

EQUATION 6.17

$$V_{periapsis} = V_{\max} = \frac{h}{R_{periapsis}} = \frac{R_{apoapsis} V_{apoapsis}}{R_{periapsis}}$$

Your minimum velocity in your orbit always occurs at apoapsis and can be computed from the following equation:

EQUATION 6.18

$$V_{apoapsis} = V_{\min} = \frac{h}{R_{apoapsis}} = \frac{R_{periapsis} V_{periapsis}}{R_{apoapsis}}$$

Flight Path Angle ϕ

As stated earlier in this chapter, the angular momentum vector constant **h** is equal to the vector product **R** × **V** (vector products are not the same as multiplication), where **R** is the spacecraft's position vector and **V** is the spacecraft's total velocity vector. **h** is constant for each orbit and is always perpendicular to the plane that defines the **R** and **V** vectors; hence all orbits are confined to a single plane. The magnitude of **h** is given by the non-vector scalar constant h in Equation 6.19.

EQUATION 6.19

$$h = RV\sin(\Psi)$$

where ψ is the angle between the vectors **V** and **R**, as shown in Figure 6.7. To simplify matters, in place of using the angle ψ, the flight path angle ϕ (also called the elevation angle) is substituted. The flight path angle is measured from the local horizon to the velocity vector and is positive in a clockwise direction away from the planet's surface. The equivalent relationship to the previous equation is

EQUATION 6.20

$$h = RV\sin(90° - \phi)$$

$$h = RV\cos(\phi)$$

Figure 6.7 also illustrates the flight path angle ϕ and its relationship to the local horizon and velocity vector.

In general, the flight path angle ϕ can be calculated from the following equation:

EQUATION 6.21

$$\phi = \cos^{-1}\frac{h}{RV} = \tan^{-1}\frac{e\sin v}{1 + e\cos v}$$

where v is the true anomaly, and e is the eccentricity.

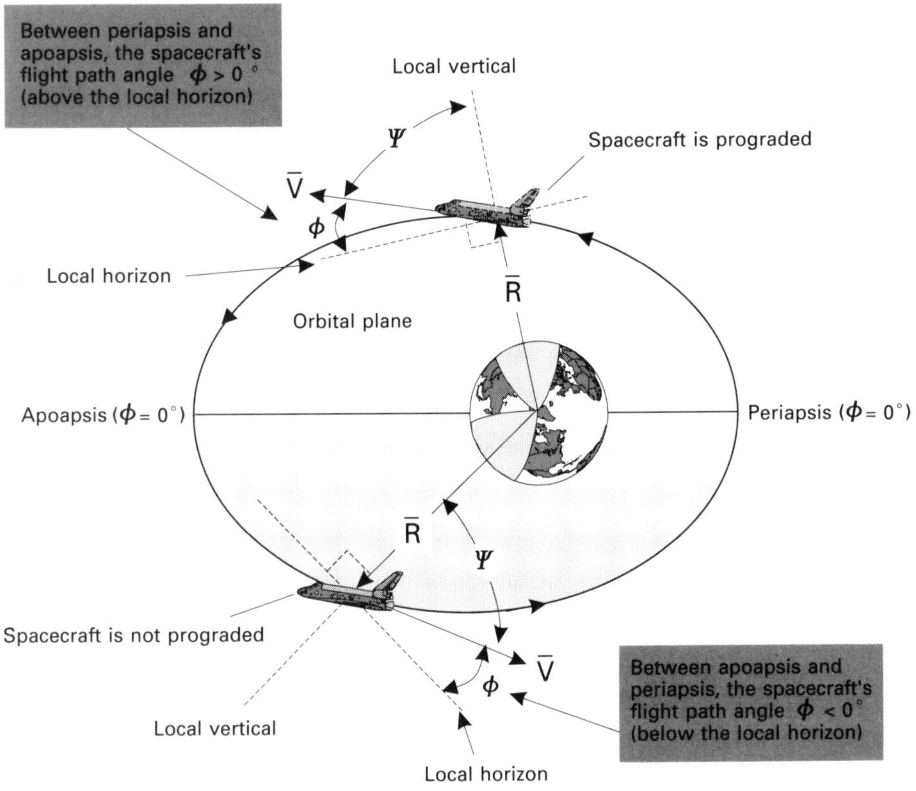

$$h = R\ V \cos \phi$$

FIGURE 6.7 *Flight path angle is measured in the orbital plane*

Predicting Future Orbital Velocities and Distances Using Equation 6.20, if you know R, V, and ϕ, you can calculate the value of h. Since h is a constant for each orbit, no matter where your spacecraft is in its orbit, once you know h, you can figure out the spacecraft's speed or distance to the planet if you know the flight path angle.

But how do you know what the value of the flight path angle is? For circular orbits, the flight path angle is always 0°, but for elliptical orbits, the angle changes at each point in your orbit. At the elliptical orbit's periapsis and apoapsis, however, the flight path angle is 0°. Thus, if you are in an elliptical orbit, and you want to figure out the value of *h*, wait until periapsis or apoapsis, then plug in the values of $R_{periapsis}$ and $V_{periapsis}$, and 0° for ϕ. The following equation summarizes this discussion for elliptical orbits.

EQUATION 6.22

$$h = R_{periapsis}V_{periapsis} = R_{apoapsis}V_{apoapsis}$$

For non-elliptical orbits, use Equation 6.21 to find the flight path angle.

> **TIP**
>
> **For elliptical orbits, the flight angle is always 0° at periapsis and apoapsis. For circular orbits, the flight angle is always 0° or very close to it. Hyperbolic and parabolic orbits have a flight angle of 0° only at periapsis.**

This is a very powerful tool you now have at your disposal. Knowing the value of *h*, you can now predict what your velocity and distance will be at periapsis and apoapsis! If $R_{periapsis}$ is less than the radius of the planet, then you'll know that the spacecraft will impact the planet's surface.

Computing the Flight Path Angle Using the Digital Attitude Display In order to figure out the magnitude of *h* it would help to know the flight path angle ϕ. Unfortunately, Space Simulator does not provide you with your computed flight path angle; you must figure it out yourself. At periapsis and apoapsis, there is no need to figure out the flight path angle since it always equals 0°. But when your spacecraft is flying elsewhere on its orbital trajectory, there is a method I have devised to figure out the flight angle. This method is similar to the procedure used to figure out your orbital inclination, and is summarized below:

1. Slow down time to .001 seconds/second so that your spacecraft's motion won't affect your measurements in this procedure.
2. Prograde your spacecraft using the Autopilot.

3. Select Chase view.
4. Press B to lock your Chase view to Absolute.
5. Pan the Chase View until you are looking from overhead down at the spacecraft with the planet centered in the middle of the screen.
6. Roll the spacecraft until the belly (where the docking hatch is) is facing towards the planet. Use only Keypad / and Keypad * to roll the spacecraft; don't touch any other controls, or you'll change the flight path angle!
7. Now you'll need to trim your pitch. As you roll the spacecraft, you'll be watching your pitch indicator on the Digital Attitude display. Roll the spacecraft clockwise or counterclockwise slightly to see how close you can get to 90°. When you've come as close as you can, write down the pitch reading.
8. Press S twice to switch back to cockpit view, and then make sure you've centered the panning bars.
9. Click the Direction button on the View 1 window until it displays Panning.
10. Press H to turn on the Head Up Display. Note whether the blue pitch ladders are upside down.
11. If the pitch ladder is right-side up, the flight path angle ϕ = pitch angle – 90° (e.g. ϕ is negative and below the local horizon). If the pitch ladder is upside down, the flight path angle $\phi = 90°$ – pitch angle (e.g. ϕ is *positive* and *above* the local horizon).

Using this method for the Galactic Explorer in the **Flight** situation, ϕ will be approximately -0.11°. Because of inaccuracies in Space Simulator, and because of the potential for error in the procedure outlined above, your calculated flight path angle will be imprecise. Due to the transcendental nature of the cosine function, the error can actually be amplified and your calculation of h will suffer accordingly.

Despite these shortcomings, it is very useful to be able to calculate h, even with only one or two digits accuracy, anywhere on your orbit's path.

Calculating Your Flight Path Angle from the Energy Equation You can also calculate your flight path angle using the energy equation and the conic equations. In order to use this method, you'll first have to find $R_{periapsis}$ in your orbit. After that, you can then find the flight path angle ϕ at any other position in your orbit. Follow these steps:

1. Find the distance $R_{periapsis}$ by accelerating time until the spacecraft makes its closest approach to the planet. When the Radial Velocity Readout displays 0 m/sec, and the TOWARD flag switches to AWAY, you'll know you are at $R_{periapsis}$. Write down the distance shown in the Distance readout (but not Altitude or Radius).
2. Write down the total velocity $V_{periapsis}$ at the moment of closest approach.
3. Solve for energy E in Equation 6.8 using $R_{periapsis}$ and $V_{periapsis}$ from Step 1 and 2 above. Be sure to use the proper value of u for the planet, moon or star you are orbiting.
4. Solve for the semi-major axis a in Equation 6.12 using E from Step 3.
5. Solve for $R_{apoapsis}$ using Equation 6.16a, plugging in the known values of a and $R_{periapsis}$ calculated previously.
6. Solve for the eccentricity e by using Equation 6.13 and the values of $R_{apoapsis}$ and $R_{periapsis}$
7. Solve for the semi-latus rectum p in Equation 6.14, using a and e that you have just calculated.
8. Now allow your spacecraft to coast to the position along its orbit where you want to measure the flight path angle. Don't use your thrusters, since this adds energy to your orbit. Also, don't advance time more than 1 minute/second or so, because this will affect accuracy. Write down the new distance R.
9. Solve for the true anomaly angle v in Equation 6.15, plugging in R from Step 8, and e, and p that you previously calculated.
10. Solve for ϕ in Equation 6.21, using e and the true anomaly angle v.

For best results, make sure precision is set to maximum, and don't accelerate time too much.

If you apply the energy equation method just described to the Galactic Explorer in the **Flight** situation, you should get the following results:

$E =$	-6.295 km^2/sec^2
$a =$	31,656 km
$e =$	0.0021
$p =$	31,656 km
$\nu =$	125°; 360°–125° = 235°
$\phi =$	±0.1°

Although the flight path angle ϕ may differ slightly with the result of the previous method, you are still getting a pretty good degree of accuracy.

Coordinate Systems, Time, and the Orbital Elements

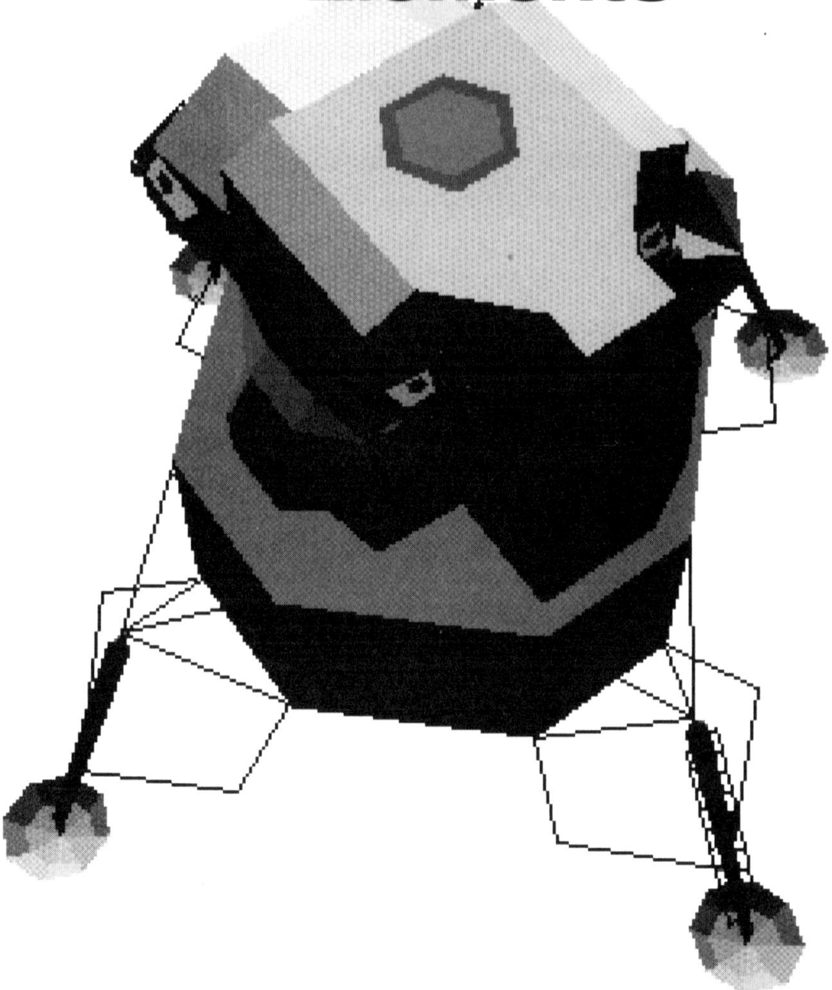

SEVEN

SEVEN

This chapter covers the topics of coordinate systems, the concept of time, and the classical orbital elements. You'll learn how to easily determine your orbital angle of inclination and how the orbital elements describe your orbit. If you are sufficiently interested, Appendix D shows you a way to precisely calculate your spacecraft's position and velocity vectors while in Earth orbit. Using this vector information, you can figure out all the orbital elements for your spacecraft and gain new insight and understanding about navigating in space.

COORDINATE SYSTEMS

In order to describe orbits, and figure out your spacecraft's position in space, you will need to understand the different coordinate systems. For orbits around the Sun, such as planets, asteroids, comets, and interplanetary spacecraft describe, the Heliocentric-Ecliptic coordinate system is convenient. For spacecraft orbiting the Earth, the Geocentric-Equatorial system is used. Astronomers use the Right Ascension-Declination system to plot objects on the celestial sphere surrounding the Earth. On Earth, the Topocentric-Horizon system is used to plot the position of objects from the local surface horizon, and this is very useful for aiming your telescope at a distant star or planet. For terrestrial navigation on the surface of the Earth, the latitude/longitude coordinate system is used.

Let's start by defining how the latitude/longitude coordinate system works. Then we'll proceed on to each of the other coordinate systems.

Latitude/Longitude Coordinates

The principal means of determining your position on the spherical Earth is to use the latitude/longitude coordinate system. This system is the foundation for all terrestrial-based navigational systems, including the aeronautical VOR/NDB stations, Loran C, Omega, Global Positioning Satellite System (called GPS), and celestial navigation.

Lines of longitude, also known as meridians, run north and south, connecting the North Pole and the South Pole. They are numbered in angular degrees from 0° to 180° east and west of the Prime Meridian, which runs through Greenwich, England.

Lines of latitude, also called parallels, run east and west, parallel to each other. They, too, are numbered in angular degrees from 0° to 90° north and south of the equator. Figure 7.1 shows the lines of latitude and longitude on the Earth.

The other planets of the solar system have also been mapped with latitude/longitude coordinate systems.

Heliocentric-Ecliptic Coordinate System

The Heliocentric-Ecliptic coordinate system is sketched in Figure 7.2. As the name implies, the Sun is the origin of this system, where the X-, Y-, and Z-axes intersect. The fundamental plane that is described by the X- and Y-axes, is the *plane of the ecliptic*, and this plane contains the heliocentric orbit of the Earth. The positive X-axis points in the direction of the vernal equinox, which occurs on the first day of Spring, March 21, when the Sun is directly along the line which connects the negative X-axis to the Earth's equator. Whenever the Earth crosses the path of the X-axis, the Sun is crossing the Equator.

The Earth is tilted 23° 27′ to the plane of the ecliptic. Thus the *equatorial plane*, which describes the plane that intersects the Earth's equator and is parallel to it, is also at an angle of 23° 27′ to the plane of the ecliptic. This gives rise to the phenomena of the seasons. When the Earth crosses the path of the positive Y-axis, it is winter in the northern hemisphere, and summer in the southern hemisphere. When crossing the negative Y-axis, the Earth experiences summer in the northern hemisphere, and winter in the southern hemisphere. The Y-axis is perpendicular to the X-axis, and the Z-axis is perpendicular to the plane of the ecliptic, as well as the X- and Y-axes.

At one time, the vernal equinox pointed towards the constellation Aries (the Ram). But since the Earth wobbles slightly, its axis of rotation has

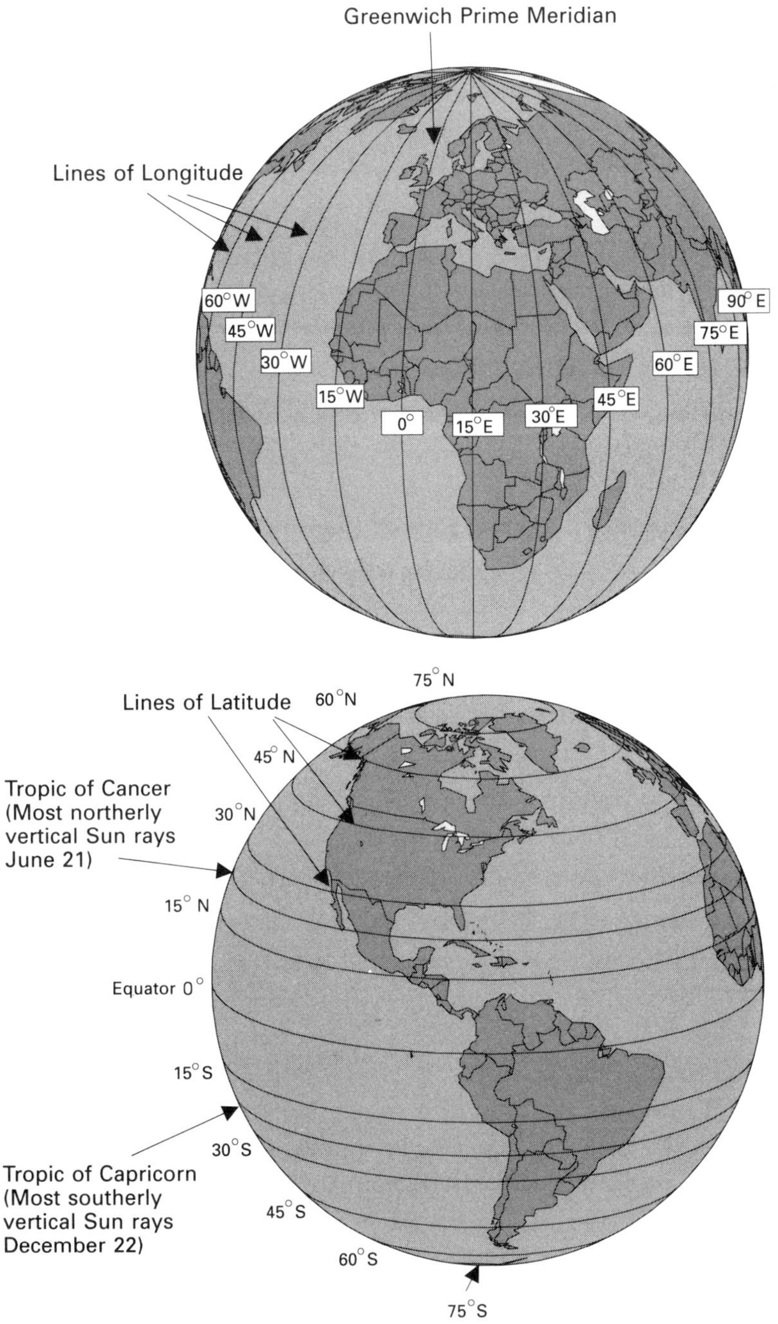

FIGURE 7.1 *Lines of longitude and latitude*

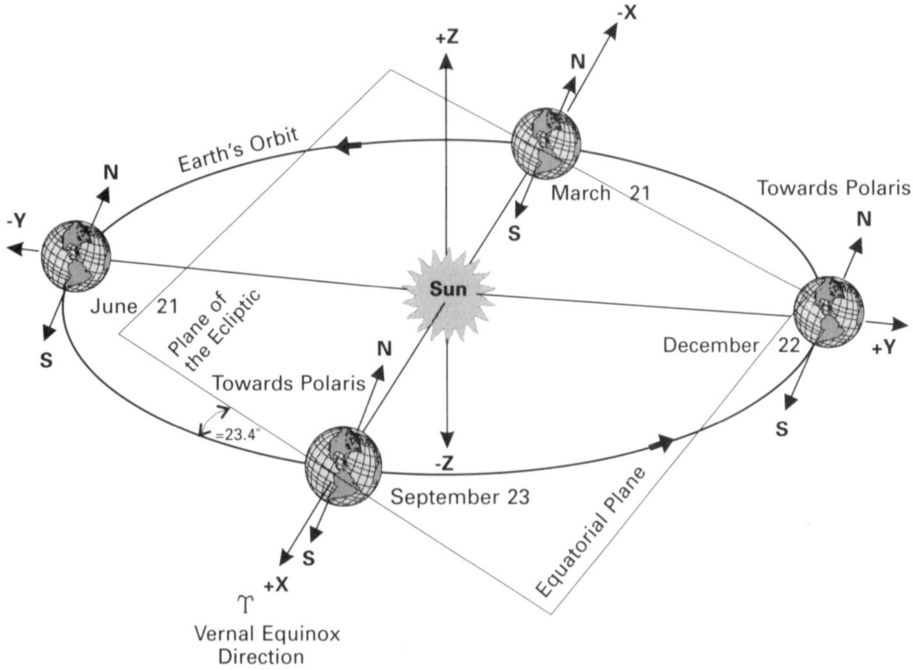

FIGURE 7.2 *Heliocentric-Ecliptic coordinate system*

shifted over the centuries. This causes the intersection of the plane of the ecliptic and the equatorial plane to move westward, in what is known as *precession* and *nutation*. This affects the Greenwich Hour Angle (GHA—the angle between Greenwich Prime Meridian and the vernal equinox), which must be recalculated yearly to adjust for this error.

Selecting a Heliocentric Map View Press the O key to bring up the Select Map Origin Object dialog box. Then click the Stars radio button, and select *Our Sun*. Click OK to return to the simulation, and then press M to bring up the map.

Map Views Space Simulator gives you three heliocentric views to choose from in Map view—Top, Front, or Side—which you select by clicking the View button in the map window. In each of the heliocentric map views, the position of the map viewer remains fixed in space in relation to the vernal equinox coordinate system. Space Simulator models the 25.38 day rotation of the Sun, and if you land your spacecraft on the Sun, it will revolve around the Sun at this rate.

Top The line of intersection of the ecliptic plane and the Earth's equatorial plane defines the X-axis of the vernal equinox, which occurs on March 21, the first day of Spring. If you were to draw a line from the Earth's center to the Sun's center on this date, the line would point towards the vernal equinox (note that the earth is on the negative portion of the X-axis on this date). On the autumnal equinox (September 23), the Earth again crosses this same equinox line, but this time it is on the positive portion of the X-axis.

The vernal equinox, or positive X-axis, points directly downward in the Top Map view, as is illustrated in Figure 7.3. The positive Z-axis points directly outward from the center of the screen towards you, while the positive Y-axis points right.

Front The vernal equinox, or positive X-axis points directly inward from the center of the map window, as is illustrated in Figure 7.4. The positive Y-axis points left, while the positive Z-axis points directly upward from the center of the screen.

Side The vernal equinox, or positive X-axis points directly to the right side of the map edge from the center of the Map window. The positive Y-axis points directly inward from the center of the map window, as is pictured in Figure 7.5, while the positive Z-axis points directly upward.

Geocentric (Earth or Any Other Planet)

The Earth is the center of intersection for the X-, Y-, and Z-axes of the Geocentric-Equatorial coordinate system shown in Figure 7.6. The fundamental plane is the equator, and the positive X-axis points in the vernal equinox direction. The Z-axis points in the direction of the North Pole. Note that this coordinate system does not rotate with the Earth. It is fixed with respect to the stars. For the purposes of measuring vector positions and velocities, the unit vectors **I**, **J**, and **K** are used to designate the X-, Y-, and Z-axes.

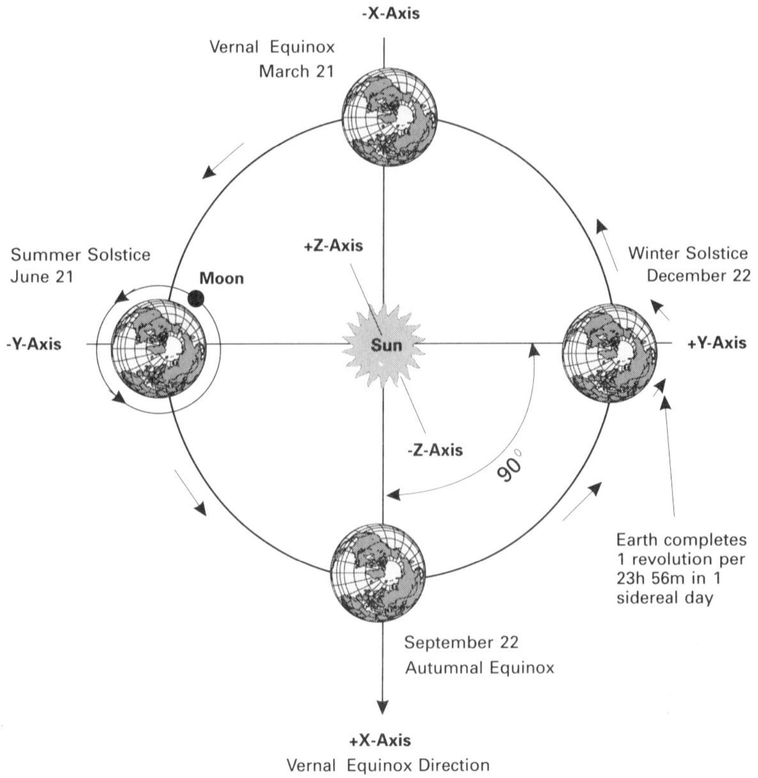

FIGURE 7.3 *Heliocentric Top Map view*

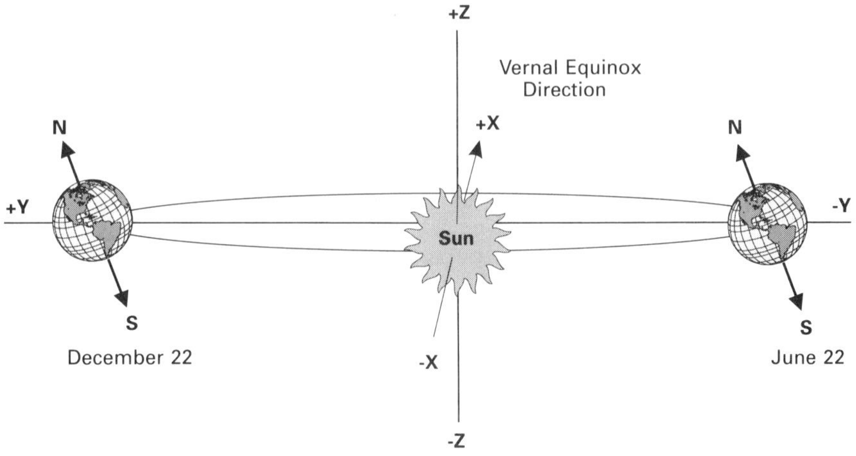

FIGURE 7.4 *Heliocentric Front Map view*

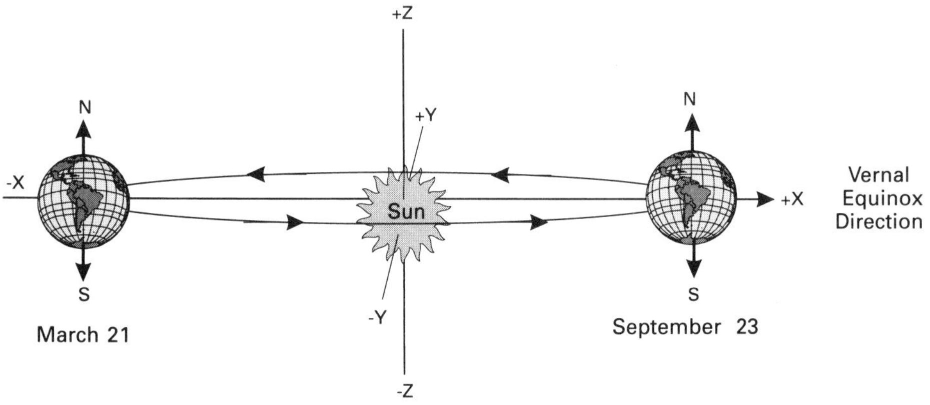

FIGURE 7.5 *Heliocentric Side Map view*

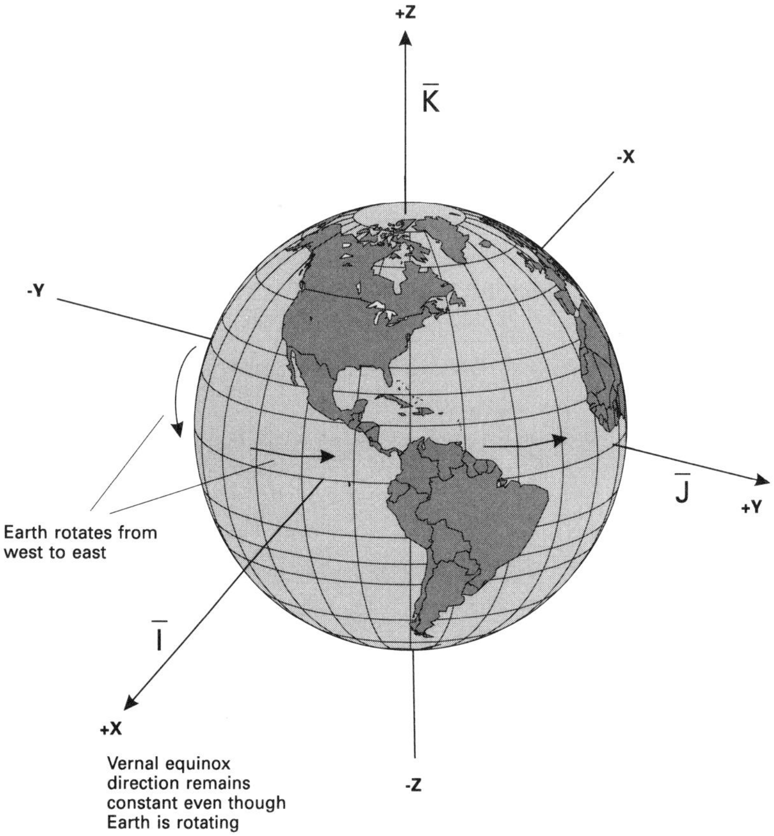

FIGURE 7.6 *The Geocentric-Equatorial coordinate system*

Selecting a Geocentric or Planetocentric Map View Press the O key to bring up the Select Map Origin Object dialog box. Then click the Planet button, and select the Earth or another planet you want to center on. Click the OK button to return to the simulation, then press M to open the Map window.

Map Views There are three Geocentric Map views: Top, Side, and Front, which you select by clicking the View button in the Map window. In each of the Geocentric Map views, the position of the map viewer remains fixed in space, in relation to the earth's geocentric vernal equinox coordinate system. The earth itself is rotating, even though you, as the map observer fixed in space, are not. You can easily verify for yourself that the Earth is rotating in the Map view by landing your spacecraft on the Earth and watching it rotate around on the surface.

Top The vernal equinox, or positive X-axis, points directly downward from the center of the map, as shown in Figure 7.7. The positive Y-axis points left, and the positive Z-axis points out of the center of the Map view window toward you.

Front The vernal equinox, or positive X-axis points directly into the Map window from the center, as shown in Figure 7.8. The positive Z-axis points upward, and the positive Y-axis points left.

Side The vernal equinox, or positive X-axis, points left. Figure 7.9 shows that the positive Y-axis points into the center of the Map view window, while the positive Z-axis points directly upward.

Viewing Epicycles from Earth If you have selected the Earth or another planet in the solar system as your map origin, you will notice that some of the planets move in odd patterns. You can best view these peculiar motions in the Top Map view window. For example, when you watch Mars, it will appear from the Earth to move in one direction, then abruptly change and move in the opposite direction, completing a small "epicyclical" circle before resuming its path around the Earth.

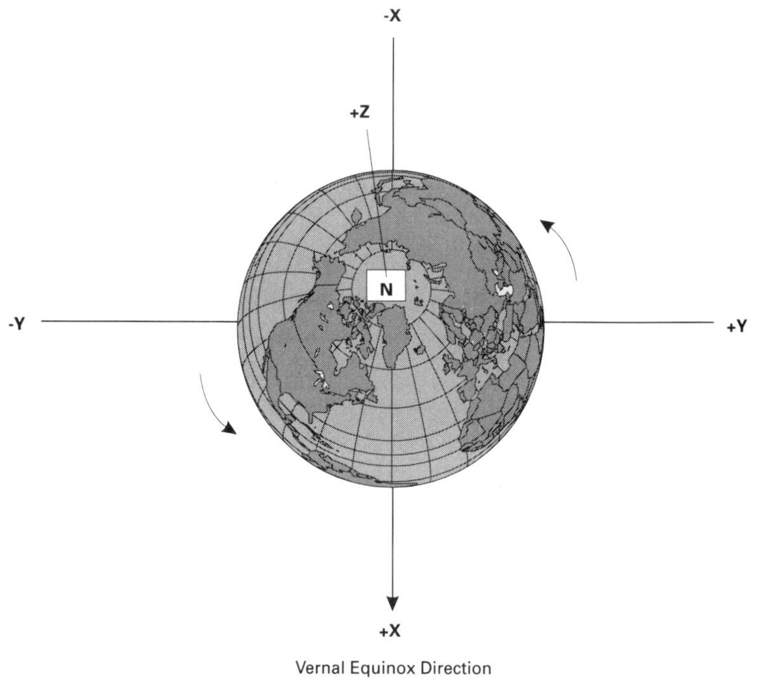

FIGURE 7.7 *Geocentric Top Map view*

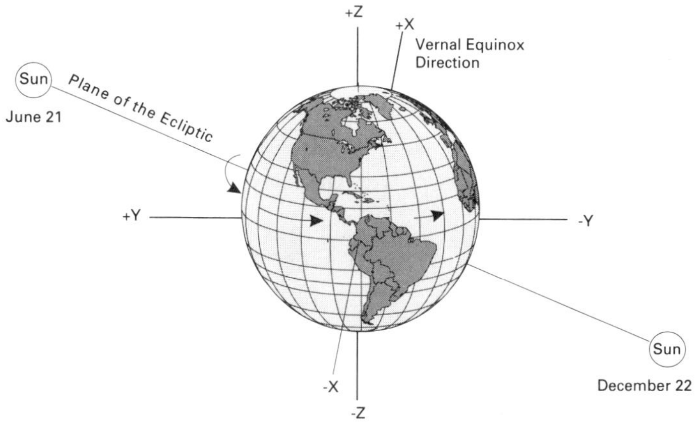

FIGURE 7.8 *Geocentric Front Map view*

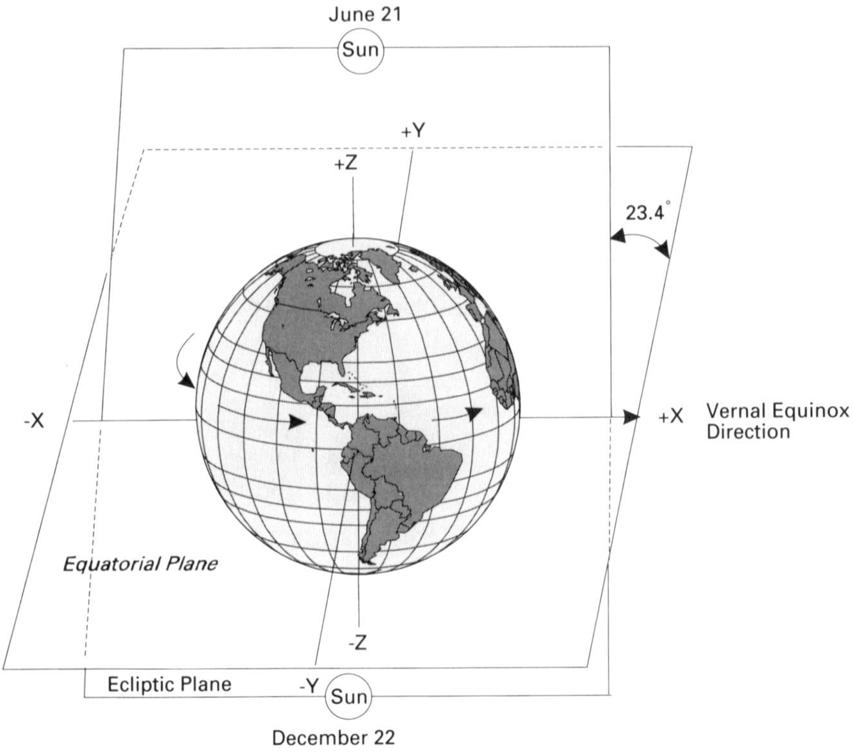

FIGURE 7.9 *Geocentric Side Map view*

Many of the other planets also experience this apparent "retrograde" motion, as viewed from the Earth.

This movement baffled early astronomers for centuries, as it defied the dogma of the time that the planets must move in "perfect" circles, because of heaven being a perfect celestial sphere. Tycho Brahe and other astronomers made many careful and accurate observations of this retrograde motion, but could not come up with an acceptable geocentric theory of the cosmos. It was left to Copernicus and Galileo to conjecture that the Earth was not, in fact, the center of the Universe, but was one of many planets orbiting the Sun. For this "crime" of contradicting church dogma of the time, Galileo was put under house arrest and forced to recant his views.

Once the geocentric theory of orbital motion was discarded, it was easy to explain the epicyclical retrograde motion of the planets as seen from Earth. The Earth travels around the Sun in the same direction as the other planets and in nearly the same plane, but it has a higher orbital speed than the outer planets. As a result, it periodically overtakes an outer planet, like a faster race car on the inside track. But as the Earth passes the outer planet, the slower orbital velocity of the outer planet causes it to appear to move backward away from the Earth, somewhat like when you pass a car on the highway. When the Earth swings back around its orbit, the outer planet will again appear to move forward as the Earth again overtakes it.

You can view these epicycles:

1. Press the O key to open the Select Map Origin Object dialog box.
2. Select the Earth as your Map Origin, and click the OK button.
3. Click the M key to open the map.
4. Click the View button until it displays Top view.
5. Zoom in or out, using the – or + keys as needed so that you can see Saturn, Jupiter, Venus, Mars, Mercury, and the Sun.
6. Accelerate time to 48 days/second.
7. As the planets rotate around the Earth in the Top Map view, they perform little *epicycles,* where they go into retrograde motion before resuming their normal counterclockwise prograde motion.

Topocentric

The Topocentric-Horizon coordinate system uses the Earth's surface as its basis. The fundamental plane is the horizon, and the positive X-axis points south. The positive Y-axis is east, and the positive Z-axis is up. To express an object's position in the sky in the Topocentric system, all you need are the range in km and the elevation and azimuth angles to the object. Azimuth (Az) is measured clockwise from the north along the X-axis, while elevation (El) is measured from the horizontal horizon to the line of sight. Figure 7.10 illustrates the Topocentric-Horizon Coordinate System.

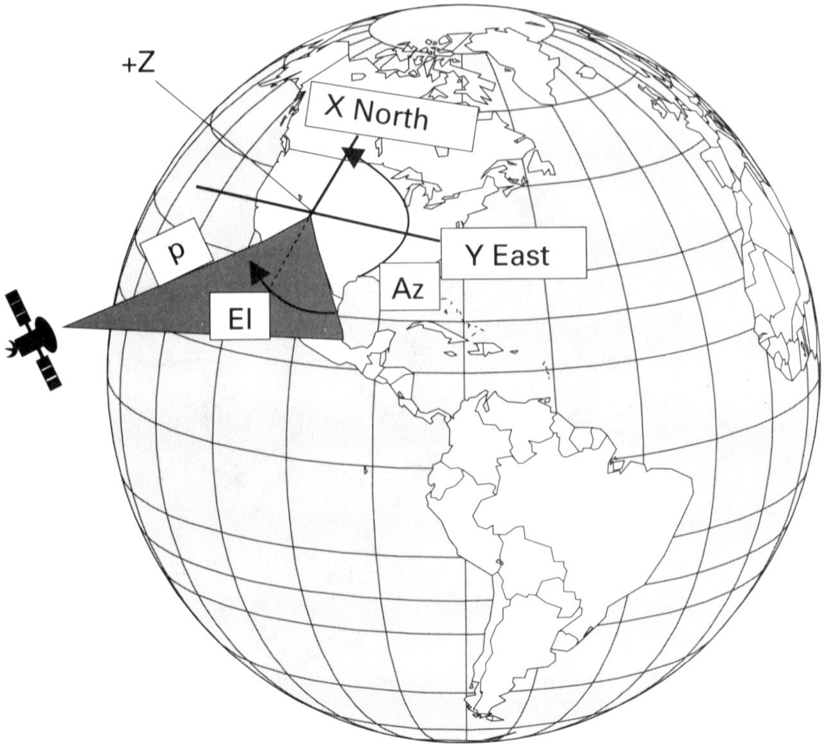

FIGURE 7.10 *The Topocentric coordinate system*

Right Ascension-Declination

This coordinate system is used by astronomers to chart the positions of all celestial objects. It is based on the Earth's sphere, using the Earth's equatorial plane and the vernal equinox as a frame of reference. As shown in Figure 7.11, the right ascension angle α is measured eastward along the equator from the vernal equinox, and it ranges from 0 to 24 hours (or equivalently 0° to 360°). The declination angle δ is measured up or down from the equator to the line of sight of the object. Declination is positive when measured northward or is negative when measured southward. Note that the Right Ascension-Declination coordinate system is an inertial frame that is fixed in space; distant stars will more or less have the same coordinates no matter what the date or time is on Earth.

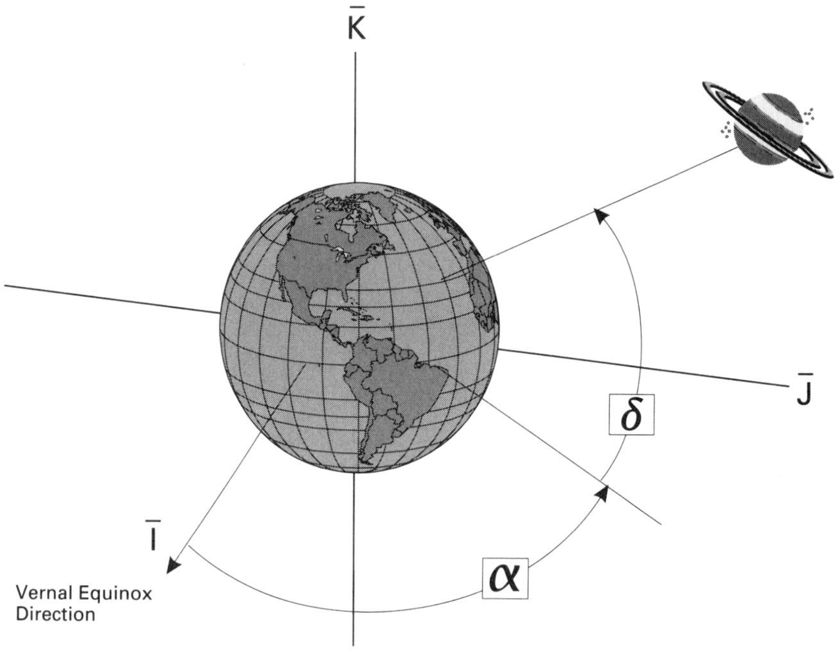

FIGURE 7.11 *The Right Ascension-Declination coordinate system*

CLASSICAL (KEPLERIAN) ORBITAL ELEMENTS

In order to quantify and describe any orbit, six classical orbital elements, also called Keplerian elements, have been defined. They are illustrated in Figure 7.12 and are described below:

1. *Semi-major axis a*—a constant defining the size of the conic orbit.
2. *Eccentricity e*—a constant defining the shape of the conic orbit.
3. *Inclination i*—the angle between the **K** unit vector (or Z-axis) and the angular momentum vector **h**. *i* always falls between 0° and 180°. Direct orbits are 0°–90°, retrograde orbits are 91°–180°.
4. *Longitude of the ascending node* Ω—the angle measured counterclockwise in the fundamental plane (equatorial or ecliptic), between the **I** unit vector (or X-axis) and the point where the spacecraft crosses the fundamental plane from south to north.

5 *Argument of periapsis* ω—the angle in the plane of the spacecraft's orbit between the ascending node and periapsis.

6 *True anomaly at epoch* ν_0—the angle in the plane of the spacecraft's orbit between periapsis and the spacecraft's current position.

Note that though Figure 7.12 shows the Geocentric Coordinate system, you can use the six classical elements to describe heliocentric orbits and orbits around other planets. However, you must use the fundamental plane and coordinate axes of the Heliocentric or other Planetocentric Coordinate system to measure a, e, i, ω, Ω. Thus if you are describing an orbit around the Sun, and you are measuring i and Ω, Ω should be measured in the plane of the ecliptic, and i should be measured between **h** and the **K** unit vector, which is now perpendicular to the plane of the ecliptic.

How do you calculate what a, e, i, ω, Ω are? If you know your **R** position and your **V** velocity vector components, then you can easily figure out all six of the classical elements! But how do you find **R** and **V**? Unfortunately, Space Simulator does not provide this data, but there is a clever method, described in Appendix D, that allows you to find the two vectors.

The next section shows you how to compute the six elements, assuming you know **R** and **V**.

Solving for the Orbital Elements

Before you can solve for the orbital elements, you'll need to form the three vectors **h**, **n**, and **e**. The vector **h** is formed by taking the cross product of **R** and **V** as the equation below shows:

EQUATION 7.1

$$\mathbf{h} = \mathbf{R} \times \mathbf{V} = \begin{vmatrix} \mathbf{I} & \mathbf{J} & \mathbf{K} \\ \mathbf{R_x} & \mathbf{R_y} & \mathbf{R_z} \\ \mathbf{V_x} & \mathbf{V_y} & \mathbf{V_z} \end{vmatrix} = (R_yV_z - R_zV_y)\mathbf{h}_x - (R_xV_z - R_zV_x)\mathbf{h_y} + (R_xV_y - R_yV_x)\mathbf{h_z}$$

It is important to remember that **h** is *always perpendicular* to the plane of the spacecraft's orbit.

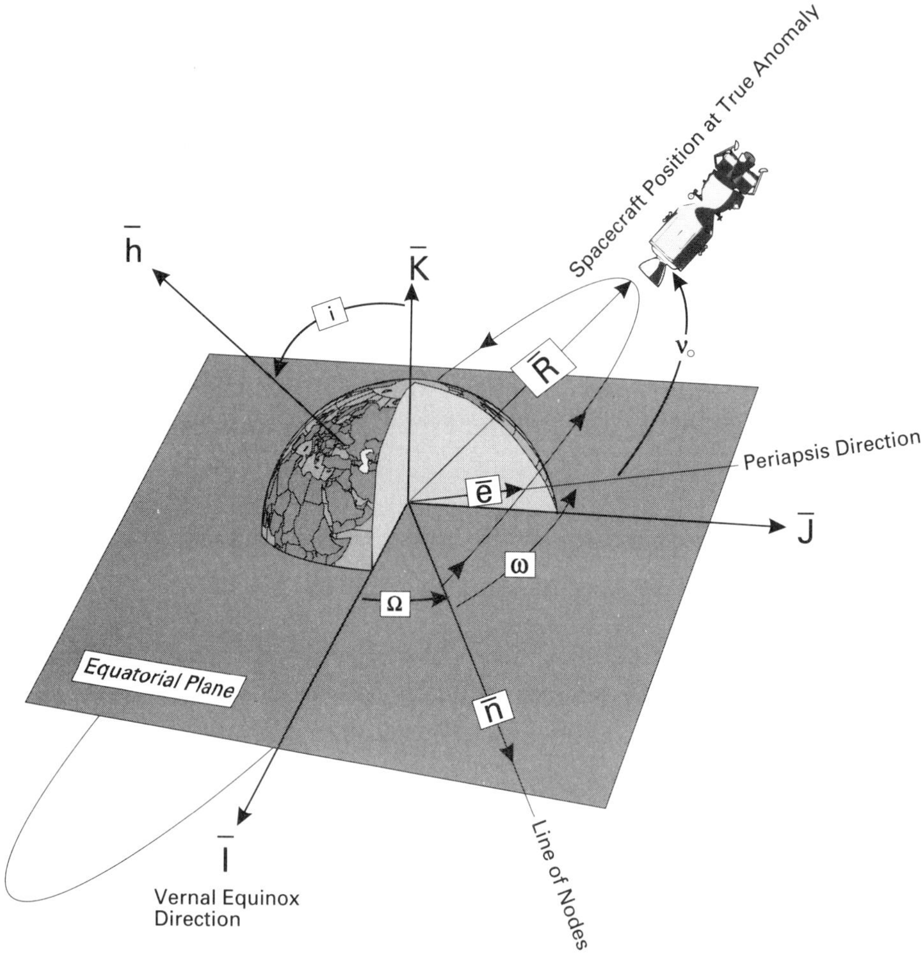

FIGURE 7.12 *The six classical orbital elements*

The node vector **n** is defined as follows:

EQUATION 7.2

$$\mathbf{n} = \mathbf{K} \times \mathbf{h} = \begin{vmatrix} \mathbf{I} & \mathbf{J} & \mathbf{K} \\ \mathbf{0} & \mathbf{0} & \mathbf{1} \\ \mathbf{h_x} & \mathbf{h_y} & \mathbf{h_z} \end{vmatrix} = (-h_y)\mathbf{n}_x + (h_x)\mathbf{n}_y + (0)\mathbf{n_z}$$

Notice that the $\mathbf{n_z}$ vector component is always zero. The **n** vector always points toward the direction of the ascending node.

The last vector **e** is the eccentricity vector, whose magnitude is equal to the eccentricity *e***.** This vector always points toward periapsis.

EQUATION 7.3

$$\mathbf{e} = \frac{1}{u}\left[\left(V^2 - \frac{u}{R}\right)\mathbf{R} - (\mathbf{R} \bullet \mathbf{V})\mathbf{V}\right]$$

where u = 398,600 km^3/sec^2 for geocentric orbits around the Earth, and $u = 1.327 \times 10^{11}$ km^3/ sec^2 for heliocentric orbits.

Semi-Major Axis *a* The semi-major axis a can be computed from one of the following formulas:

EQUATION 7.4

$$a = \frac{R_{periapsis} + R_{apoapsis}}{2}$$

$$a = \frac{-u}{2E} \qquad E = \frac{V^2}{2} - \frac{u}{R}$$

where u is the same constant used previously.

Eccentricity *e* The eccentricity can be computed from one of the following formulas:

EQUATION 7.5

$$e = \frac{R_{apoapsis} - R_{periapsis}}{R_{apoapsis} + R_{periapsis}}$$

$$e = \sqrt{1 + \frac{2Eh^2}{u^2}}$$

$$e = |\mathbf{e}| = \sqrt{\mathbf{e}_x^2 + \mathbf{e}_y^2 + \mathbf{e}_z^2}$$

Inclination *i* Inclination is the angle between the **K** and **h** vectors:

EQUATION 7.6

$$i = \cos^{-1} \frac{\mathbf{h_z}}{h}$$

where $\cos^{-1}$ is the inverse cosine function and $h = sqrt(\mathbf{h_x}^2 + \mathbf{h_y}^2 + \mathbf{h_z}^2)$.

If $i = 0°$ or 180°, the orbit is equatorial; if $i = 90°$, then the orbit is polar.

Finding Inclination Using Your Spacecraft's Instruments You can use your Digital Attitude Indicator to find *i* without knowing **R** and **V**! To prepare for the exercise, follow these steps:

1. For best accuracy using this method, you must wait until your spacecraft is crossing the equator of the planet.
2. As soon as the spacecraft crosses the equator, slow down the time rate to .001 seconds/second so that you'll have time to perform the next few steps.
3. Open the Autopilot (Alt A), select the Prograde button, and then click the Execute button to return to the simulation. Your spacecraft will rotate to the orbital velocity vector direction it is currently traveling in.

Now you are ready to find your inclination angle by following these steps:

1. Roll the spacecraft counterclockwise by pressing Keypad /, or clockwise by pressing Keypad *, and try to get the pitch angle as close to 90° as possible, with the Earth below you in your view window. During this step, *don't dare touch any control other than the Roll controls*, or you'll ruin the whole inclination measurement procedure. You won't be able to get the pitch all the way to 90°, but the closer the better.
2. Now press Keypad 8 to pitch the spacecraft down to 0° pitch, as shown on your Digital Attitude Pitch display. If you pass the 0° mark and need to backtrack, press Keypad 2 to pitch up. But don't touch any other controls!

3 Record the Roll readout on the Digital Attitude Indicator.

4 If the roll angle is between 0° and 180°, perform this step, otherwise go to step 5. Orbits that are direct (easterly) will have a roll angle between 0° and 180°. If the roll angle is between 0° and 90°, inclination angle $i = 90° - \text{roll angle}$. If the roll angle is between 90° and 180°, inclination angle $i = \text{roll angle} - 90°$. Thus, for example, if you were measuring the Galactic Explorer's orbital inclination in the **Flight** situation, and the spacecraft were crossing the equator from south to north, you would measure a roll angle of 30°. Hence, $i = 90° - 30° = 60°$, and the Galactic Explorer's orbital angle of inclination would be 60° in a direct easterly orbit. Likewise, if the Galactic Explorer were crossing the equator from north to south in the same orbit, the roll angle would be 150°, and $i = 150° - 90° = 60°$.

5 If the roll angle is between 0° and –180°, perform this step. Orbits that are retrograde (westerly) have a roll angle between 0° and –180°. If the roll angle is between 0° and –90°, inclination angle $i = |\text{roll angle}| + 90°$, where the roll angle inside the brackets indicates an absolute value (meaning negative values should be converted to positive values). If the roll angle is between –90° and –180°, inclination angle $i = 180° - |\text{roll angle} + 90°|$.

Longitude of the Ascending Node Ω

Since Ω is the angle between **I** (X-axis) and **n**:

EQUATION 7.7

$$\Omega = \cos^{-1} \frac{\mathbf{n}_x}{n}$$

where $n = sqrt(\mathbf{n_x}^2 + \mathbf{n_y}^2 + \mathbf{n_z}^2)$. Note that if $\mathbf{n_y} < 0$, then for proper quadrant resolution, $360° - \Omega = \Omega$.

If the $\Omega = 0°$, then the ascending node is at the vernal equinox (the X-axis); if $\Omega = 90°$, then the ascending node is at the Y-axis.

Argument of Periapsis

Since ω is the angle between **n** and **e**:

EQUATION 7.8

$$\omega = \cos^{-1}\left(\frac{\mathbf{n} \bullet \mathbf{e}}{ne}\right) = \cos^{-1}\left(\frac{\mathbf{n}_x\mathbf{e}_x + \mathbf{n}_y\mathbf{e}_y + \mathbf{n}_z\mathbf{e}_z}{ne}\right)$$

Note that ω is undefined for circular or equatorial orbits. For proper quadrant resolution, if $\mathbf{e_z} < 0$, then $360° - \omega = \omega$. When $0° < \omega < 180°$, periapsis is in the northern hemisphere, and when $\omega = 0°$ or $180°$, periapsis occurs along the equator.

True Anomaly v_O Since the true anomaly v_O is the angle between **e** and **R**:

EQUATION 7.9

$$v_0 = \cos^{-1}\left(\frac{\mathbf{e} \bullet \mathbf{R}}{eR}\right) = \cos^{-1}\left(\frac{\mathbf{e}_x\mathbf{R}_x + \mathbf{e}_y\mathbf{R}_y + \mathbf{e}_z\mathbf{R}_z}{eR}\right)$$

For proper quadrant resolution, if **R dot V** < 0, then $360° - v_O = v_O$.

THE MEASUREMENT OF TIME

There are several time measurement standards that are used in science. For day-to-day activities, we use *local mean solar time*, but since this time varies from time zone to time zone, a standard time called Universal Time (UT) is defined to coordinate the different time zones. UT is the mean solar time that occurs at the Greenwich Prime Meridian. Often UT is called Greenwich Mean Time (GMT) or Zulu (Z) Time. Universal Coordinated Time, or UTC, is derived from International Atomic Time (TAI)(based on the number of vibrations of a cesium atom) such that it differs by less than 0.9 seconds of UT and by a whole number of seconds from TAI. UTC is the time that is broadcast on national radio stations such as WWV, and is now the basis of legal time-keeping on Earth.

Sidereal Time vs. Mean Solar Time

Ordinary time is reckoned by daily motion of the Sun across the sky. A complete solar day is defined as the time that it takes for the Sun to reappear at the same location in the sky where it was seen the day before. However, the Earth has to turn on its axis slightly more than one revolution relative to the fixed stars during this interval. The reason is that the Earth travels 1/365th of the way around its orbit in one day.

This extra angular rotation per day means that it takes only 23 hours 56 minutes 4 seconds of ordinary solar time to complete one revolution, relative to the fixed stars. A *sidereal day*, consisting of 24 *sidereal hours*, is defined as a measure of the Earth's actual rotation relative to the fixed stars. The following relationship governs sidereal time and ordinary solar time:

1 Day of Mean Solar Time =	1.0027379093 Days of Mean Sidereal Time
1 Day of Mean Solar Time =	24h 03m 56s of Sidereal Time
1 Day of Mean Sidereal Time =	0.9972695664 Days of Mean Solar Time
1 Day of Mean Sidereal Time =	23h 56m 04s of Mean Solar Time

When it is 00:00:00 Greenwich Sidereal Time (GST), the Greenwich Prime Meridian is facing the vernal equinox. When it is 06:00:00 (GST), Greenwich has rotated 90° east of the vernal equinox. Each additional hour of sidereal time that elapses causes the Earth to rotate east by another 15°. Thus, the sidereal hours correspond to the right ascension angles that are measured in the Right Ascension Coordinate system.

GROUND TRACK OF YOUR SPACECRAFT

Your spacecraft's ground track over the Earth is often sinusoidal, when plotted on a Mercator projection of the Earth. As you change your orbit's characteristics, your ground track will change dramatically.

Earth's Rotation Affects Ground Track of Spacecraft

Since the Earth is rotating right by approximately 15°/hr (as measured in degrees longitude) in the same general direction the Galactic Explorer is traveling, your ground track over the Earth will take a lot more time to arrive over the same region on the Earth that you started your orbit from. This is why a sine-shaped ground track will shift west, as the Earth rotates east. For example, if the period of the Galactic Explorer's orbit is 15 hours 38 minutes, the Earth will have revolved by 234.5° (because converting to Hours-Minutes-Seconds (HMS) to decimal hours: 15.633 hours × 15°/hr = 234.5°). Therefore, you will be 234.5° longitude further *west* of your original position, even though you've completed one entire 360° orbit! This is because while you have revolved 360° around the Earth, the Earth has itself revolved 234.5° *east* putting your spacecraft's ground displacement 234.5° *west* of its initial position. If your orbital period were only 90 minutes, then your ground displacement after 1 orbit would be only about 22.5° west of your present longitude, neglecting perturbative effects of the Earth (which are not modeled in Space Simulator). We know that the Earth is non-spherical and that the center of gravity is not coincident with the center of mass. The Earth bulges outward at the equator and this causes spacecraft in low Earth orbit to experience a perturbative torque that displaces the ground track by up to 9° per day farther westward than would be the case due to the Earth's rotation alone.

TIP

There is an excellent shareware DOS program by David Ransom called STSPLUS that plots the ground track of any satellite or spacecraft in Earth orbit. The program displays a Mercator Projection of the Earth, or a 3-D Orthographic Projection and, as the satellite/spacecraft moves, it plots the circular area in which the spacecraft is visible from the ground. This program is found on CompuServe's Space Flight Forum, in the Software Library 2, under the name "STS Orbit Plus." The program is also available on the Internet, and if you want the absolute latest version, you should call the RPV Astronomy BBS at (310) 541-7299 in Southern California.

Ground Track for Different Orbits

Contrary to what you might think, geosynchronous orbits that have high inclination orbits do not stay put over a single spot over the Earth. Instead they weave a figure 8 pattern that crosses the equator and goes up or down in latitude. Geosynchronous orbits that have a 0° inclination, on the other hand, will stay pretty much over the same spot on the Earth, unless perturbed by the Earth's oblate spheroidal gravity field. Figure 7.13 shows the ground tracks for various orbits.

Effect of Launch Site on Orbital Inclination

Due to spherical trigonometry constraints, the inclination of an orbit *cannot be less than the latitude of the launching site.* The minimum orbital inclination can be achieved only with a due east launch. When taking off from Kennedy Space Center, you will never be able to launch directly into an orbit with an inclination of less than 28°. For the Russians the effect is far worse; they cannot launch into any orbit less than 45° inclination because none of their launch sites are located at less than 45° N latitude. What's more, it is very costly energy-wise to make plane changes. Thus, to achieve an equatorial orbit from Russia would take almost 75 percent of the energy needed to achieve orbit! Because the Russians are partners in the construction of America's space station Freedom, the space station will have to be put into a higher inclination orbit than is desirable for the Space Shuttle. The Space Shuttle can launch heavier payloads when it takes advantage of the Earth's rotation by a direct launch east. The Shuttle must go up with a lighter payload because launching the Shuttle northeast, in an orbit that the Russians need, will rob it of some of the Earth's rotational velocity assist.

CALCULATING YOUR SPACECRAFT'S FIELD OF VIEW

The altitude of a circular geocentric spacecraft orbit determines the amount of the Earth's surface that is visible from space. This field of view ranges from near 0 percent at the Earth's surface, to 2.4 percent at 322 km altitude (175 miles), all the way up to 49.9 percent at 3,189,000 km. The Galactic Explorer, in the default **Flight** situation with its circular orbit of 31,696 km, can see only 39.94 percent of the Earth's surface. Figure 7.14 illustrates how Equation 7.10 is figured.

EQUATION 7.10

$$\textit{Field of View}\ \% = 50(1 - \frac{R_E}{R})$$

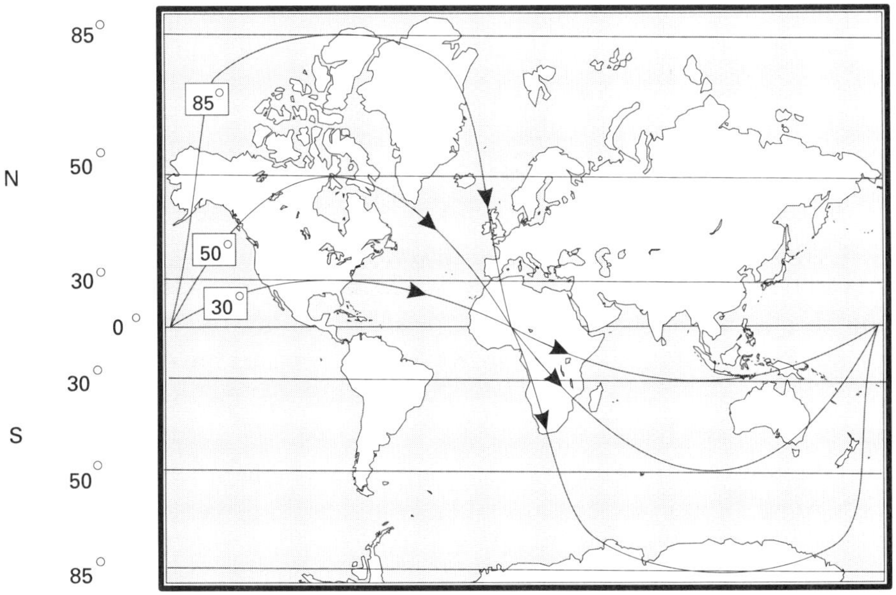

Ground track for circular orbit with different inclination angles

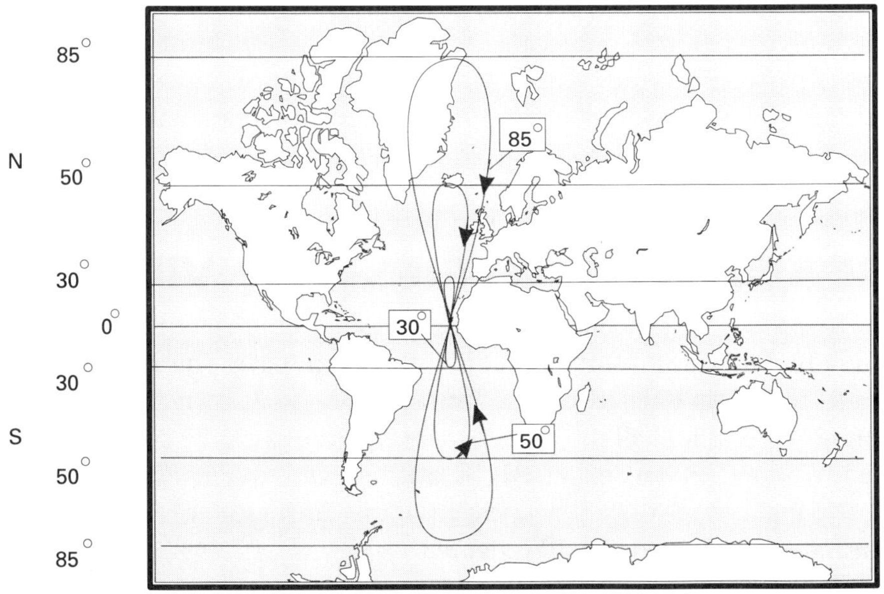

Ground track for geosynchronous orbits with different inclination angles

FIGURE 7.13 *Ground tracks for circular orbit (above) and geosynchronous orbits (below)*

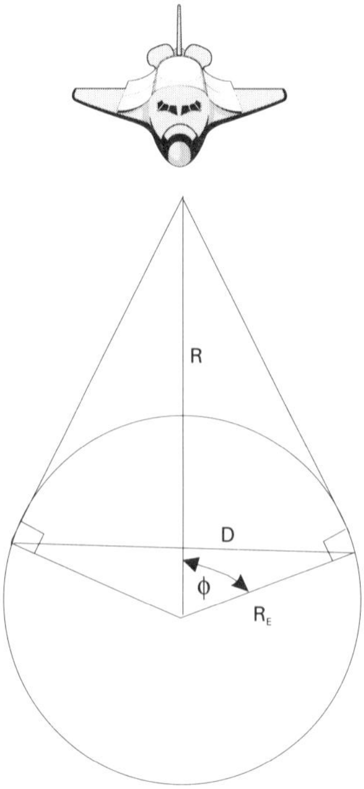

$$\phi = \cos^{-1} \frac{R_E}{R}$$

$$FOV = 50(1 - \cos^{-1} \phi) = 50(1 - \frac{R_E}{R})$$

FIGURE 7.14 *The field of view*

PART THREE

MISSIONS YOU CAN FLY MANUALLY

Performing Basic Orbital Maneuvers

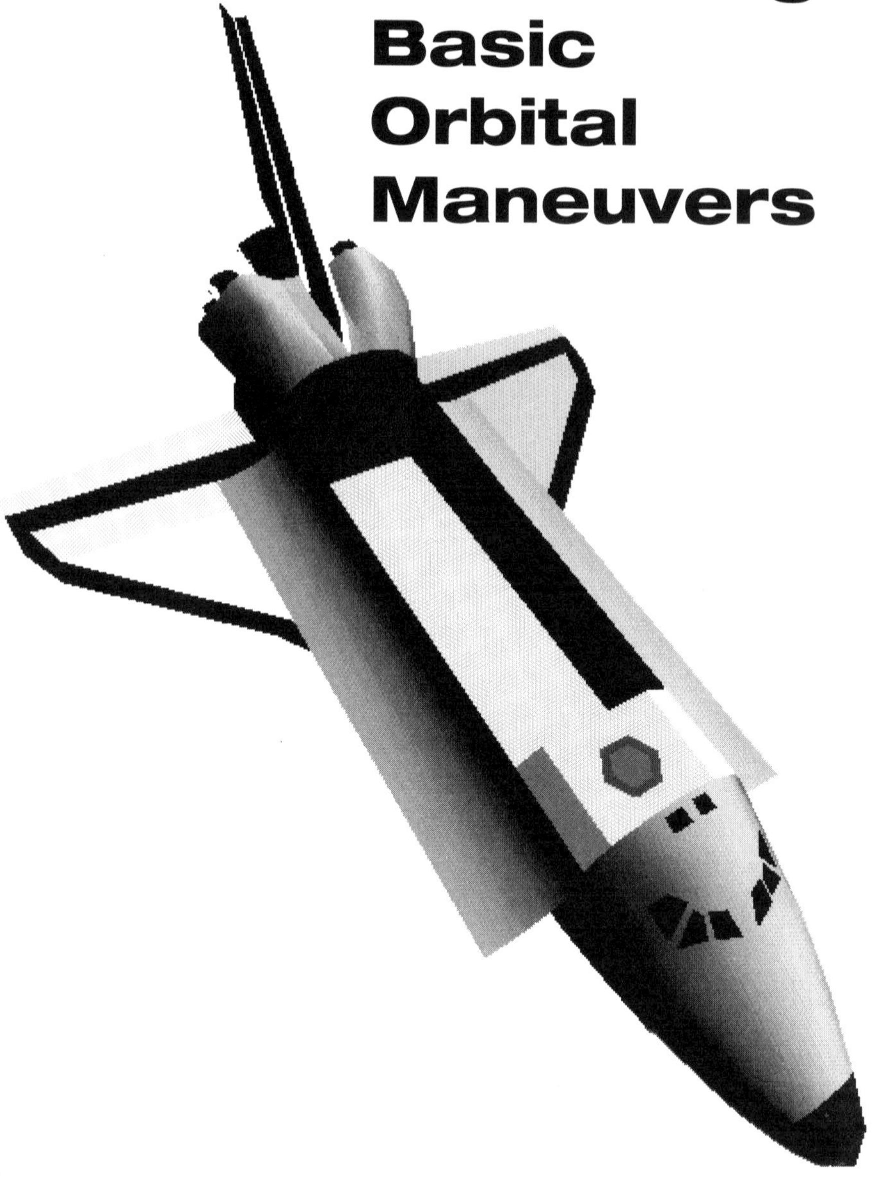

EIGHT

E I G H T

Now that you have been introduced to some of the basic concepts for orbital mechanics, let's apply this knowledge in some example trajectories. We'll use the following constants for the remainder of this chapter:

$u_{\text{Earth}} = 3.986 \times 10^5 \text{ km}^3/\text{sec}^2$
$R_{\text{Earth}} = 6378$ km (Earth's center-to-surface distance)
$u_{\text{Mars}} = 4.297 \times 10^4 \text{ km}^3/\text{sec}^2$
$R_{\text{Mars}} = 3380$ km (Mars' center-to-surface distance)

CREATING CONIC ORBITS

In this section, you'll learn how to create circular, elliptical, parabolic, and hyperbolic orbits. For the examples that follow, you can substitute your own orbits around the Sun or any planet in the solar system, as long as you plug in the appropriate gravitational parameter value of u and the correct R distance for the Sun or planet in question. In Appendix C, you'll find a list of the gravitational parameters for the Sun and each planet of the solar system.

The Circular Orbit (Eccentricity = 0, Energy < 0)

The circular orbit, shown in Figure 8.1, has eccentricity e equal to zero, and the semi-major axis a equal to the radius R of the orbit. The orbital velocity is constant, the elevation angle ϕ is always 0°, and the energy E is always less than zero.

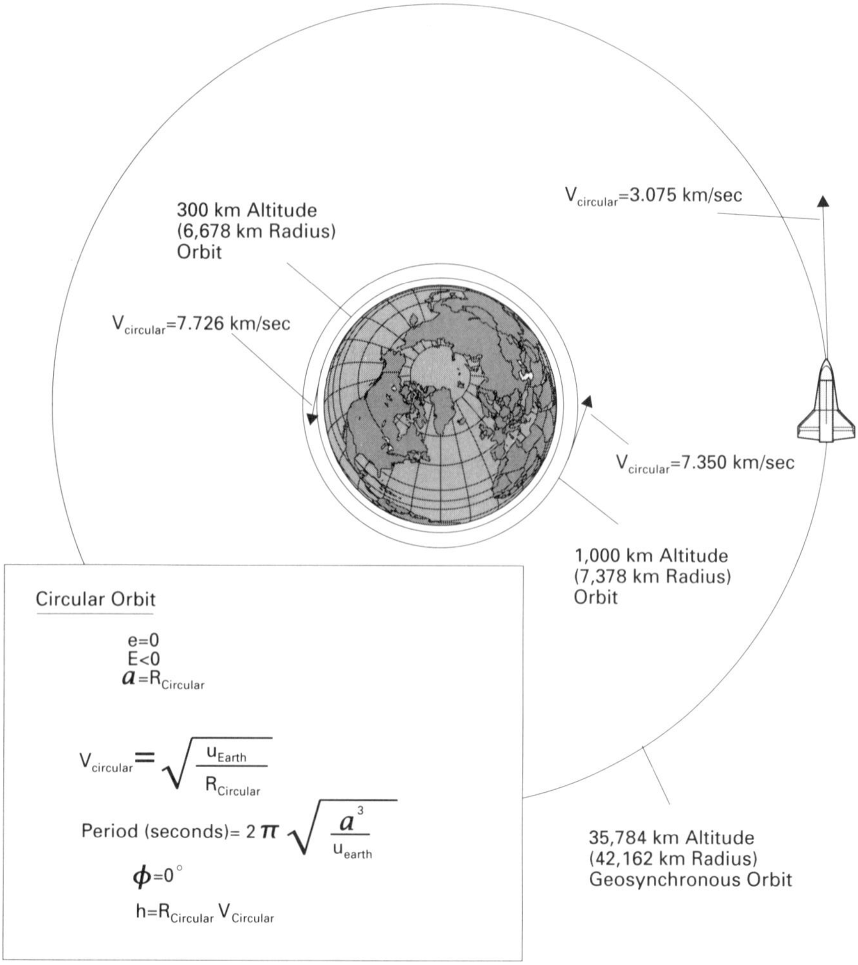

FIGURE 8.1 *Circular orbit*

With this in mind, it is possible to use the energy equation from Chapter 6 to calculate circular orbital velocity for any distance from the Earth.

EQUATION 8.1

$$V_{Circular} = \sqrt{\frac{u}{R_{Circular}}}$$

Creating a Circular Orbit To circularize your orbit around any planet, moon or sun, follow these steps:

1. Move the spacecraft to the $R_{Circular}$ distance you wish.
2. Select the planet, moon, or star you wish to orbit as your Reference Object (press Alt R to open the Select Reference dialog box).
3. Use the Autopilot's Orient command to orient the spacecraft towards the planet, moon, or star.
4. Pitch the spacecraft so that the Digital Attitude display shows ±90° pitch or as close as you can get. The closer you are to 90°, the better. This will put your elevation angle ϕ close to 0°, which is necessary for circular orbits.
5. Plug $R_{Circular}$ into Equation 8.1, using the appropriate gravitational parameter value of u for the planet, moon, or star you are orbiting, and solve for $V_{Circular}$.
6. Press F4 to rid your spacecraft of any velocity it now has.
7. Fire your Main Thrusters (Keypad +) until your tangential velocity is equal to the calculated $V_{Circular}$. Your orbit will now be circular.

For more accuracy in changing your velocity to $V_{Circular}$, use the Autopilot's Thrust Duration control.

The above method cheats a little because it makes use of the F4 "cut all velocity" command, which ordinarily would not be available to you in a real spacecraft. If you want to be super-realistic and avoid Step 6 above, you must wait until your present orbit reaches apoapsis or periapsis, then use the Autopilot's Prograde or Retrograde command to achieve $V_{Circular}$. For example, if your velocity at apogee is less than $V_{Circular}$, you must prograde the spacecraft and accelerate until $V_{Circular}$ is achieved. Or, if your velocity at periapsis is greater than $V_{Circular}$, you must retrograde the spacecraft and decelerate until $V_{Circular}$ is achieved.

Example Problem: Find the circular velocity for the Galactic Explorer when it is 500 km above the Earth's surface. Then create the orbit.

Solution: The radius of the circular orbit is $R_{Circular} = R_{Earth}$ + Altitude of Orbit = 6378 km + 500 km = 6878 km. Plugging this into Equation 8.1, along with $u_{Earth} = 3.986 \times 10^5$ km^3/sec^2, we find that $V_{Circular}$ = 7.613 km/sec. Thus, to create a circular orbit at 500 km, position the spacecraft at 500 km altitude, then press F4 to cancel any previous velocity. Next, pitch the spacecraft to ±90° and fire the thrusters until tangential velocity equals $V_{Circular}$, or 7.613 km/sec.

The Elliptical Orbit (0 < Eccentricity < 1, Energy < 0)

Elliptical orbits always have eccentricities between 0 and 1, and energy E less than zero, as shown in Figure 8.2. The distance R varies along the orbit, as does velocity V and the flight angle ϕ. With regard to ϕ, it is always 0° at periapsis and apoapsis, and is positive when the true anomaly v is between 0° and 180° (the spacecraft's velocity direction points above the local horizontal horizon). During the other half of the orbit when the true anomaly v is between 180° and 360°, ϕ is negative (i.e., spacecraft's velocity direction is below the local horizontal horizon).

> **NOTE**
>
> **For elliptical orbits, at periapsis the tangential velocity is at a maximum. At apoapsis, tangential velocity is at a minimum.**

Creating an Elliptical Orbit

Example Problem: Determine the orbital characteristics of an elliptical orbit around the Earth with a perigee altitude of 300 km and an apogee altitude of 32,000 km. Then create the orbit.

Solution:

$R_{perigee} = R_{Earth} + 300\text{ km} = 6378\text{ km} + 300\text{ km} = 6678\text{ km}$

$R_{apogee} = R_{Earth} + 32{,}000\text{ km} = 6378\text{ km} + 32{,}000\text{ km} = 38{,}378\text{ km}$

$2a = R_{perigee} + R_{apogee} = 45{,}056\text{ km}$ and $a = 22{,}528$ km.

$e = (R_{apogee} - R_{perigee})/(R_{apogee} + R_{perigee}) = 0.7036$

$E = (-u_{Earth})/(2a) = -8.8468\text{ km}^2/\text{sec}^2$

$p = a(1-e^2) = 11{,}375\text{ km}$

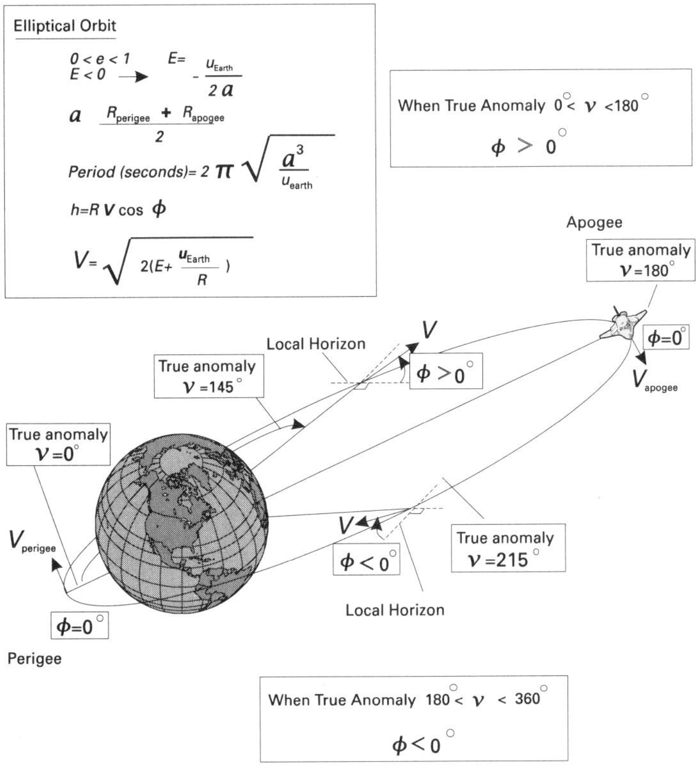

FIGURE 8.2 *Elliptical orbit and the flight angle relationship to true anomaly*

$h = 67{,}335\ \text{km}^2/\text{sec}$ since $p = h^2/u_{\text{Earth}}$

$V_{\text{perigee}} = h/R_{\text{perigee}} = 10.083\ \text{km/sec}$

$V_{\text{apogee}} = h/R_{\text{apogee}} = 1.755\ \text{km/sec}$

Therefore, to create this elliptical orbit, move your spacecraft to an R_{perigee} distance of 6678 km and then increase or decrease your tangential velocity until it equals V_{perigee} of 10.083 km/sec. Similarly, you could create this same orbit by moving your spacecraft to R_{apogee} of 38,378 km, then increasing or decreasing your tangential velocity until it equals V_{apogee} of 1.755 km/sec. After reaching R_{perigee} or R_{apogee}, you must cancel your previous velocity (press F4), then pitch the spacecraft to ±90° before using your thrusters to achieve the desired tangential velocity.

The Parabolic Orbit (Eccentricity = 1, Energy = 0)

In contrast to the closed circular and elliptical orbits, the parabolic orbit is open, and represents a trajectory which escapes from the Earth or other body. It can also represent the orbit of a comet or meteor approaching the Earth. The parabolic orbit, shown in Figure 8.3, has eccentricity *e* exactly equal to one and energy *E* equal to zero. There is no apoapsis since the orbit is open and the spacecraft escapes from the Earth or other body on a one-way trip to infinity. As the spacecraft recedes from the Earth, velocity drops to zero.

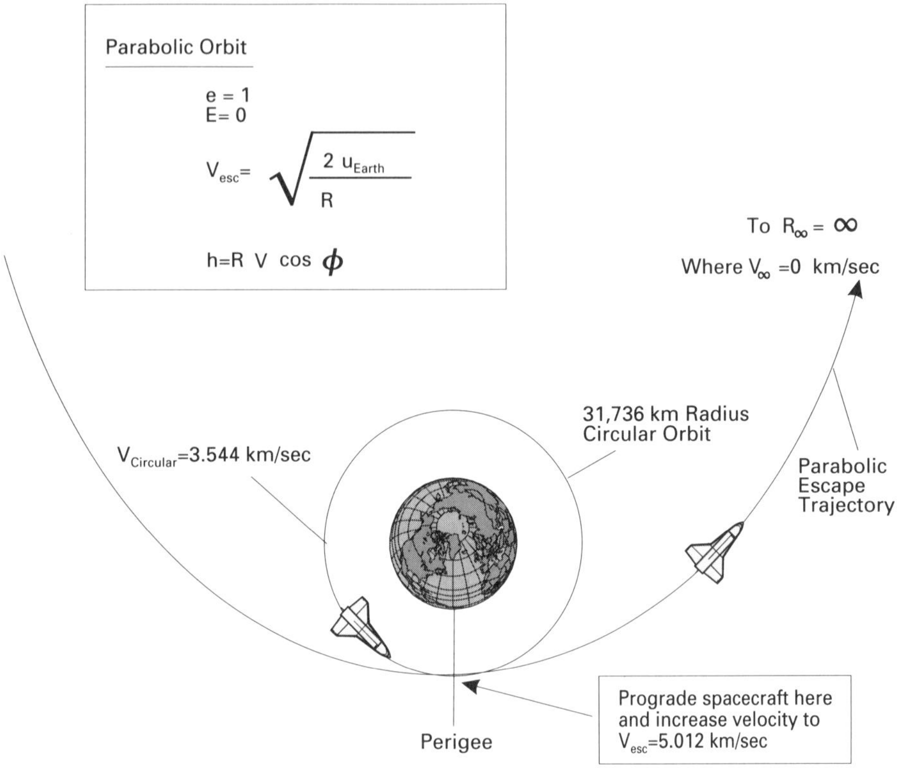

FIGURE 8.3 *The parabolic orbit*

The minimum velocity necessary to escape the gravitational SOI of a star, planet or moon is called the *escape velocity*, or V_{esc}. From the energy equation, when $E = 0$, V_{esc} is calculated as

EQUATION 8.2

$$V_{esc} = \sqrt{\frac{2u}{R}}$$

> **TIP**
>
> **In the escape velocity equation, the farther your spacecraft is from the Earth, the lower the escape velocity. Thus you can escape from the Earth's gravitational SOI more easily when you are in a higher orbit than you can from a lower orbit. For example, V_{esc} at 300 km altitude is 10.926 km/sec, while V_{esc} at 32,000 km altitude is 4.558 km/sec. Thus, if you are in an elliptical orbit, it takes less fuel to escape from the Earth if you fire your thrusters at apogee rather than at perigee.**

Note that V_{esc} is equal to exactly (sqrt2) × $V_{Circular}$.

Using Equation 8.2, you can also compute escape velocities for other planets. For example, if you want to calculate the escape velocity from Mars' surface, you would plug into the equation the values of $u_{Mars} = 4.297 \times 10^4$ km^3/sec^2, and $R_{Mars} =$ 3380 km. V_{esc} from Mars' surface turns out to be 5.042 km/sec (ignoring Mars' equatorial surface rotation velocity of 0.24 km/sec which would reduce by 0.24 km/sec the needed V_{esc} velocity by the spacecraft if it were taking off from the equator). Note that this orbit would be parabolic, since the velocity would drop to zero outside of Mars' SOI.

Creating a Parabolic Orbit

Example Problem: Create a parabolic orbit that just escapes from the Earth's SOI, when the Galactic Explorer is in a circular orbit 31,736 km away from the Earth's center, and the spacecraft has a tangential velocity of 3.544 km/sec.

Solution:

$R = 31{,}736$ km

$V = 3.544$ km/sec

EQUATION 8.3

$$V_{esc} = \sqrt{\frac{2u_{Earth}}{R}} = \sqrt{\frac{2 \times 3.986 \times 10^5 \dfrac{km^3}{sec^2}}{31{,}736\ km}} = 5.012\ \frac{km}{sec}$$

Since the Galactic Explorer already has a tangential velocity of 3.544 km/sec, you need only increase this speed by 1.468 km/sec (5.012 km/sec – 3.544 km/sec = 1.468 km/sec), to put the spacecraft on a parabolic escape trajectory away from the Earth. Be sure to prograde the spacecraft before firing your thrusters!

Notice that as your spacecraft escapes from the Earth's gravitational SOI, your velocity will drop. Your radial velocity should drop to 0 m/sec eventually, but due to Space Simulator's time approximation errors you may not see it drop all the way to zero. The reason your speed drops to zero is that the parabolic orbit represents the least-energy escape, and you have no excess energy to allow for excess escape velocity.

The Hyperbolic Orbit (Eccentricity > 1, Energy > 0)

Spacecraft sent from the Earth on interplanetary trajectories travel on hyperbolic paths relative to the Earth. The eccentricity of such orbits is always greater than 1, and the energy E is positive, meaning that the spacecraft will leave the Earth with excess escape velocity, unlike the parabolic orbit. Once the spacecraft has left the Earth's SOI, however, the orbit becomes elliptical with respect to the Sun. Like the parabolic orbit, the hyperbolic orbit has no apoapsis since the orbit is open and the spacecraft escapes from the Earth or other body on a one-way trip to infinity.

In Equation 8.4 below, a hyperbolic excess speed V_∞ is defined as the velocity of the spacecraft after it has escaped the Earth's SOI. The injection velocity $V_{injection}$ is the speed of the spacecraft after you have finished thrusting while still in the Earth's SOI. V_{esc} was defined in Equation 8.2.

EQUATION 8.4

$$V_\infty = \sqrt{V_{injection}^2 - V_{esc}^2}$$

Thus if you want to leave the Earth's gravitational SOI on a hyperbolic trajectory, you would need to fire your thrusters until your V_{bo} is greater than the V_{esc} for your current orbital altitude. Note that if V_{bo} is exactly equal to V_{esc}, then your orbit will be parabolic.

Example Problem: Find V_∞ if your spacecraft is on a hyperbolic trajectory leaving the Earth. At present, the spacecraft is 50,000 km from the Earth, and its velocity is 5.200 km/sec.

Solution: First calculate V_{esc} for a distance $R = 50{,}000$ km using Equation 8.2. V_{esc} at this distance turns out to be 3.993 km/sec. Next, in Equation 8.4, plug in the value of $V_{esc} = 3.993$ km/sec and $V_{bo} = 5.200$ km/sec. Solving for V_∞, we find that after escaping from the Earth's SOI, the spacecraft will reach a terminal velocity of $V_\infty = 3.331$ km/sec.

The Gravity Assist Maneuver (Hyperbolic Flyby)

The gravity assist maneuver increases or decreases the energy of a spacecraft's hyperbolic orbit by using the gravitational field of a nearby planet, moon or star to slingshot the spacecraft in a different direction, as shown in Figure 8.4. You can change the velocity magnitude and direction of a spacecraft with no energy input by the spacecraft, although it robs the planet, moon, or star of the energy used to change the orbit. Note that the incoming hyperbolic velocity of a spacecraft using the planetary assist maneuver equals the hyperbolic exit velocity of the spacecraft relative to the planet, moon, or star around which the hyperbolic orbit exists. This is because, in relation to the planet, moon, or star, conservation of energy dictates that the speed of the approaching spacecraft, relative to the planet, must exactly equal the speed of the spacecraft leaving the planet. However, after exiting the gravitational SOI of the body used for the hyperbolic orbit, the heliocentric speed and the direction of the spacecraft both change!

Thus, for example, the Voyager spacecraft used Jupiter's mass to swing by in a hyperbolic gravity assist maneuver. The hyperbolic approach velocity *relative to Jupiter* was exactly the same as the hyperbolic exit velocity *relative to Jupiter*. However, the heliocentric velocity and direction changed substantially, which allowed the Voyager spacecraft to gain energy *relative to the Sun (but not to Jupiter!)* and to travel on to Saturn.

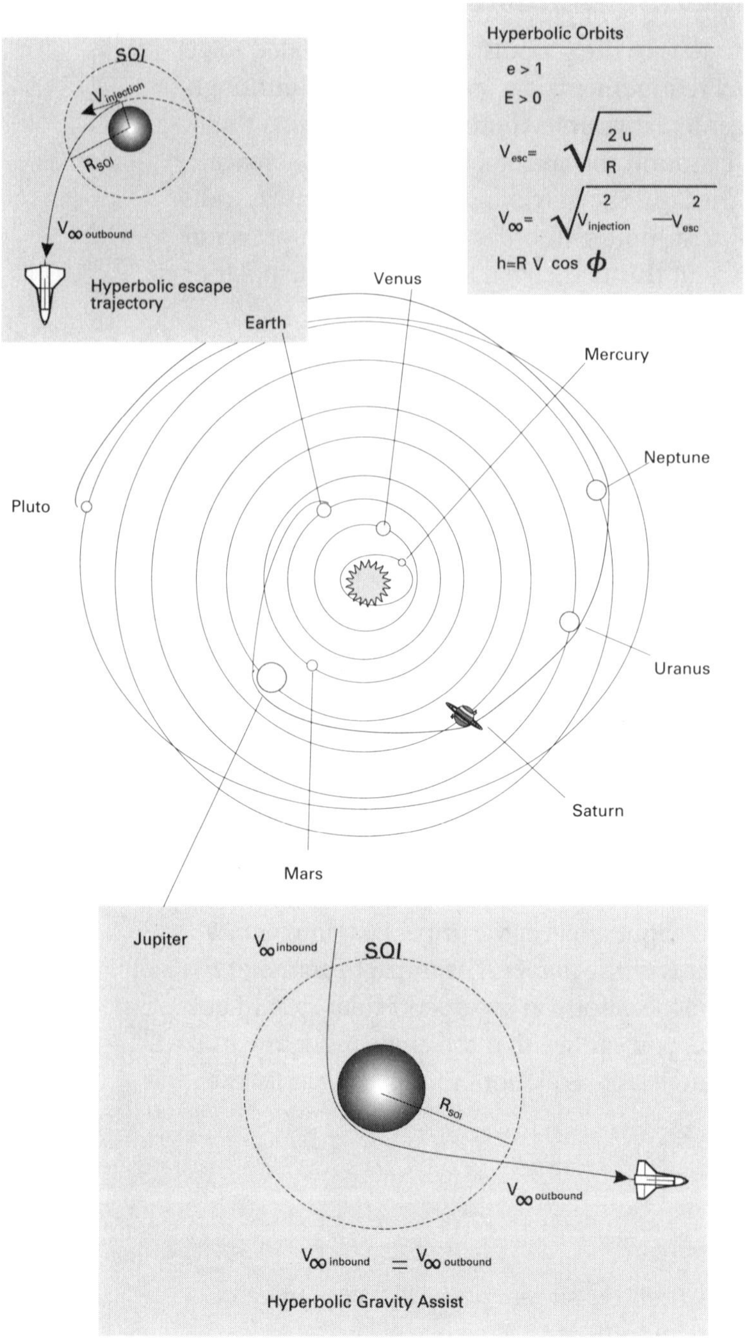

FIGURE 8.4 *Gravity assist maneuver for hyperbolic orbits*

The use of hyperbolic flyby orbits is of great interest to mission planners because it allows spacecraft to reduce the propulsive velocity needed to get to a planet. The costs and fuel requirements are greatly reduced, although the spacecraft may take longer to arrive at its destination. For orbits that leave the plane of the ecliptic around the Sun, such as the Ulysses space probe in polar orbit around the Sun, the gravity assist maneuver was indispensable. Ulysses was hurled past Jupiter, in order to deflect the spacecraft out of the ecliptic plane. Without this maneuver, the heliocentric polar orbit would have been prohibitive in terms of fuel and cost.

The terms *pumping* and *cranking* are used with the gravity assist maneuver. *Pumping* refers to changing the energy of a trajectory, while *cranking* refers to changing the angular deflection of the orbit. From Earth, a Mercury swingby produces the largest energy change because of its closeness to the Sun and its high heliocentric velocity. Hence you can pump your spacecraft's orbit through a Mercury flyby. A Jupiter swingby produces the largest trajectory deflection for a given hyperbolic approach velocity, because of the planet's large mass. Thus, you can crank your spacecraft's orbit through a Jupiter flyby.

Creating Hyperbolic Orbits When a spacecraft is on a hyperbolic trajectory towards a planet, it will either hit the planet, graze the planet's surface, or execute a flyby. To help determine whether the spacecraft is on a collision course, or whether it will fly by the planet, two terms have been developed: *the impact parameter b* and *the approach distance d*. Let us define the impact parameter geometrically, as shown in Figure 8.5.

In Figure 8.5, you'll notice the flight angle ϕ, the impact parameter b, V_∞, R_∞, and R_{planet}, which is the radius of the planet. The impact parameter b is perpendicular to V_∞; likewise the local horizon is perpendicular to R_∞. Looking at the geometry of the figure, you can see that top angle inside the impact parameter triangle is the same angle as ϕ. Equation 8.5 defines b as follows:

EQUATION 8.5

$$b = R_{planet}\sqrt{1+\frac{V_{esc}^2}{V_\infty^2}}$$

where V_{esc} is *the escape velocity from the surface of the planet.* (To calculate V_{esc} use Equation 8.2, but be sure to plug in R_{planet}!).

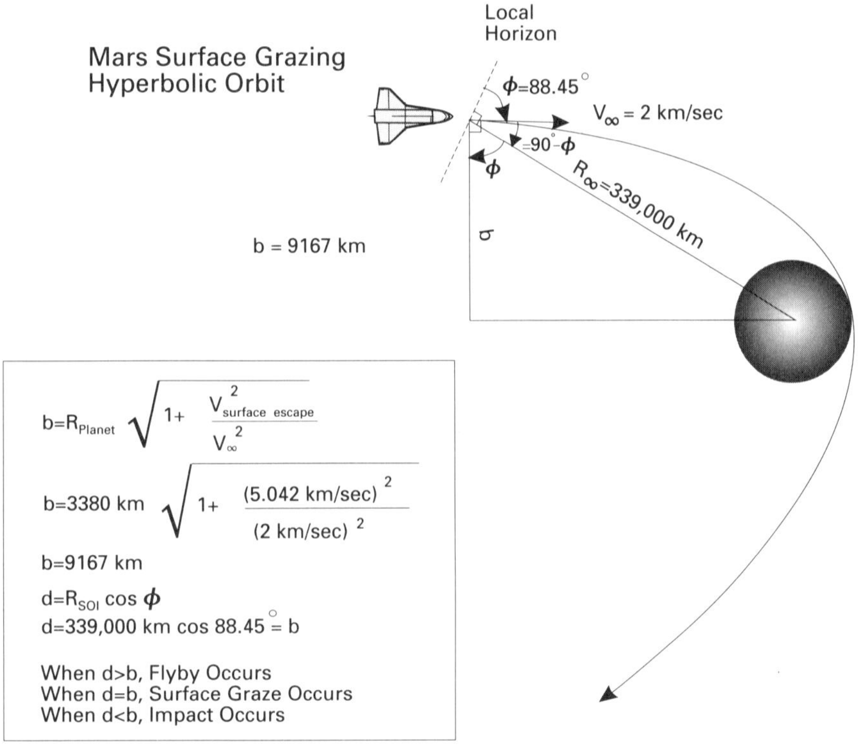

FIGURE 8.5 *The impact parameter b and a grazing hyperbolic orbit*

The approach distance is defined by Equation 8.6, follows:

EQUATION 8.6

$$d = R_{SOI} \cos\phi$$

where R_{SOI} is the planet's gravitational SOI radius (see Chapter 6), and ϕ is the flight path angle at R_{SOI}.

Once you have calculated the values of b and d, you can use one of the following relations to determine the nature of the hyperbolic orbit:

1. If $d > b$, the spacecraft will flyby the planet.
2. If $d = b$, the spacecraft will graze the planet's surface.
3. If $d < b$, the spacecraft will impact on the planet's surface.

Example Problem: The Galactic Explorer is just outside of Mars' SOI at a distance of 339,000 km. (Due to compromises made to increase Space Simulator's performance, the R_{SOI}'s for the planets and moons are different than the real R_{SOI}'s. The real R_{SOI} for Mars is 578,100 km, but we'll use the artificial value here). Create a hyperbolic orbit that just grazes the surface of Mars.

Solution: Using the Set Location menu option under the Location menu, set the Galactic Explorer's position to Mars' R_{SOI} of 339,000 km. Since the spacecraft will just barely graze the surface, the approach distance d equals the impact parameter b ($d = b$). We need to figure out an appropriate velocity and flight angle to create this orbit. Let's arbitrarily choose 2 km/sec as our V_∞ speed and then figure out what the flight path angle needs to be at R_{SOI}. Plug in the value of 2 km/sec for V_∞, the value of 5.042 km/sec for V_{esc} (surface escape velocity of Mars), and the value of 3380 km for $R_{Mars} = R_{planet}$ in Equation 8.5, then solve for the impact parameter b. You should get a value of 9167 km for b. Since $d = b$ for this exercise, you can solve for the flight path angle ϕ in Equation 8.6. The angle ϕ turns out to be 88.45°.

"How critical is this flight angle for this particular velocity?" You may wonder. Looking at Equation 8.6, you see that if your spacecraft's flight path angle is *greater than* 88.45°, you'll impact Mars because $d < b$. If your spacecraft's flight path angle is *less than* 88.45°, then you'll flyby Mars because $d > b$. If the flight path angle is *exactly equal* to 88.45°, then the spacecraft will just graze Mars' surface.

Since our objective here is to graze Mars' surface, all you need to do is aim the spacecraft so that the flight angle is 88.45°, than accelerate to 2 km/sec!

To create this orbit now, follow these steps:

1. Place the Spacecraft 339,000 km from the center of Mars (be sure to click the Distance from Center radio button!).
2. Set the Reference Object to Mars.
3. Click the Velocity indicator so that it shows the Total Velocity/Lightspeed Indicator.
4. Orient the Spacecraft towards Mars using the Autopilot.

5. Set the Track view to Mars.
6. Pitch the spacecraft up (or down) as close as you can to 1.55°. (Remember that your flight path angle is measured from the local horizontal, so 90° – 88.45° = 1.55° on your pitch readout).
7. Accelerate to 2 km/sec, as measured on your Total Velocity/Lightspeed readout (but not radial or tangential velocity!).
8. Accelerate time no faster than 17.1 minutes/second, and then slow down time as the spacecraft comes closer to Mars.

Using the above orbit, you can come within 100 km of Mars' surface. But beware, if you are sloppy in creating the initial flight angle and velocity, you'll crash!

Example Problem: Create a hyperbolic flyby of the Moon.

Solution: Using the method described in the previous example, the flight path angle $\phi = 74.38°$ for a velocity of 1 km/sec at an R_{SOI} distance of 19,950 km from the Moon. Therefore, if you locate your spacecraft 19,950 km from the moon and pitch the spacecraft up by 15.62° (90° – 74.38° = 15.62°), then accelerate to 1 km/sec, you'll just flyby the Moon's surface. At this velocity, if your pitch angle drops below 15.62° you'll impact on the moon, but if your pitch is greater than 15.62°, you'll flyby at a greater altitude.

Setting Your Hyperbolic Turning Angle The turning angle is the angle by which your spacecraft is deflected from its original path around the planet. If you know the eccentricity of your orbit, you can accurately predict the turning angle with the following equation:

EQUATION 8.7

$$\sin\frac{\delta}{2} = \frac{1}{e}$$

where δ equals the turning angle, and e is the eccentricity. From this equation you should note that the greater the eccentricity of the orbit (which also corresponds to a greater energy E of the orbit, as seen in

Equation 8.9), the smaller the turning angle. Figure 8.6 depicts the turning angle.

To solve for the angle δ, use this equation:

EQUATION 8.8

$$\delta = 2\sin^{-1}\frac{1}{e}$$

To find the eccentricity *e* of your hyperbolic orbit, use this equation:

EQUATION 8.9

$$e = \sqrt{1 + \frac{2Eh^2}{u_{planet}^2}}$$

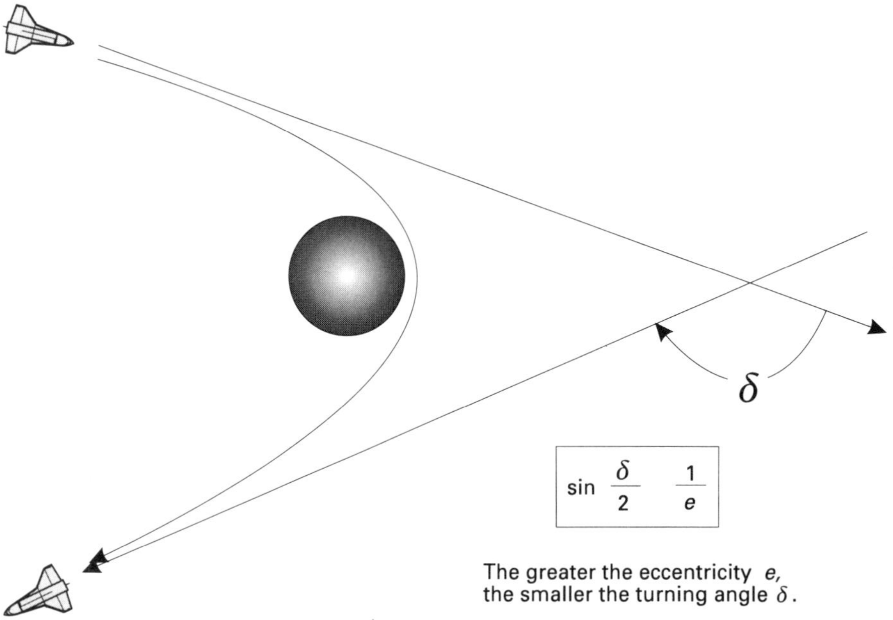

FIGURE 8.6 *The turning angle for the hyperbolic flyby*

The energy E of the orbit can be determined from the energy equation,

EQUATION 8.10

$$E = \frac{V_\infty^2}{2} - \frac{u_{planet}}{R_\infty}$$

where R_∞ and V_∞ are your distance and velocity to the planet at the edge of the gravitational SOI. V_∞ in this equation is simply the velocity relative to the planet that you see on your total velocity readout when you are outside or at the planet's SOI. Don't confuse this with the V_∞ described in Equation 8.4, since their other V_∞ is associated with leaving the planet's SOI. Notice that when R_∞ is a large number, u/R_∞ approaches zero, and so the equation reduces to $E = V^2_\infty/2$ when the spacecraft is far from the planet's SOI. However, for Space Simulator purposes, you'll need to use the value of u/R_∞ in the equation.

The angular momentum h and flight path angle ϕ are related to R_∞, V_∞, e, and E, by the following equations.

EQUATION 8.11

$$h = R_\infty V_\infty \cos\phi$$

$$\phi = \cos^{-1}\frac{h}{R_\infty V_\infty}$$

EQUATION 8.12

$$h = u\sqrt{\frac{(e^2 - 1)}{2E}}$$

Example Problem: Create a hyperbolic flyby around Mars which has a turning angle of 170° for a V_∞ of 527 m/sec when the spacecraft is at R_{SOI} (the spacecraft bounces back from Mars in almost exactly the reverse direction from which it initially approached the planet).

Solution: Since you know the turning angle δ is 170°, you can figure out the eccentricity from Equation 8.7. The eccentricity turns out to be 1.00382. Next, calculate the energy of the orbit using Equation 8.10.

With $V_\infty = 0.527$ km/sec, $R_\infty = R_{SOI} = 339{,}000$ km, and $u_{Mars} = 4.297 \times 10^4$ km^3/sec^2, the energy $E = 0.012109$ km^2/sec^2. Now that you know e and E, you can solve for the angular momentum h in Equation 8.12. Solving for h, $h = 24{,}157$. *Next, use h* in Equation 8.11 to solve for the flight path angle ϕ; which turns out to be $\phi = 82.23°$. Therefore, to create this orbit, you locate the spacecraft 339,000 km from Mars, then pitch the spacecraft up by 7.77° (90° – 82.23° = 7.77°). Next you fire your thrusters until your total velocity equals 527 m/sec.

To create this orbit, as shown in Figure 8.7, follow these steps:

1. Using the Set Location command, place the Spacecraft 339,000 km away from the center of Mars (be sure to click the Distance from Center radio button!).
2. Set the Reference Object to Mars.
3. Click the Velocity indicator so that it shows the Total Velocity/Lightspeed Indicator.
4. Orient the Spacecraft towards Mars using the Autopilot.
5. Set the Track view to Mars.
6. Pitch the spacecraft up (or down) as close as you can get to 7.77°.
7. Accelerate to 527 m/sec, as measured on your Total Velocity/Lightspeed readout (but not radial or tangential velocity!).
8. Accelerate time no faster than 1.1 hours/second, and then slow down time as the spacecraft comes closer to Mars.

You can observe the 170° turn best when the Top Map view is centered on Mars.

LAUNCHING YOUR SPACECRAFT

Manually launching your spacecraft into a stable orbit is not so easy. This is a very complex topic that cannot be adequately addressed in a book of this length. However, you can launch your spacecraft into a stable orbit using this simplified procedure:

1. Using the Set Location command, place the Galactic Explorer on the Earth's surface.

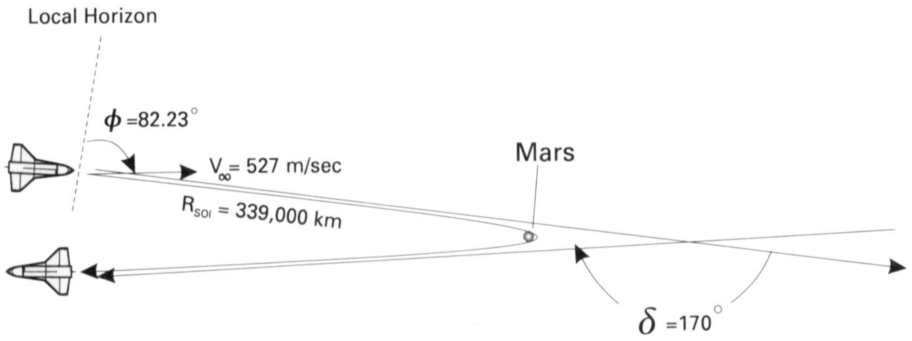

$$\sin\frac{\delta}{2} = \frac{1}{e}$$

$$\sin\frac{170^\circ}{2} = \frac{1}{e} = \frac{1}{1.00382}$$

FIGURE 8.7 *Hyperbolic flyby of Mars with turning angle of 170°.*

2. Accelerate the spacecraft with maximum thrust.
3. At 511 km altitude, shut off the engines.
4. Pitch the spacecraft down to 90° (or as close as possible) in preparation for acquiring tangential orbital velocity.
5. Press F4 to rid the spacecraft of all velocity.
6. Accelerate the spacecraft at maximum thrust for about 184 seconds or until the tangential velocity has increased to 7.726 km/sec. This is circular velocity for a 300 km orbit.
7. As the spacecraft is accelerating tangentially to the Earth's surface, it is also falling towards the Earth and gaining unwanted radial velocity. To cancel this radial velocity, pitch the spacecraft up to 0°, so that the nose is facing away from the Earth, then fire your thrusters until the radial velocity is reduced to 0 m/sec.

Your spacecraft will now be in an elliptical orbit around the Earth. Notice that to reduce radial velocity, you orient your spacecraft's engines toward the Earth (pitch = 0° with nose pointing away from Earth). To gain radial velocity, just do the reverse—that is, point the nose toward the Earth (pitch = 0°) and accelerate. To gain tangential velocity, point the nose at pitch = 90° and accelerate.

IN-PLANE ORBIT CHANGES

When you need to change orbits, you can use the in-plane Hohmann transfer ellipse to bridge the initial and final orbit. The two-impulse Hohmann transfer is named after Walter Hohmann, who in 1925 discovered that these orbits were the most economical in terms of ΔV and energy requirements. Interplanetary probes and geosynchronous satellites make use of the Hohmann transfer ellipse because it is often the most fuel-efficient method of traveling in space.

Hohmann Transfer from Inner to Outer Orbit

In a Hohmann transfer from an inner orbit to an outer orbit, as shown in Figure 8.8, there are two impulsive ΔV's required. The first ΔV_1 is made to increase the spacecraft's velocity when the spacecraft is prograded at periapsis along the inner orbit. This increases the energy of the orbit so that it becomes elliptical and at the new apoapsis, the spacecraft is tangent to the outer orbit. At this point, the velocity is too slow to maintain the outer orbit, so the spacecraft is again prograded and a second ΔV_2 is made to increase velocity. Once this is done, the spacecraft will remain in the outer orbit.

Hohmann Transfer from Outer to Inner Orbit

A Hohmann transfer from an outer orbit to an inner orbit, as shown in Figure 8.9, is accomplished in much the same way as the previous example. However, instead of increasing ΔV, ΔV must be *decreased* for the two impulsive velocity changes. This means you must *retrograde* the spacecraft at the outer orbit's apoapsis before firing the thrusters to produce a negative ΔV_1.

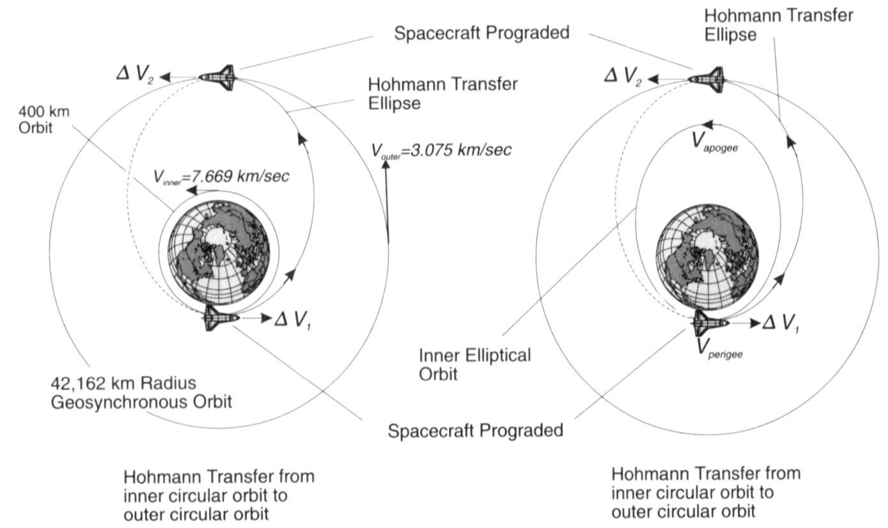

FIGURE 8.8 *Hohmann transfer from inner to outer orbit*

Likewise, when the spacecraft is tangent to the inner orbit at the transfer orbit's periapsis it is traveling too fast to stay in the inner orbit, and so you must again retrograde the spacecraft for a negative ΔV_2.

Hohmann Example: Establishing Geosynchronous Orbit

In this example, we will demonstrate how to achieve a geosynchronous (GSO) orbit from an inner orbit using a Hohmann transfer ellipse. Your spacecraft will initially be in a circular orbit of 400 km altitude. In Chapter 6, we discovered that a circular geosynchronous orbit around the Earth requires an altitude of 35,784 km, or a distance of 42,162 km from the Earth's center. Because this Hohmann transfer is from an inner to an outer orbit, two *positive* ΔV's are required to achieve GSO.

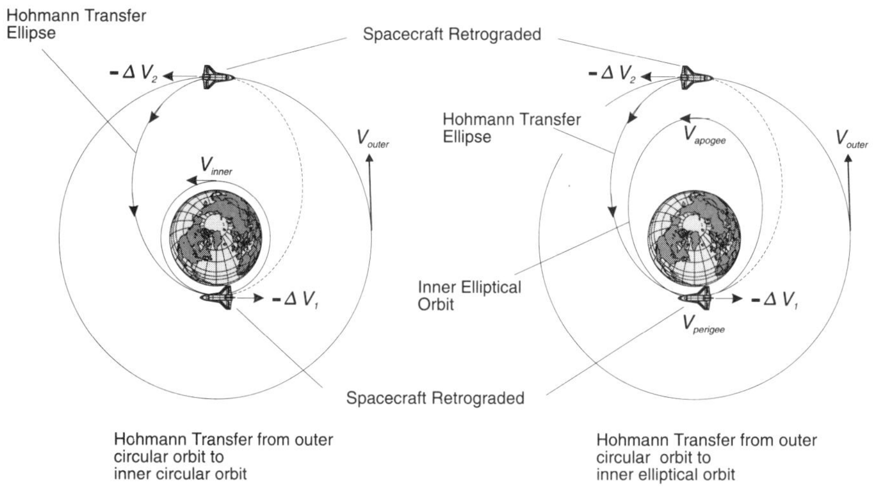

FIGURE 8.9 *Hohmann transfer from outer to inner orbit*

Before you can use the transfer orbit, you'll have to find the orbital characteristics for the inner, outer, and transfer orbits.

Inner Orbit:

$$R_{inner} = 6,378 \ + \ 400\,km = 6,778\ km$$

$$V_{inner} = \sqrt{\frac{u}{R_{inner}}} = 7.669\ km/\ sec$$

Outer Orbit:

$$R_{outer} = 42,162\ km$$

$$V_{outer} = \sqrt{\frac{u}{R_{outer}}} = 3.075\ km/\ sec$$

Transfer Orbit:

$$2a_{transfer} = R_{inner} + R_{outer} = 48,940\ km$$

$$E_{transfer} = -\frac{u}{2a_{transfer}} = -8.145\ km^2\ /\ sec^2$$

$$V_{transfer\ periapsis} = \sqrt{2\left(E_{transfer} + \frac{u}{R_{inner}}\right)} = 10.066\ km\ /\ sec$$

$$V_{transfer\ apoapsis} = \sqrt{2\left(E_{transfer} + \frac{u}{R_{outer}}\right)} = 1.618\ km\ /\ sec$$

$$\Delta V_1 = V_{transfer\ periapsis} - V_{inner} = 2.397\ km/\ sec$$

$$\Delta V_2 = V_{outer} - V_{transfer\ apoapsis} = 1.457\ km/\ sec$$

To create this Hohmann transfer orbit, follow these steps:

1. Using the Autopilot's Orbit command, create a circular orbit of 400 km altitude with an inclination of 0°. Executing this command will take several minutes, so be patient.
2. Set the Track view to the Earth.
3. Prograde the spacecraft.

4. Accelerate the spacecraft to the transfer orbit's periapsis velocity of 10.066 km/sec ($\Delta V_1 + V_{inner} = V_{transferapoapsis} = 10.066$ km/sec)
5. Accelerate time until your spacecraft reaches an apoapsis distance of approximately 42,000 km (your radial velocity will drop to 0 m/sec at apoapsis).
6. Prograde the spacecraft.
7. Accelerate the spacecraft to the outer orbit's velocity ($\Delta V_2 + V_{transferapoapsis} = V_{outer} = 3.075$ km/sec)

If you've done everything correctly, you are now in GSO orbit! If your inclination is 0°, your ground track will be stationary over a specific location over the Earth, and your orbital period will be synchronized with the 23h 56m diurnal rotation of the Earth. However, if your inner orbit was not inclined to 0° before you started, your ground track will weave a figure eight pattern over the Earth. Unfortunately, the Autopilot is none too reliable when setting the inclination angle, so this may happen to you.

Now that you know how to transfer from an inner to an outer orbit, you can try your hand at transferring from an outer to an inner orbit. Using the previous example, transfer the spacecraft back to its original circular 400 km altitude orbit from GSO. All that you need to do is *retrograde* the spacecraft and apply the *same* ΔV_1 and ΔV_2, but in the reverse order!

OUT-OF-PLANE ORBIT CHANGES

Many times it is necessary to change the plane of your orbit, as shown in Figure 8.10. For example, if your launch is from Kennedy Space Center (KSC) in Florida, you cannot create an equatorial orbit of 0° inclination without a plane change. (For equatorial orbits, the launch site must be located on the equator).

Plane changes require large ΔV's and are therefore extremely expensive in terms of fuel consumption, as can be seen in the following equation:

EQUATION 8.13

$$\Delta V = 2V_{initial} \sin\frac{\theta}{2}$$

where θ is the plane change angle, $V_{initial}$ is the initial spacecraft velocity before the plane change, and ΔV is the required velocity change. Because plane changes are so costly, they are best made when $V_{initial}$ is at a minimum (at apogee for elliptical orbits) and when crossing the equator.

As can be seen in the equation, a plane change of 60° makes ΔV equal to $V_{initial}$! Thus if your spacecraft blasted off from the Earth with a velocity of 17,000 km/hr, and you wanted a plane change of 60°, it would require that you burn the same amount of fuel that was needed for the takeoff!

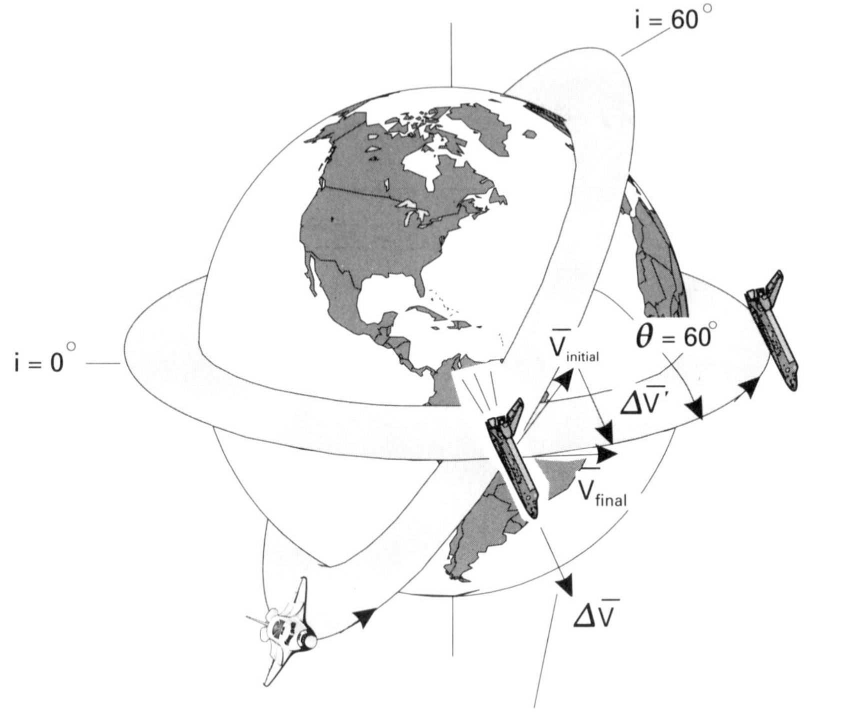

FIGURE 8.10 *Plane change from 60° inclination to a 0° equatorial orbit (θ = 60°)*

Changing Your Orbital Angle of Inclination

To change your orbital angle of inclination, you first need to know your present angle of inclination *i* and the angular difference to the new orbit. For example, if i is 60°, and you want to create a 0° equatorial orbit, the angular difference θ is equal to 60°. Plugging 60° into Equation 8.13, we found that $\Delta V = V_{initial}$.

Now that you know how much ΔV is required, you'll need to figure out which direction to point your spacecraft before firing its thrusters. The ΔV must be applied when the spacecraft crosses the equator, so you should use the Front and Side Map views of your spacecraft and wait until it crosses the equator. The directional angle α you'll need to point the spacecraft for the ΔV is illustrated in Figure 8.11, and can be calculated from the Law of Cosines. However, the angle you will actually use in the example is the complementary angle of α (180° – α), which we will call β. All you need to do is figure out the angle α, then turn your spacecraft β degrees before firing your thrusters to achieve the new orbit's $\mathbf{V_{final}}$ velocity vector. Note that the magnitude of $V_{initial} = V_{final}$ (but not the directions!)

From the Law of Cosines,

EQUATION 8.14

$$V_{final}^2 = \Delta V^2 + V_{initial}^2 - 2\Delta V\, V_{initial} \cos a$$

you can solve for the angle α using this equation:

EQUATION 8.15

$$\alpha = \cos^{-1} \frac{(\Delta V^2 + V_{initial}^2 - V_{final}^2)}{2\Delta V\, V_{initial}} \quad ; \quad if\ V_{initial} = V_{final}\ then \quad \alpha = \cos^{-1} \frac{\Delta V}{2\, V_{initial}}$$

The complementary angle β that you'll use to turn the spacecraft is calculated from α as follows:

EQUATION 8.16

$$b = 180° - a$$

To illustrate the geometry involved when you increase or decrease the angle of inclination, see Figure 8.11.

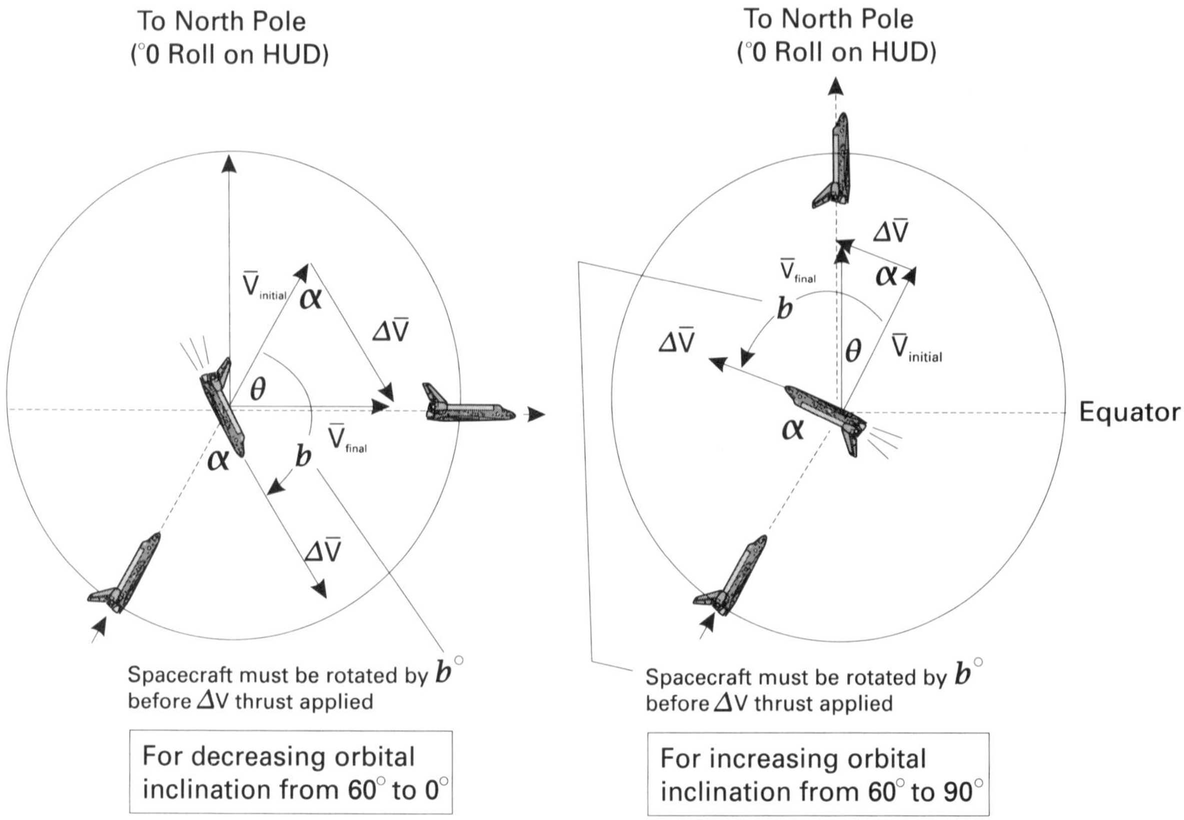

FIGURE 8.11 *Plane change schematic for decreasing orbital inclination angle (left) and for increasing orbital inclination angle (right)*

As shown in Figure 8.12, you can use the Front and Side Map views of the Earth (or another body) to get a rough fix on your angle of inclination.

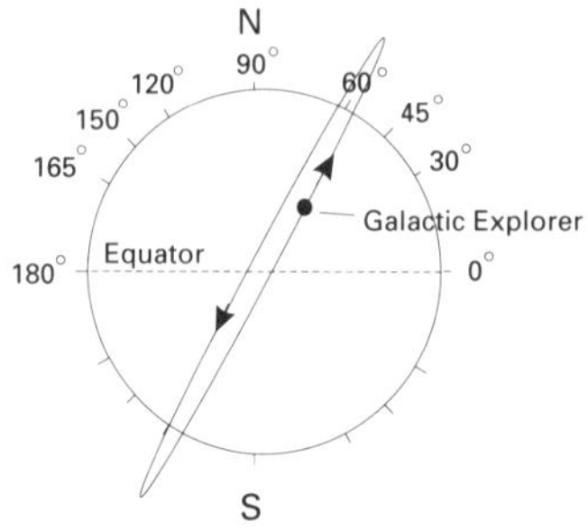

FIGURE 8.12 *Eyeballing your orbital angle of inclination on the Front and Side Map views*

The next two examples use the Galactic Explorer in the **Flight** situation to demonstrate some plane changes.

Example: From 60° Orbit to Equatorial 0° Orbit

Follow these steps to execute a plane change from 60° inclination to an equatorial 0° inclination:

1. Using Equation 8.13, we learn that for the Galactic Explorer's $V_{initial}$ of 3.544 km/sec, a 60° plane change requires a $\Delta V = 3.544$ km/sec.
2. Using Equation 8.15, we find that the angle $\alpha = 60°$ (because $V_{initial} = V_{final}$). Therefore from Equation 8.16, $\beta = 180° - 60° = 120°$. You'll use this angle $\beta = 120°$ in step 6.
3. When the spacecraft crosses the equator, as displayed on your Front or Side Map view, slow time to 0.001 second/second so you'll have time to complete the maneuver.
4. Use the Autopilot to orient the spacecraft towards the Earth.
5. Roll the spacecraft until it arrives at +30° as shown on your Roll readout. This is equivalent to your current angle of inclination i, corrected for a 90° phase difference on the readout ($90° - i = 30°$).
6. Roll the spacecraft right by β degrees. Since β in this example equals 120°, roll right by 120° until the roll readout displays +150°.
7. Pitch the spacecraft up until the Digital Pitch readout is as close to 90° as possible. Your spacecraft is now oriented properly for the ΔV thrust.
8. Increase time to 1 second/second.
9. Take note of your current tangential velocity; we'll call this $V_{initial}$. Fire your Main Thrusters and watch as your tangential velocity decreases, and then starts to increase again. When the tangential velocity again equals $V_{initial}$ (i.e., if $V_{initial} = 3.544$ km/sec, then $V_{final} = 3.544$ km/sec), cut all thrust. This is your V_{final}.

After the burn is complete, your spacecraft will be in an equatorial orbit of 0° inclination!

For greater accuracy, you should use the Autopilot's Thrust Duration controls and time the burn for precisely 90.4 seconds.

Example: From 60° Orbit to Polar 90° Orbit To execute a plane change from 60° to a polar 90° orbit, follow these steps:

1. Since 90° – 60° is a 30° plane change, ΔV calculated from Equation 8.13 is 1.835 km/sec.
2. We know from Equations 8.15 (use $V_{initial} = V_{final}$ to simplify) and 8.16, $\alpha = 75°$, and $\beta = 105°$.
3. Follow steps 3, 4, and 5 of the previous example.
4. Roll the spacecraft *left* by β degrees. Since β in this example is 105°, rolling left from the +30° roll that you're currently at means that you should stop the roll when the readout shows –75° (30° – 105° = –75°).
5. Follow steps 7, 8, and 9 of the previous example. Note that, if you use your Autopilot's Thrust Duration control, the burn time for this example will be 46.8 seconds, for a $\Delta V = 1.835$ km/sec.

After the burn is completed, your spacecraft will be in a polar orbit of 90° inclination!

Changing Your Inclination Angle for Any Orbit

You can perform any plane change angle you like using the two examples above as your guide. Be sure to use the *first* example if you are *decreasing* your inclination angle *i*. Use the *second* example if you are *increasing* your inclination angle *i*. For example, if you wanted to increase *i* from an equatorial orbit ($i = 0°$) to an ecliptic orbit ($i = 23.45°$), you would use the second example. In this instance, if your $V_{initial} = 3.544$ km/sec, $\Delta V = 1.440$ km/sec, $\alpha = 78.28°$, and $\beta = 101.72°$. Since your starting angle of inclination is 0°, in step 3 you must first roll the spacecraft to $(90° - i) = +90°$. In step 4, you finish the left roll of $\beta = 101.72°$ degrees when the roll readout shows –11.72° (because 90° – 101.72° = –11.72°). Then follow the remainder of the steps as given.

RE-ENTRY INTO THE ATMOSPHERE

Re-entry into the atmosphere is a very complex topic; a complete treatment of the subject is far beyond the purview of this book. Nonetheless, some elementary concepts will prove useful in your efforts to land your spacecraft. We will use the Shuttle to demonstrate re-entry.

Instrument Panel Mode Change

While in a planet's atmosphere, or when you are within close range of a planet's surface, your cockpit instrumentation and HUD will automatically shift to a different mode. Pitch is based on the planet's surface, with 0° meaning the spacecraft nose is pointing parallel to the horizontal surface below, and 90° meaning the spacecraft nose is pointing vertically upwards from the ground (this is different from the space-based mode). Negative pitch means your spacecraft's nose is pointing downwards towards the ground.

Roll is based on the local horizontal horizon; 0° means your spacecraft is horizontal to the ground, while ±180° means the spacecraft is upside down. Positive roll means your spacecraft is banked right, while negative roll means your spacecraft is banked left.

Yaw is based on the currently selected reference object. If your reference object is the Earth, yaw is based on the magnetic compass heading, with 0° pointing north, 90° pointing east, 180° pointing south, and 270° pointing west. But if you select a surface object as your reference object, such as the Shuttle Landing Facility or San Francisco, the yaw angle's 0° marker will be centered on that surface point.

Your velocity gauges are replaced by ground speed and vertical speed, while your distance readouts show altitude and ground distance to the selected reference object.

TIP

To fly towards the Shuttle Landing Facility or any other surface location, after re-entering the atmosphere, select one of the locations as your surface reference object, than yaw the spacecraft until the yaw angle is 0°.

Landing the Shuttle

Normally, when the Space Shuttle is in a 320 km orbit above the Earth, it is traveling at a velocity of 7.714 km/sec (27,771 km/hr or 17,256 mph). It can re-enter the atmosphere if you reduce the velocity by only 88.88 m/sec! The entire re-entry procedure should take about an hour of real time.

Follow these steps to bring in the Space Shuttle from a 320 km circular orbit:

1. Begin the de-orbit over the Indian Ocean at 93° E. longitude. This puts you half way around the world from Kennedy Space Center (KSC). (Use the Set Location command to determine spacecraft longitude.)
2. To execute the de-orbit burn, retrograde the shuttle, and fire your thrusters until tangential velocity is reduced by 88 m/sec.
3. Just before atmospheric entry at 63 km altitude, prograde the spacecraft.

> **TIP**
>
> **To practice landing the Shuttle, use the Shuttle landing situations Aproach.stn, Tuchdown.stn, On-Final. You'll see some spectacular photo-realistic scenery of Kennedy Space Center.**

4. Position the Orbiter for the correct re-entry angle of attack for the nose. For re-entry your pitch angle should be –28° *below the local horizon*. This means you should pitch the spacecraft to 90° – 28° = +62° pitch. But when you re-enter the atmosphere at around 63 km altitude, the pitch readouts change. Your new pitch angle should vary between –10° to –30° on the readout. If you pitch up too high, you'll skip off the atmosphere back into space; if you pitch down too low, you'll enter the atmosphere too quickly and not have sufficient altitude to get to KSC.
5. At 63 km altitude, you'll note that atmospheric drag appears, as displayed on your acceleration gauge. Adjust pitch angle up or down to maintain a uniform descent velocity.
6. Select the Shuttle Landing Facility as your current reference object. Yaw, pitch, roll, velocity, and distance readouts will change to reflect your spacecraft's orientation to the Shuttle Landing Facility.
7. Yaw the spacecraft to a course of 0° as displayed on the Yaw readout. This is the direction you'll need to go to get to the landing site.

8. Perform S-shaped turns to bleed off excess speed, but keep the spacecraft headed towards 0° yaw.
9. Descend on a 22° glideslope to the runway.
10. Near the runway, perform a nose-up flare maneuver to reduce glide angle to 1.5°.
11. At 27 meters altitude, deploy the landing gear.

Aero-Braking

The use of the atmosphere to modify orbital trajectories is referred to as *aerobraking*. When the atmosphere is used to slow down a spacecraft so that it can enter a parking orbit, this is called *aerocapture*.

By using the atmosphere as a brake, considerable fuel can be saved that would otherwise be needed to slow the spacecraft down. Aerobraking requires high precision, though, since the spacecraft's angle of attack determines the amount of braking and heating the spacecraft experiences. In general, the steeper the angle of attack, the greater the heat friction and braking.

Skipping Off the Atmosphere If your angle of attack while entering the atmosphere is too small, your spacecraft will skip off the atmosphere like a pebble that is skipped off of a pond's surface. However, if your angle of attack is too steep, your spacecraft can burn up. Note that if you enter with an angle of attack of 90° from the local horizontal horizon, you could experience up to 300 *g*'s of deceleration! This would mean that before you burned up, you would be killed by the tremendous *g* forces.

If your spacecraft loses enough velocity after the first skip, it will again skip off the atmosphere. In general, the exit velocity from a single skip maneuver will be 68 percent of the entry velocity, if the angle of attack is –22° or less. This skipping method of re-entry was used by the Apollo spacecraft (although with a different angle of attack) in order to bleed off excess velocity and avoid overheating. During the skip, the Apollo Command Module's heat shield was able to cool down sufficiently for the final re-entry.

Plotting a Lunar Trajectory to the Moon

NINE

N I N E

Plotting a lunar trajectory to the Moon is a complex task, one made all the harder by the fact that the Moon experiences irregularities in its orbital motion due to perturbations by the Sun and the Earth's tidal forces. In fact, the orbital elements for the Moon are constantly changing and must be recalculated for each year. Therefore, when planning lunar missions, you must use up-to-date lunar ephemeris data for the date and times of the lunar interception. Fortunately for Space Simulator pilots, the principal perturbations of the Moon's orbit are not modeled, so you can assume that the orbit is fixed in space, relative to the stars.

TIDAL FRICTION AND THE EFFECT ON THE MOON'S ORBIT

The Moon's gravitational pull on the Earth's oceans causes a tidal bulge on the side of the Earth facing the Moon. Since the Earth rotates daily, the tidal bulge moves and causes the diurnal high and low tides that we experience on Earth. As the Earth rotates, the ocean tides flow back and forth across the ocean floors and coastal shallows. The resulting friction between the water and the solid Earth causes a loss of kinetic energy from the daily rotation of the Earth, which is expended in the form of heat. Consequently, the Earth's rotation is slowing, and atomic clocks measuring atomic time must be readjusted yearly to match the actual solar time. This time loss is not inconsequential; if an atomic clock were keeping time over the last 2000 years, it would be out of step with today's solar time by about 3 hours! Hence, as the Earth slows down, the length of the solar day increases.

According to a theory advanced by Sir George Darwin (the son of the naturalist), the Moon was at one time much closer to the Earth than at present. The slow spiral of the Moon away from the Earth is caused by the fact that the tidal bulge of the Earth's oceans is carried eastward by the Earth's rotation. This shifts the center of gravity of the Earth east of the line joining the centers of mass of the Earth and Moon. Because of this, a small force is exerted on the Moon in the direction of its orbital motion, causing it to speed up and slowly spiral outwards. Eventually, over billions of years, this will cause the Moon to escape from the Earth.

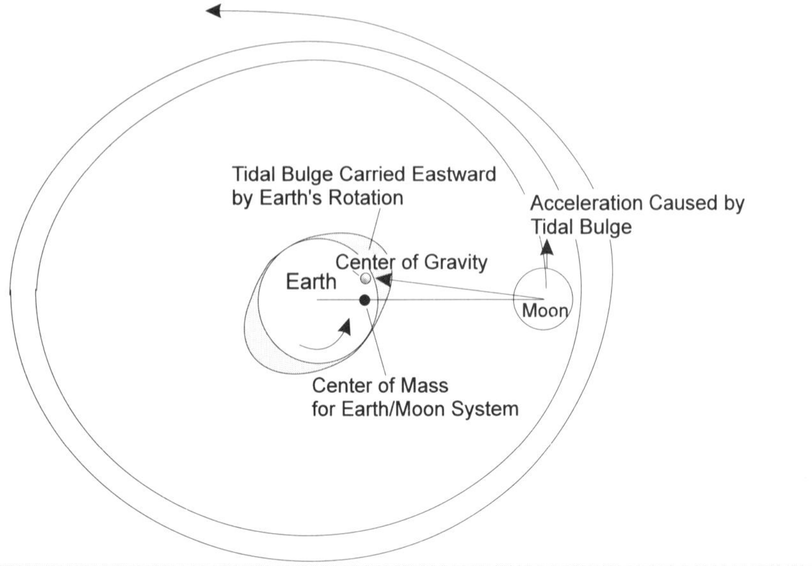

ORBITAL ELEMENTS OF THE MOON

The six classical Keplerian elements for the Moon are described as follows:

Semi-Major Axis *a*: The mean value of a for the real Moon is 384,400 km. In Space Simulator, however, a = 387,088 km.

Eccentricity *e*: The mean eccentricity e is 0.054900489.

Inclination Angle i: In Space Simulator, the Moon's angle of inclination is fixed at 23.45° to the equatorial plane. However, the real Moon's angle of inclination varies from 28° 35′ to 18° 19′ with a period of 18.6 years, due to the rotation of the line of nodes. The line of nodes is defined as the intersection of the Moon's orbital plane with the ecliptic plane. The inclination angle to the plane of the ecliptic stays relatively constant with a mean value of 5° 8′.

Longitude of the Ascending Node Ω: Because the line of nodes rotates westward, it causes the angle Ω to rotate 360° around the Earth once every 18.6 years.

Argument of Perigee ω: The line of apsides (the semi-major axis of the orbit) rotates in the direction of the Moon's orbital motion, thereby causing to increase by 360° every 8.9 years.

Right Ascension at Epoch α: The hour angle is measured eastward from the vernal equinox to the projection of the Moon's current position vector on the equatorial plane. The Moon completes a single orbit around the Earth once every 27.32166 days (± 7 hours per revolution due to solar and tidal perturbations). In Figure 9.1, α is approximately 9:00 hours and as the Moon orbits, the hour angle increases to 23:59 (just before the vernal equinox direction), then sweeps through 0:00 back to 9:00 hours after 27.32166 days.

Because the Moon's period of revolution around the Earth (27.32166 days) is exactly equal to its equatorial rotation rate, the Moon always keeps the same face turned towards the Earth. It wasn't until the '60s, when lunar space probes were dispatched to the far side of the Moon, that we were able to observe and map the Moon's entire surface. If the Moon's orbit were circular, and its axis of rotation were perpendicular to its orbit, we would see exactly 50 percent of its surface. Because the Moon's orbit is slightly elliptical ($e = 0.0549$) and its equator is inclined 6.7° to the plane of its orbit, an effect known as *lunar libration* (rocking motion in both latitude and longitude) allows us to see about 59 percent of its surface.

SIMPLE EARTH-MOON TRAJECTORIES

The presence of the Earth and the Moon in close proximity to a spacecraft in orbit is referred to as the *restricted three-body problem*. We have already seen the simple two-body differential equation of motion for the

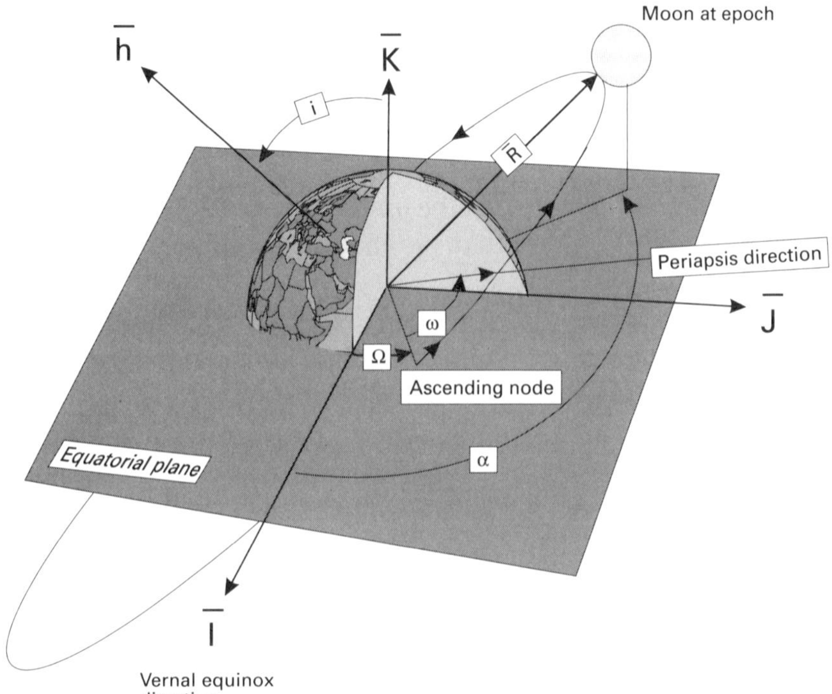

FIGURE 9.1 *Lunar orbital elements*

Earth-spacecraft system (Equation 6.6), from which the energy equation and conic equations are derived. Unfortunately, the *n-body problem* for more than two bodies defies a complete analytical solution, and the spacecraft's guidance can only be solved by using a computer to integrate Equation 6.6 each second of time for every gravitational body (this is how Space Simulator works). This is a computationally intensive task that suffers from an exponential increase in the number of calculations needed as the number of bodies increases. Thus, even with a high speed computer, it can take hours to calculate a single translunar orbit. Since it is a trial-and-error method, the initial spacecraft velocity and position vectors are varied until the computer comes up with the correct arrival conditions. The computation of precision lunar trajectories for the Apollo spacecraft was performed in such a manner, taking into account the oblate shape of the Earth, solar perturbations, and solar pressure, as well as the attraction of the Earth and Moon.

Fortunately, a less cumbersome analytical method, called *the patched conic approximation*, can be used to approximate the spacecraft's initial trajectory conditions, as well as its arrival conditions. These conditions, though only approximations, can be used to narrow down the choice of initial velocity and position vectors so that the computer can work more efficiently.

THE PATCHED CONIC METHOD

The patched conic approximation avoids the three-body problem of the Earth-Moon-spacecraft system by assuming that while the spacecraft is in the Earth's SOI, it is experiencing only the two-body forces of the Earth-spacecraft. Then when the spacecraft leaves the Earth's SOI and encounters the Moon's SOI, it experiences only the two-body forces of the Moon-spacecraft. The transition between the Earth's SOI and the Moon's SOI is called the *patch*, since it describes the patching of two conic-shaped orbits (hence the term *patched conic)*.

With these assumptions, you can use the Earth's gravitational parameter u for the Energy equation, the time of flight (derived from Kepler's Third Law), and the conic equations, to figure out all the necessary aspects of the spacecraft's orbit while it is in the Earth's SOI. Then, when the spacecraft enters the Moon's SOI, you substitute the gravitational parameter u for the Moon, and use the same equations to calculate the orbital characteristics around the Moon. Figure 9.2 shows trajectories of varying shapes.

Establishing a Geocentric Orbit that is Coplanar to the Moon's Orbit

We will use an in-plane Hohmann transfer ellipse between a spacecraft in a 300 km circular parking orbit around the Earth and the Moon's SOI. In order to be in the same orbital plane as that of the Moon, the spacecraft must have the same angle of inclination of 23.45° as the Moon's

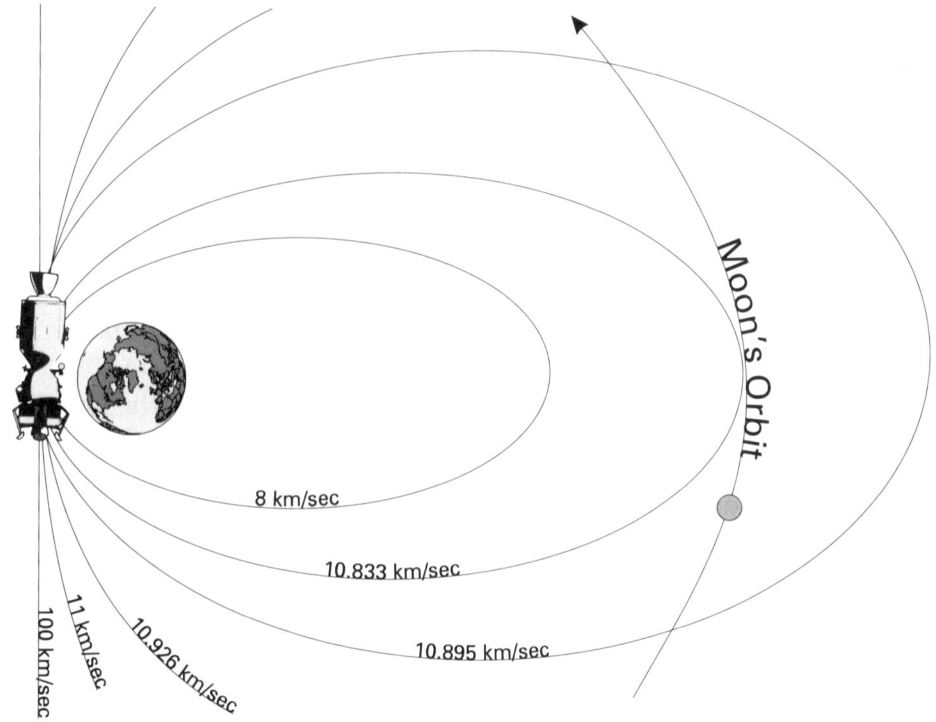

FIGURE 9.2 *Varying injection speed varies the trajectory shape*

orbit. To accomplish this tricky task, you'll need to perform these steps:

1. Set the Spacecraft's location to 23.45° North latitude on the Earth's surface (don't worry about longitude).
2. Select the Window/View Controls menu command, and in the dialog box click the Map View button and then the Moons button. This allows you to see the Moon displayed in the Map window.
3. Select the Earth as your Map Reference (press O key and select Earth), then open the Front Map view and zoom out 1.1 million km.

4 Accelerate time until the Moon has moved as far away from the Earth as it will go toward the upper left corner of the map, then reduce time acceleration to 1 second/second.

5 Now zoom in the Map to 17,180 km. You should see the spacecraft slowly rotating around the Earth's surface at 23.45° North latitude.

6 Accelerate time until the spacecraft appears on the left edge of the Earth's spherical outline in the Front Map view, then reduce time acceleration to 1 second/second (See Figure 9.3).

7 Use the Autopilot Launch command to launch the spacecraft into a 300 km altitude circular orbit, with a launch azimuth of +90°. (Remember due to spherical trigonometry constraints, the *lowest* orbital angle of inclination from latitude 23.45° is 23.45°).

After a few minutes, the Autopilot will finish its work, and the spacecraft's orbit will be coplanar with that of the Moon, as shown in Figure 9.3.

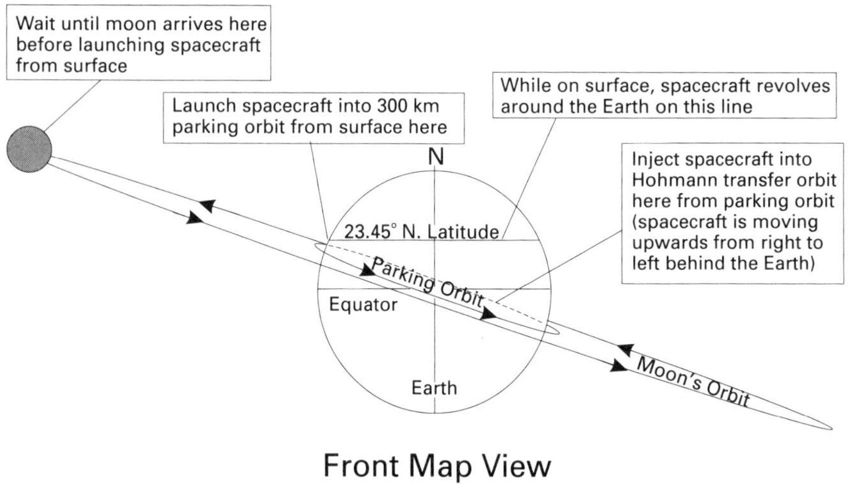

FIGURE 9.3 *Establishing a parking orbit around the Earth before translunar injection orbit.*

Figuring Out the Hohmann Transfer Orbit

We now need to figure out the Hohmann transfer orbit characteristics, which are summarized on the following page.

Hohmann Transfer Orbit at Injection from Geocentric Orbit

$$R_0 = R_{perigee} = 300\ km + R_{Earth} = 6{,}678\ km$$

$$R_{apogee} = R_{DistancetoMoon} = 387{,}088\ km$$

$$a = \frac{R_{perigee} + R_{apogee}}{2} = \frac{6{,}678 + 387{,}088}{2} = 196{,}883\ km$$

$$E = -\frac{u_{Earth}}{2a} = -\frac{3.986 \times 10^5}{2 \times 196{,}883} = -1.012279\ km^2 / sec^2$$

$$V_0 = \sqrt{2\left(E + \frac{u_{Earth}}{R_0}\right)} = 10.833\ km / sec$$

$$\phi_0 = 0°$$

$$h = R_0 V_0 = 72{,}342\ km^2 / sec$$

$$p = \frac{h^2}{u_{Earth}} = 13{,}129\ km$$

$$e = \sqrt{1 + \frac{2Eh^2}{u^2}} = \sqrt{1 - \frac{p}{a}} = 0.96608$$

Hohmann Transfer Orbit at Patch Point of Moon' s SOI

$$R_1 = \sqrt{R^2_{Distance\ to\ Moon} + R^2_{SOI} - 2R_{Distance\ to\ Moon} R^2_{SOI} \cos\lambda_1}$$

$$= \sqrt{(387{,}088\ km)^2 + (20{,}000 km)^2 - 2(387{,}088\ km)^2 (20{,}000 km)^2 \cos 30°}$$

$$= 369{,}903\ km$$

$$V_1 = \sqrt{2\left(E + \frac{u_{Earth}}{R_1}\right)} = 0.361\ km / sec$$

$$\phi_1 = \cos^{-1}\frac{h}{R_1 V_1} = 57°$$

$$v_1 = \cos^{-1}\left[\frac{1}{e}\left(\frac{p}{R_1} - 1\right)\right] = 177°$$

Note that we use a mean distance of 387,088 km for the Moon's orbit only in Space Simulator, which is different than the real value of 384,400 km.

Calculating the Proper Phase Angle of the Moon Before Departure

Next, we need to figure out when the next departure window will occur in order for interception with the Moon to occur. We will be using a Hohmann transfer velocity of 10.833 km/sec, and the time of flight is a little less than 1/2 of the period of the transfer ellipse, or 82.33 hours. Since the Moon moves through an angle of 1.51776×10^{-4} degrees/sec in its orbit, the Moon's phase angle at departure with that of the spacecraft is determined from the following equation:

EQUATION 9.1

$$\gamma_0 = v_1 - \gamma_1 - 1.51776 \times 10^{-4} \frac{Degrees}{sec} (t_1 - t_0)$$

$$\gamma_0 = 177° - 1.5° - \left(1.51776 \times 10^{-4} \frac{Degrees}{sec}\right)\left(88.33\ hours \times 3600 \frac{seconds}{hour}\right) = 127°$$

where γ_0 is the phase angle at departure, γ_1 is the phase angle at arrival, v_1 is the true anomaly of the transfer orbit at the Moon's SOI interception, t_1 is the time at arrival, and t_0 is the time at departure. The geometry is illustrated in Figure 9.4.

If we assume that the angle λ_1 is equal to 30° at arrival, we can use the Law of Sines to calculate λ_1, which turns out to be 1.5°.

EQUATION 9.2

$$\sin\gamma_1 = \frac{R_{SOI\ of\ Moon}}{R_1} \sin\lambda_1$$

$$\gamma_1 = \sin^{-1}\left(\frac{R_{SOI\ of\ Moon}}{R_1} \sin\lambda_1\right) = \sin^{-1}\left(\frac{20{,}000km}{369{,}903km} \sin 30°\right) = 1.5°$$

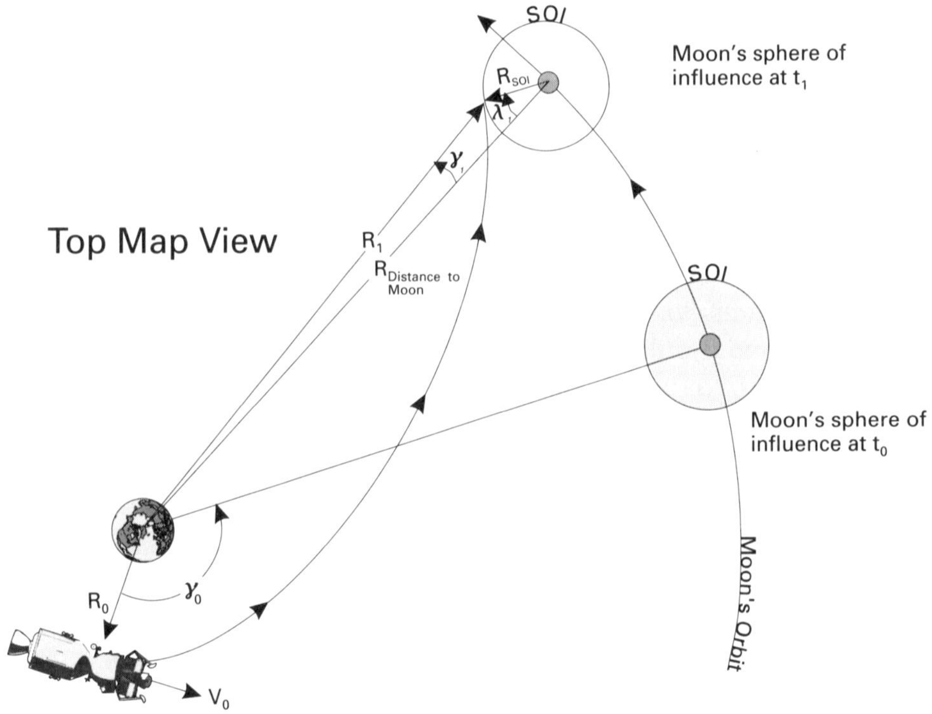

FIGURE 9.4 *The patched conic transfer to the lunar sphere of influence*

Assuming that t_0 is at time zero, and knowing the true anomaly v_1 is 177° at interception, if we plug the value of $\gamma_1 = 1.5°$ into Equation 9.1, we find that the proper phase angle γ_0 at departure should be 127°.

Therefore, you should wait until the spacecraft leads the moon by 127° before firing your thrusters. To get the spacecraft to the proper phase angle position, accelerate time and watch the Front Map view until the spacecraft orbits behind the Earth (at the right side of the Earth's spherical edge), and then stop time acceleration before the spacecraft appears to reach the center of the Map display. This angle is illustrated in Figure 9.3, which depicts the Front Map view where the spacecraft is on the *opposite side of the Earth* in the coplanar parking orbit. If you want better phase angle precision, you could derive a method based on Space Simulator's built-in Observatory's measurement of the Moon's Right Ascension angle (RA), and then convert the RA to the Moon's current longitude position over the Earth. Then you would check the spacecraft's current longitude versus the Moon's longitude until the proper phase angle was reached. To simplify things, we will not use this method here, but you can see it demonstrated in the next chapter for the Mars mission.

NOTE

If you have difficulty setting up the initial translunar injection conditions, you may want to try the special Space Simulator situation I've created, titled MOON.STN, that you can download from the Sybex CompuServe forum or, via ftp, on the Internet at 2ftp.iup.edu in the Flight Simulator directory. This situation has the spacecraft located in the proper position and phasing angle; all you'll need to do is apply thrust!

Injecting the Spacecraft Into the Transfer Orbit

Now that your spacecraft is positioned correctly for the proper phase angle at departure, follow these steps:

1. Prograde the spacecraft using the Autopilot.
2. Fire your thrusters until your tangential velocity reaches 10.833 km/sec.
3. Accelerate time to *no more than 17 minutes/second* to speed up the time of interception.
4. Switch to the Top Map view and then zoom out so that you can watch the spacecraft's interception trajectory.
5. When you are about 340,000 km from the Earth, switch your reference object to the Moon, and note your new lunar distance. When your spacecraft reaches 20,000 km from the Moon, you have entered the Moon's SOI!
6. Reduce time acceleration and switch the Map reference object to the Moon as you approach the Moon.

If your spacecraft misses the Moon, you should adjust your phase angle from the parking orbit. Note that *if your spacecraft leads the Moon, then your phase angle needs to increase (the spacecraft is closer to the Earth's right spherical edge in the Front Map view)*, and *if your spacecraft trails the Moon, the phase angle needs to decrease (the spacecraft is closer to the Earth's center in the Front Map view).*

Selenocentric Patch Conditions at the Moon's SOI

Since we are now in the Moon's SOI, we need to apply the patch conditions for the Moon to find out the selenocentric (Moon-centered) orbital characteristics. Examining Figure 9.5, we see that the spacecraft's orbital velocity vector $\mathbf{V_2}$ relative to the moon is

EQUATION 9.3

$$\overline{\mathbf{V}_2} = \overline{\mathbf{V}_1} - \overline{\mathbf{V}_{Moon}}$$

Applying the Law of Cosines, we find the magnitude of the spacecraft's velocity relative to the Moon at the patch point is:

EQUATION 9.4

$$V_2 = \sqrt{V_1^2 + V_{Moon}^2 - 2V_1V_{Moon}\cos(\phi_1 - \lambda_1)} = 0.715\ km/sec$$

where the orbital speed V_{Moon} of the Moon is given as 1.1018 km/sec, ϕ_1 is the flight path angle relative to the Earth at the patch point (from $h = R_1V_1\cos(\phi_1)$), and λ_1 is 30°.

The spacecraft's flight path angle relative to the Moon at the patch point can be found from this expression:

EQUATION 9.5

$$\phi_{Relative\ to\ Moon\ at\ Patch\ Point} = 90° - \sin^{-1}\left[\frac{V_{Moon}}{V_2}\cos\lambda_1 - \frac{V_1}{V_2}\cos(\lambda_1 + \gamma_1 - \varphi_1)\right] = 90° - 51° = 39°$$

For lunar impact to occur at the spacecraft's patch velocity of 0.715 km/sec, the flight path relative to the Moon would have to be 72° or greater (using the impact parameter $b = 6{,}029$ km, impact occurs when $d < b$ with $d = R_{SOI} \cos\phi$). Since this is not the case, we know that the spacecraft will flyby the Moon and not impact.

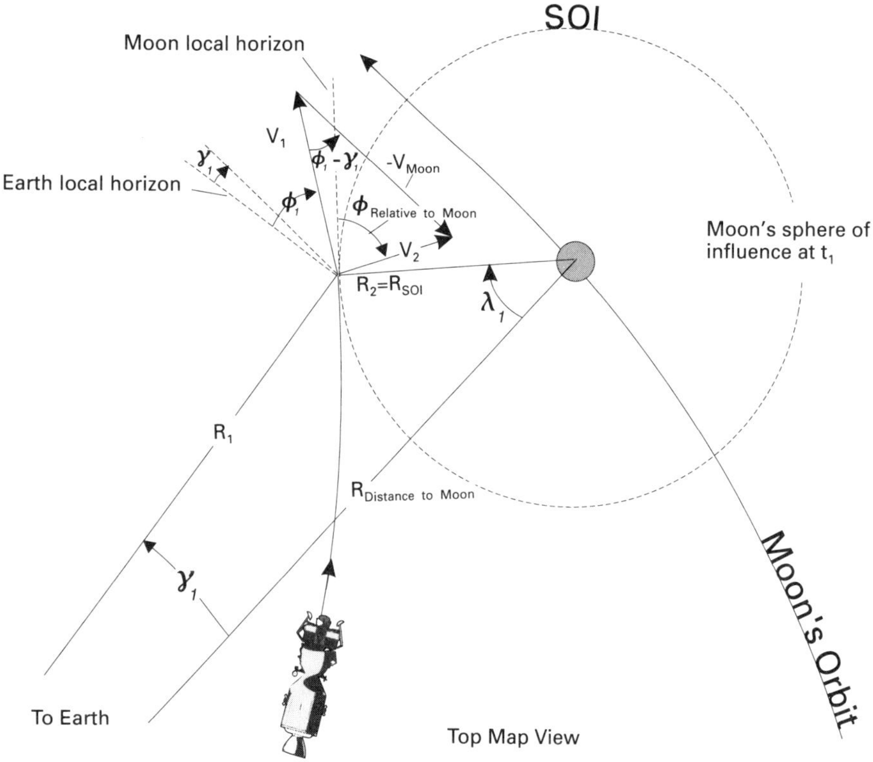

FIGURE 9.5 *The selenocentric patch conditions*

The Selenocentric Arrival Orbit

Because we now know the selenocentric spacecraft velocity to be $V_2 =$ 0.715 km/sec, the distance $R_2 = R_{SOI} = 20{,}000$ km, and the flight path angle of 39° relative to the Moon, we can use the gravitational parameter

u_{Moon} = 4.90287 × 10^3 km^3/sec^2 and calculate the spacecraft's selenocentric orbital characteristics as follows:

Selenocentric Orbit

$$R_2 = R_{SOI} = 20{,}000\ km$$

$$V_2 = 0.715\ km/sec$$

$$\phi_{Relative\ to\ Moon\ at\ Patch\ Point} = 39°$$

$$E = \frac{V_2^2}{2} - \frac{u_{Moon}}{R_2} = \frac{(0.715\ km)^2}{2} - \frac{4.90287 \times 10^3\ km^3/sec^2}{20{,}000\ km} = 0.01047\ km^2/sec^2$$

$$h = R_2 V_2 \cos\phi_{Relative\ to\ Moon\ at\ Patch\ Point} = 11{,}113\ km^2/sec$$

$$p = \frac{h^2}{u_{Moon}} = 25{,}189\ km$$

$$e = \sqrt{1 + \frac{2Eh^2}{u^2}} = 1.0524$$

$$R_{Periselenium} = \frac{p}{1+e} = 12{,}272\ km$$

$$V_{Periselenium} = \frac{h}{R_{Periselenium}} = 0.906\ km/sec$$

$$\sin\frac{\delta_{Turning\ Angle}}{2} = \frac{1}{e};\quad \delta_{Turning\ Angle} = 2\sin^{-1}\frac{1}{e} = 143°$$

Note that the selenocentric orbit is a hyperbola ($e > 1$, $E > 0$) with a turning angle δ of 143°, and that periselenium is at 12,272 km. Your actual results may vary considerably from the calculated results shown in this example, due to uncertainties in your launch position and velocity, as well as Space Simulator's time acceleration errors. In the **MOON.STN** situation I created, the spacecraft actually impacted with the Moon's surface. The other selenocentric orbit values were as follows: R_2 = 19,998 km, V_2 = 1.239 km/sec, E = 0.5223 km^2/sec^2, h = 1417, p = 409 km, e = *1.0427*, and $R_{periselenium}$= 200 km (meaning that impact occurred since $R_{periselenium} < R_{Moon's\ Radius}$ (1738 km).

The Apollo spacecraft flew on trajectories similar to the one described here. However, the Apollo trajectory was designed as a "free-return," meaning that the orbit passed around the Moon in such a manner that it could return to the Earth with no additional power as shown in Figure 9.6. This added margin of safety ensured that the spacecraft would return to the Earth, even if the service module engines failed.

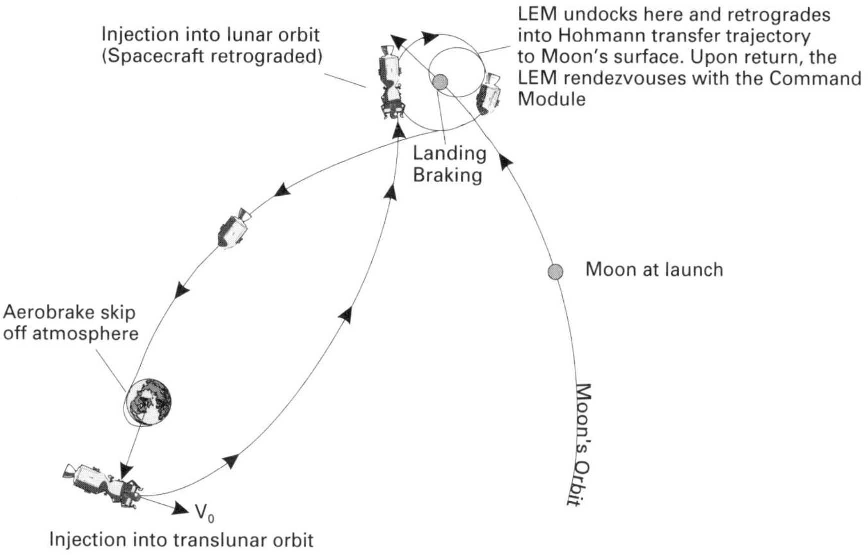

FIGURE 9.6 *The free-return trajectory used by Apollo*

LEM THRUST AND TRANSLATION CONTROLS

When using the LEM to land on the Moon, you may be confused by the orientation of the spacecraft with regard to the thrust and rotation controls. Just remember that the front of the LEM is where the hatch is, and the bottom of the spacecraft is where the windows and ladder are. In Figure 9.7, you'll see the rotational and translation directions for the LEM. The best way to practice using these controls is to open the **1972** situation, then undock the LEM from the Apollo Service Module. Next, using the Moon and the Apollo Service Module as your reference points, rotate and translate the LEM until you get the hang of using the controls.

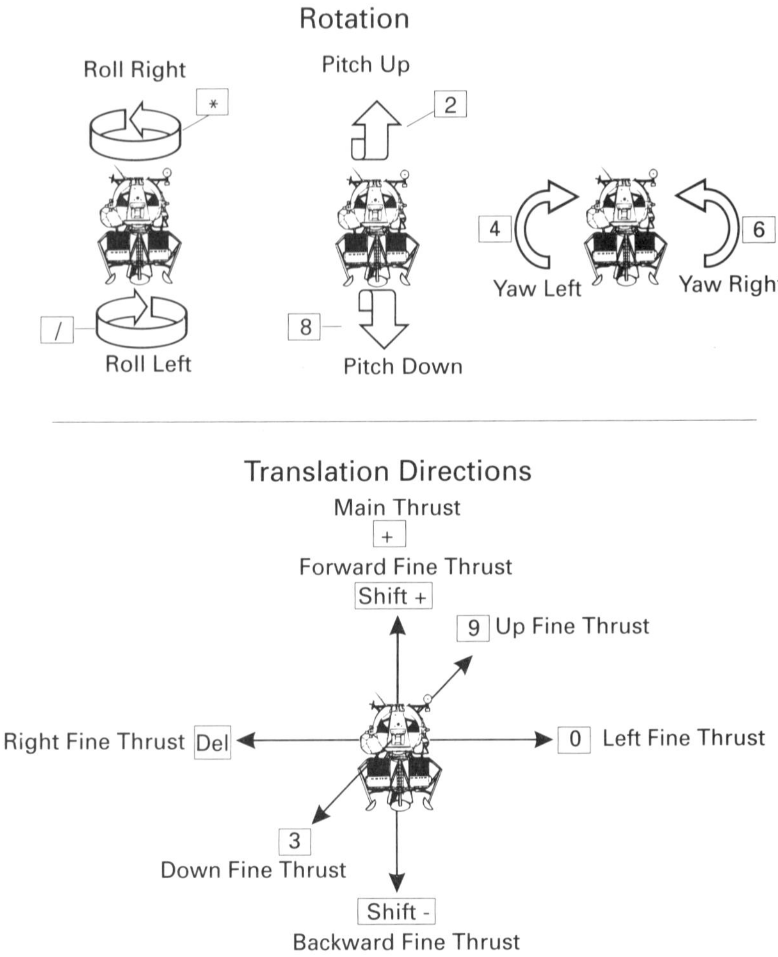

FIGURE 9.7 *Rotation and translation directions for the LEM*

Landing on the Moon is a tricky procedure, and you'll need to slow the spacecraft's vertical *and* ground velocity to less than 10 m/sec. The Main Thrusters (Keypad +) must be used to slow your vertical speed, but only the Left/Right (Keypad 0 and Keypad .) and the Up/Down (Keypad 9 and Keypad 3) Fine Thrusters are needed to control your ground speed.

When you are ready to take off from the Moon, apply the Main Thrusters and the LEM's upper ascent stage will blast off leaving the lower descent stage behind. You can see this all happen in Chase view.

Flying to Mars and Other Interplanetary Destinations

TEN

TEN

In this chapter, you'll learn how to dispatch your spacecraft on a Hohmann transfer trajectory to Mars, and in the process, learn how to plot orbits to any of the other planets. Unfortunately, Space Simulator doesn't have the capability of plotting high precision interplanetary orbits, and so your calculated trajectory will deviate from what you see on screen.

Despite this shortcoming, you can still have some fun calculating your trajectories and watching as Space Simulator plots your flight path. Although you won't be able to reliably predict where and when interplanetary interception will occur, you can play around with the initial launch conditions and by experimentation find an intercept path that will work for you. At the very least, you'll learn how real spacecraft trajectories are planned.

THE SOLAR SYSTEM

All the physical and orbital data for the nine planets are listed in Appendix C. Except for Mercury and Pluto, the orbits of the planets are nearly circular (but still elliptical in accordance with Kepler's First Law), with eccentricities of 0.0068 for Venus and 0.0934 for Mars. Mercury and Pluto have highly elliptical orbits, and their eccentricities are higher: 0.2056 for Mercury and 0.2583 for Pluto. In Figure 8.4 in Chapter 8, you can see that Pluto's orbit is so eccentric that its perihelion is inside the orbit of Neptune.

Also, with the exception of Mercury and Pluto, the orbital inclination i of each planet's orbit with respect to the plane of the ecliptic strays no farther than 3.4°. Mercury is inclined by 7°, and Pluto by 17.136° to the ecliptic plane. Thus, *to simplify our model of the solar system, we can say that the major planets move in coplanar circular orbits.*

Because the major planets move more or less in the plane of the ecliptic, spacecraft interception trajectories must also travel in the plane of the ecliptic. The only exception to this rule is when a spacecraft deliberately uses a planetary gravity assist to perform an out-of-the-ecliptic-plane intercept.

The asteroids, or minor planetoids, lie mostly between the orbit of Mars and Jupiter in a region of space called the *asteroid belt*. Of the 100,000 that are larger than 1 km, Ceres, Pallas, Vesta, and Hygiea are the largest, with Ceres having a radius of 500 km. Not all the asteroids are in the main asteroid belt, however. There are an estimated 2000 *Earth-approaching asteroids* that are larger than 1 km across, and at least 1 million asteroids that are larger than 10 m. In 1993, one such asteroid passed the Earth within 150,000 km!

BODE'S LAW

There is a simple relationship known as Bode's Law which has a curious resemblance to the known distances of the planets from the Sun. If you write down the numbers 0, 3, 6, 12,... (and continue the series by doubling the last number of the sequence), then add 4 to each number and divide by 10, the numbers obtained give the approximate distances of the planets from the Sun in Astronomical Units (AU). The law works quite well for the inner planets, but breaks down entirely for Neptune and Pluto, as can be seen in Table 10.1. There is at present no explanation of whether this law is a pure coincidence or has some bearing on the theory of the evolution of the solar system.

APPLYING THE PATCHED CONIC METHOD TO INTERPLANETARY TRAJECTORIES

In the previous chapter, we saw how the patched conic works for a single patch condition, namely transferring from the Earth's SOI to the Moon's SOI. For interplanetary missions, two patch conditions are applied: the first patch occurs when the spacecraft leaves the Earth's SOI and enters the Sun's SOI, and the second patch occurs when the spacecraft transfers from the Sun's SOI to the destination planet's SOI.

TABLE 10.1: *Bode's Law and Actual Distances to the Sun*

Planet	Bode's Law Distance to Sun (AU)	Actual Distance to Sun (AU)
Mercury	0.4	0.3871
Venus	0.7	0.7233
Earth	1.0	1.0000
Mars	1.6	1.5237
Asteroids	2.8	2.6500 (Average)
Jupiter	5.2	5.2028
Saturn	10.0	9.5380
Uranus	19.6	19.1910
Neptune	38.8	30.0610
Pluto	77.2	39.5290

For example, the spacecraft leaves on a hyperbolic trajectory with respect to the Earth so that at launch only the Earth and spacecraft are considered. Then, when the spacecraft reaches the Earth's SOI, we apply the *first patch* and calculate the orbit based only on the Sun and the spacecraft, ignoring all other planets. We find that, after leaving the Earth's SOI, the orbit is now an ellipse with respect to the Sun's SOI. If we choose a Hohmann least energy transfer orbit, we can figure out the appropriate heliocentric velocities and planetary phase angles needed for interception.

After the spacecraft reaches the destination planet's SOI, we apply the *second patch* and convert the heliocentric velocities to planetocentric velocities. If we carefully choose our angles and velocities, we can calculate the impact parameter, and then predict whether the spacecraft will flyby the destination planet on a hyperbolic orbit, be captured in an elliptical orbit, or impact the planet. With some fine tuning, we can save fuel by targeting the spacecraft's planetocentric orbit to include an aerobrake maneuver in the atmosphere.

ORIENTING YOUR SPACECRAFT FOR INNER AND OUTER PLANET PASSAGE

The method by which spacecraft are placed in heliocentric Hohmann transfer orbits differs depending on whether passage is to an inner or outer planet. If you are transferring to a planet in an outer orbit, such as from the Earth to Mars, you aim the spacecraft's residual escape velocity vector with respect to the Earth ($\mathbf{V}_\infty$) in the direction of the departure planet's orbital velocity ($\mathbf{V}_{\mathbf{Earth}}$) to take advantage of the planetary velocity assist. Thus, $\mathbf{V}_\infty + \mathbf{V}_{\mathbf{Earth}} = \mathbf{V}_{\mathbf{perihelion}}$, where $\mathbf{V}_{\mathbf{perihelion}}$ is the spacecraft's Hohmann velocity *with respect to the Sun at perihelion.* On the

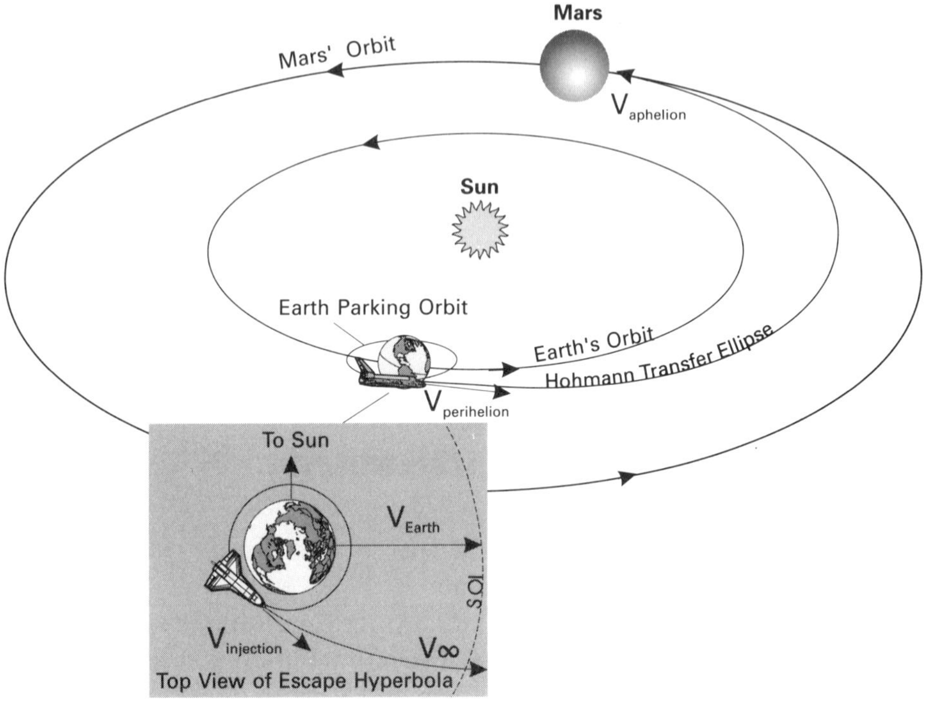

FIGURE 10.1 *Planetary escape from Earth parking orbit to outer planet using Hohmann transfer ellipse*

other hand, if you are transferring to an inner planet, such as from the Earth to Venus, you would aim $\mathbf{V}_\infty$ of the spacecraft in the direction *opposite to* $\mathbf{V}_{\mathbf{Earth}}$, so that $\mathbf{V}_{\mathbf{Earth}} - \mathbf{V}_\infty = \mathbf{V}_{\mathbf{aphelion}}$, where $\mathbf{V}_{\mathbf{aphelion}}$ is the spacecraft's Hohmann velocity *with respect to the Sun at aphelion*. The two methods of passage are illustrated in Figures 10.1 and 10.2.

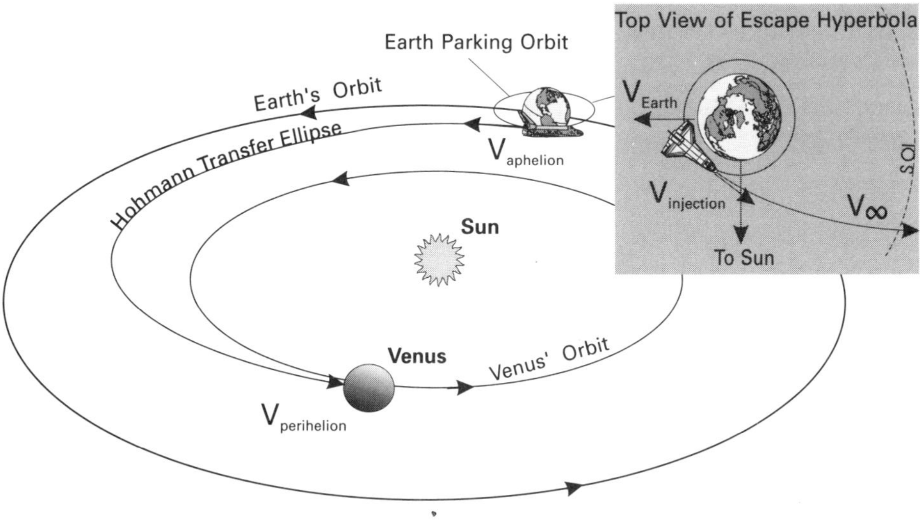

FIGURE 10.2 *Planetary escape from Earth parking orbit to inner planet using Hohmann transfer ellipse*

CALCULATING THE HOHMANN TRANSFER ORBIT TO MARS

Before we can determine what $V_{\text{injection}}$ is needed from parking orbit around the Earth, we need to calculate the heliocentric velocities required for a Hohmann transfer to Mars. Since the Hohmann transfer orbit's perihelion is at the Earth's orbit and the aphelion is at Mars' orbit, we can use the semi-major axis of Earth and Mars to calculate the semi-major axis $a_{\text{Earth-Mars Hohmann orbit}} = (a_{\text{Earth}} + a_{\text{Mars}})/2$. Using the familiar Energy equation $E = -u/2a$, we can then determine the energy of the transfer orbit, and then the heliocentric velocity $V_{perihelion}$ needed at departure from the Earth's SOI. The transfer orbit's characteristics are calculated as follows:

$$\underline{\textit{Hohmann Transfer Orbit Departure From Earth's SOI (Perihelion)}}$$

$$R_{perihelion} = a_{Earth} = 149{,}600{,}000\ km$$

$$R_{aphelion} = a_{Mars} = 227{,}900{,}000\ km$$

$$a_{Earth-Mars\ Hohmann\ orbit} = \frac{R_{perihelion} + R_{aphelion}}{2} = \frac{149{,}600{,}000\ km + 227{,}900{,}000\ km}{2} = 188{,}750{,}000\ km$$

$$E = -\frac{u_{Sun}}{2a_{Earth-Mars\ Hohmann\ orbit}} = -\frac{1.327 \times 10^{11}}{2 \times 188{,}750{,}000} = -351.523\ km^3 / sec^2$$

$$V_{perihelion} = \sqrt{2\left(E + \frac{u_{Sun}}{R_{perihelion}}\right)} = 32.726\ km / sec$$

$$\underline{\textit{Hohmann Transfer Orbit Arrival at Patch Point of Mars' SOI (Aphelion)}}$$

$$R_{aphelion} = a_{Mars} = 227{,}900{,}000\ km$$

$$V_{aphelion} = \sqrt{2\left(E + \frac{u_{Sun}}{R_{aphelion}}\right)} = 21.483\ km / sec$$

Note however, that $V_{perihelion}$ and $V_{aphelion}$ are the velocities of the spacecraft *with respect to the Sun, not to the Earth.* In order to get to Mars, your spacecraft must accelerate to $V_{perihelion}$ = 32.726 km/sec, and once your spacecraft reaches Mars, it will have a $V_{aphelion}$ = 21.483 km/sec.

Table 10.2 lists the Hohmann velocities and time of flights for trajectories from Earth to the planets.

SYNCHRONIZING ARRIVAL WITH THE DESTINATION PLANET'S POSITION

If the spacecraft is to intercept the destination planet at the same time it crosses the planet's orbit, you will need to figure out the correct angular

TABLE 10.2: *Hohmann Trajectories from Earth*

Planet	Heliocentric Speed at Earth Departure	Time of Flight
Mercury	22.280 km/sec	105.5 days
Venus	27.280 km/sec	146.1 days
Mars	32.730 km/sec	258.8 days
Jupiter	38.570 km/sec	2.74 years
Saturn	40.050 km/sec	6.04 years
Uranus	41.070 km/sec	16.16 years
Neptune	41.420 km/sec	30.780 years
Pluto	41.600 km/sec	46.03 years

relationship between the Earth and target planet at departure. This angle, called the lead or phase angle γ, is shown in Figure 10.3 for a Hohmann transfer from the Earth to Mars.

The total sweep angle, or true anomaly v_O, from departure to arrival along the spacecraft's Hohmann ellipse is 180° (i.e., ½ the ellipse). At departure, the proper phase angle between the Earth and the destination planet can be determined by the following equation:

EQUATION 10.1

$$\gamma = v_0 - \omega_{Destination\ Planet} \times (Time\ of\ Flight\ in\ Years)$$

where $\omega_{DestinationPlanet}$ is the angular velocity of the destination planet along its orbit, v_O is the angle between departure and arrival along the spacecraft's orbit, and *Time of Flight in Years* is the time the spacecraft takes to reach the destination planet. *For outer planet passages, such as*

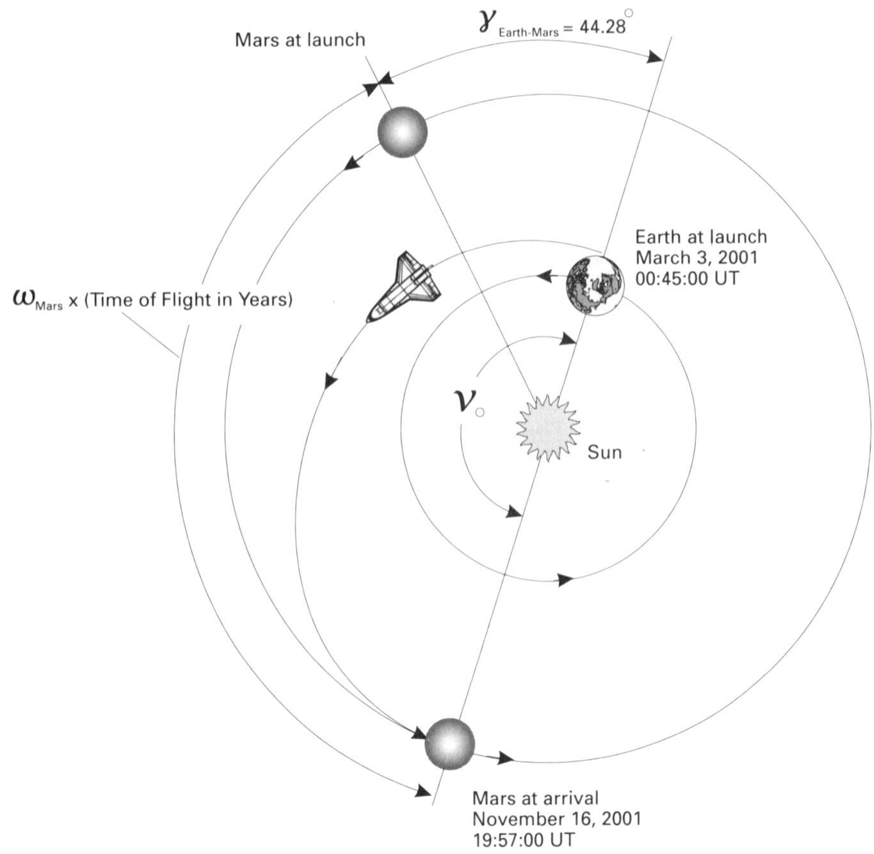

FIGURE 10.3 *Phase angle at departure*

Earth to Mars, γ is the angle by which the slower moving, outer destination planet (Mars) leads the faster moving, inner planet (Earth) at launch. For inner planet passages, such as Earth to Venus, the angle γ is the angle by which the slower moving Earth leads the faster moving Venus at launch.

Calculating the Time of Flight

Before you can figure out the planetary phase angle γ, you need to know the spacecraft's time of flight to reach the destination planet.

The time of flight can be calculated from Kepler's Third Law once you know the semi-major axis *a* of the Hohmann transfer orbit:

EQUATION 10.2

$$a_{semi-major\ axis\ of\ Hohmann\ orbit} = \frac{a_{Earth} + a_{Destination\ Planet}}{2}$$

$$Time\ of\ Flight\ (in\ seconds) = \pi\sqrt{\frac{a^3_{semi-major\ axis\ of\ Hohmann\ orbit}}{u_{Sun}}}$$

$$Time\ of\ Flight\ (in\ days) = \frac{Time\ of\ Flight\ (in\ seconds)}{1} \times \frac{1\ day}{24\ hours} \times \frac{1\ hour}{3{,}600\ seconds}$$

$$Time\ of\ Flight\ (in\ years) = \frac{Time\ of\ Flight\ (in\ days)}{1} \times \frac{1\ year}{365\ days}$$

For example, to calculate the time of flight for a Mars mission, you would perform the following calculations:

$$a_{semi-major\ axis\ of\ Earth\text{-}Mars\ Hohmann\ orbit} = \frac{a_{Earth} + a_{Mars}}{2} = \frac{149{,}600{,}000\ km + 227{,}900{,}000\ km}{2} = 188{,}750{,}000\ km$$

$$Time\ of\ Flight\ (in\ seconds) = \pi\sqrt{\frac{a^3_{semi-major\ axis\ of\ Earth\text{-}Mars\ Hohmann\ orbit}}{u_{Sun}}} = 22{,}363{,}761\ seconds$$

$$Time\ of\ Flight\ (in\ days) = \frac{Time\ of\ Flight\ (in\ seconds)}{1} \times \frac{1\ day}{24\ hours} \times \frac{1\ hour}{3{,}600\ seconds} = 258.8\ days$$

$$Time\ of\ Flight\ (in\ years) = \frac{Time\ of\ Flight\ (in\ days)}{1} \times \frac{1\ year}{365\ days} = 0.7092\ years$$

where $u_{Sun} = 1.327 \times 10^{11}\ km^3/sec^2$.

Refer back to Table 10.2 for a listing of flight times.

> **NOTE**
>
> **The time of flight for a Hohmann transfer ellipse where the spacecraft intercepts the destination planet at perihelion or aphelion is *always* ½ *the period of the entire orbit.* (Note the absence of a 2 before the π in Equation 10.2).**

Calculating the Planetary Phase Angle γ for Earth-Mars

To calculate the planetary phase angle between the Earth and Mars for the Hohmann transfer, use Equation 10.1 and plug in the values of $v_O = \pi$ (180°), $\omega_{Mars} = 3.340$ radians/year (from Table 10.3), and *Time of Flight(in years)* = 0.7092 years (calculated from the previous example):

$$\gamma_{Earth-Mars} = \pi - 3.340 \frac{radians}{year} \times (0.7092\, years) = 0.7729\ Radians = 44.28°$$

The optimum lead angle $\gamma = 44.28°$ for a Mars interception severely limits the times when a launch may take place. In fact, once the optimum phase angle has been reached, there won't be another launch window for 2.135 years, in what is known as the *synodic period*. Table 10.3 shows the synodic periods, as well as the angular velocity Δ, or each of the planets.

TABLE 10.3: *Angular Velocities and Synodic Periods of the Planets with Respect to the Earth*

Planet	ωPlanet (radians/year)	Synodic Period (year)
Mercury	26.11	0.3169 years
Venus	10.217	1.600 years
Mars	3.340	2.135 years
Jupiter	0.5297	1.092 years
Saturn	0.2132	1.035 years
Uranus	0.0748	1.012 years
Neptune	0.0381	1.006 years
Pluto	0.0254	1.004 years

You can estimate the angular position of the planets in Space Simulator using one of two methods described below.

Plotting γ on the Map Using the heliocentric Top Map view, you can roughly determine when the Earth and the destination, Mars, have the correct phase angle. Simply accelerate time and watch the Earth and Mars orbit the Sun; when Mars leads Earth by approximately 44°, stop the time acceleration, note the time and date, and then launch the spacecraft when it has reached the correct hyperbolic angle *n to the* $\mathbf{V}_{\mathbf{Earth}}$ direction.

Plotting γ by Using RA Angles in the Observatory For a more precise determination of γ, you can compare the heliocentric right ascension (RA) angle between the Earth and Mars using Space Simulator's Observatory. All you need to do is modify the date and time until the difference in the two RA hour angles between the Earth and Mars equals $\gamma = 44.28°$ (Mars leads the Earth by 2h 57m 07s of RA). To do this:

1. From the Options menu, select Observatory. A new Instrument Panel will open.
2. For this example, change the date on the Instrument Panel clock to **01 Mar 2001** and the time to **00:00:00** UT. You can change this later to other dates and times.
3. Click the Observatory Location label on the Instrument Panel and in the dialog box that opens, click the Planet button and choose the Earth as your observatory location (it doesn't matter where the surface location of the observatory is). Click OK twice to return to the simulation.
4. Click the Target label on the Instrument Panel and, in the dialog box that opens, select *Our Sun*. Click OK. This will aim the observatory telescope at the Sun.
5. On the Instrument Panel, note the Right Ascension readout of 22h 47m 36s. This is the RA angle to the Sun from the Earth, as shown in Figure 10.4. However, we need the RA angle to the Earth from the Sun which *is always exactly 12 hours different.*

To get this heliocentric RA, simply subtract (or add, if necessary) 12 hours to the RA angle on the readout so that it will remain between 0 and 24 hours. Thus, we *subtract* 12 hours from 22h 47m 36s to get a heliocentric Earth RA of 10h 47m 36s.

6 Repeat Step 3 but instead of the Earth, choose Mars. The new RA angle of the Sun from Mars will appear on the RA readout as 1h 48m 41s. However, we need the RA angle to Mars from the Sun which is, again, *exactly 12 hours different*. To get the heliocentric Mars RA we *add* 12 hours (because subtracting would make the RA < 0h) to get 13h 48m 41s.

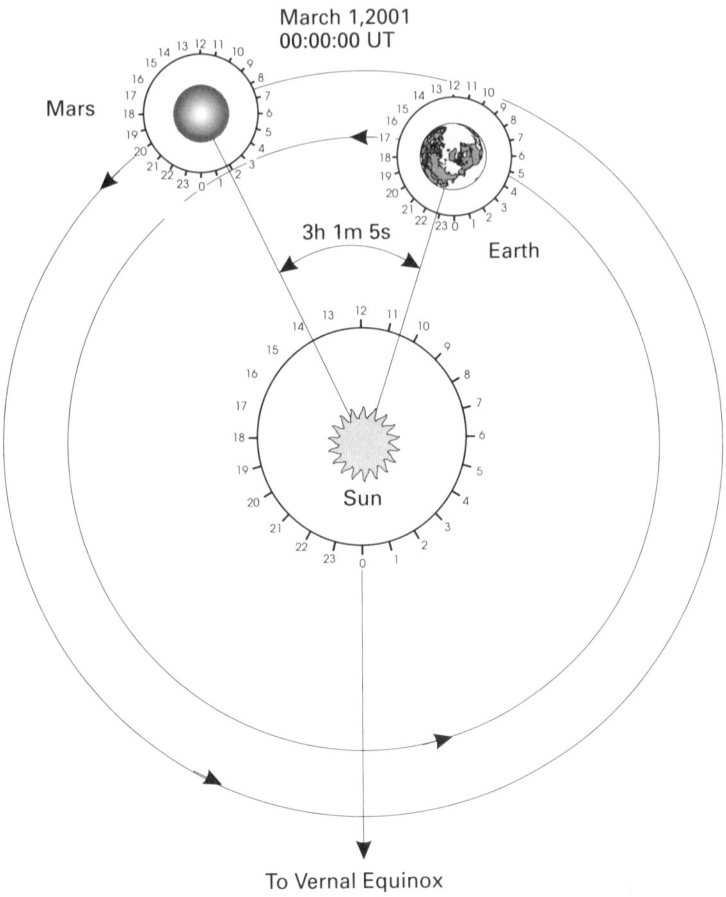

FIGURE 10.4 *The Right Ascension (RA) angular relationships of the Sun, Earth, and Mars.*

7 Open the Top Map view (press M), while still in Observatory mode, and zoom in or out to see the RA angular relationship between the Sun-Earth-Mars system. You should see something like Figure 10.4.

Now to find the *exact* angle γ between the Earth and Mars follow these steps:

1 The planetary phase angle γ is equal to the absolute value of Mars' RA – Earth's RA. This is your angle of γ_{RA} measured in hours-minutes-seconds of arc instead of degrees.

$$\gamma_{RA} = \left| Mars_{RA} - Earth_{RA} \right|$$

Example:

$$\gamma_{RA} = \left| 13h\ 48m\ 41s - 10h\ 47m\ 36s \right| = 3h\ 1m\ 5s$$

2 You'll need to convert γ_{RA} = 3h 1m 5s to decimal degrees ($\gamma_{Decimal\ Degrees}$) to see how close it is to the required angle of γ = 44.28°. To do this:

A First convert the RA angle of γ_{RA} to decimal RA ($\gamma_{Decimal RA}$) using this formula:

$$\gamma_{Decimal\ RA} = HH + \frac{MM}{60} + \frac{SS}{3600}$$

where

$$HH = \gamma_{RA}\ Hour$$

$$MM = \gamma_{RA}\ Minute$$

$$SS = \gamma_{RA}\ Second$$

Example:

$$\gamma_{RA} = 3h\ 1m\ 5s$$

$$\gamma_{Decimal\ RA} = 3 + \frac{1}{60} + \frac{5}{3600} = 3.0181\ hours$$

B Then convert the γ Decimal RA to γ Decimal Degree by multiplying by 15:

$$\gamma_{Decimal\ Degree} = \gamma_{Decimal\ RA} \times 15$$

Example:

$$\gamma_{Decimal\ Degree} = 3.0181\ hours \times 15 = 45.2715°$$

> **TIP**
>
> **Using the RA method described here, you will find that the best time for departure from the Earth to Mars falls on 03 Mar 2001 at 00:45:00 UT (γ Decimal Degree = 44.28°).**

Since γ Decimal Degree ≠ 44.28°, you need to advance the time until the RA of γ Decimal Degree agrees with 44.28°.

Applying the First Patch: Escaping the Earth's SOI

We have already calculated what the spacecraft's heliocentric Hohmann velocity must be from the Earth for a Mars mission ($V_{perihelion}$= 32.726 km/sec). Now we must figure out the geocentric velocities $V_{injection}$ and V_{∞} needed to send the spacecraft on the Mars trajectory at the spacecraft's current orbital radius $R_{injection}$. If we assume that the spacecraft is in a 320 km altitude geocentric circular orbit, $R_{injection} = R_{altitude} + R_{Earth}$ = 320 km + 6378 km = 6698 km, and we can calculate the circular velocity $V_{circular}$ as:

EQUATION 10.3

$$V_{Circular} = \sqrt{\frac{u}{R_{injection}}} = \sqrt{\frac{u_{Earth}}{R_{altitude} + R_{Earth}}} = \sqrt{\frac{3.986 \times 10^5}{(320\ km + 6378\ km)}} = 7.714\ km / sec$$

The escape velocity V_{esc} from the Earth's SOI for this 320 km altitude orbit can be calculated by:

EQUATION 10.4

$$V_{esc} = \sqrt{\frac{2u_{Earth}}{R_{injection}}} = \sqrt{2}\ V_{Circular} = \sqrt{2} \times 7.714\ km / sec = 10.909\ km / sec$$

When the spacecraft has escaped the Earth's SOI, it should have a hyperbolic excess velocity V_∞ with respect to the Earth of:

EQUATION 10.5

$$V_\infty = V_{perihelion} - V_{Earth} = 32.726\ km/sec - 29.790\ km/sec = 2.936\ km/sec$$

since the spacecraft will take advantage of the Earth's orbital velocity V_{Earth} of 29.790 km/sec to reach the needed Hohmann transfer velocity $V_{perihelion}$ of 32.726 km/sec.

The geocentric injection velocity from a 320 km orbit ($V_{injection}$) can be calculated by the following expression:

EQUATION 10.6

$$V_{injection} = \sqrt{V_{esc}^2 + V_\infty^2} = \sqrt{(10.909\ km/sec)^2 + (2.936\ km/sec)^2} = 11.297\ km/sec$$

Thus, when leaving from a 320 km altitude orbit, you'll need to accelerate the spacecraft to $V_{injection}$ = 11.297 km/sec in order to reach V_∞ = 2.936 km/sec at the Earth's SOI edge. At this point, your heliocentric Hohmann $V_{perihelion}$ should be approximately 32.726 km/sec.

> **WARNING**
>
> **A 1 percent error in your $V_{injection}$ velocity will cause a 15.2 percent error in V_∞. This means that if your $V_{injection}$ for Mars is off by 112 m/sec, V_∞ will deviate by 440 m/sec!**

For transfer to an outer planet, such as Mars, the vector $\mathbf{V}_\infty$ should be parallel to the Earth's orbital velocity vector $\mathbf{V}_{\mathbf{Earth}}$, as shown in Figure 10.5. Because the departure orbit is a hyperbola, the spacecraft will turn through an angle n before reaching the asymptotes of the escape hyperbola, with which $\mathbf{V}_\infty$ will be parallel. Our job is to make sure that the spacecraft is at an angle n with $\mathbf{V}_{\mathbf{Earth}}$, *before* prograding the spacecraft for the $V_{injection}$ burn.

The angle n is governed by the following relationship:

EQUATION 10.7

$$\cos n = -\frac{1}{e}$$

where e is the eccentricity of the hyperbola. The eccentricity of the hyperbola can be obtained from the injection conditions:

EQUATION 10.8

$$\underline{Departure\ \ Hyperbola\ \ Inside\ \ Earth's\ \ SOI}$$

$$V_{injection} = 11.297\ km / sec$$

$$R_{injection} = R_{altitude} + R_{Earth} = 320\ km + 6378\ km = 6698\ km$$

$$E = \frac{V^2_{injection}}{2} - \frac{u_{Earth}}{R_{injection}} = 4.301\ km^2 / sec^2$$

$$h = V_{injection} R_{injection} = 75{,}667\ km^2 / sec$$

$$e = \sqrt{1 + \frac{2Eh^2}{u^2_{Earth}}} = 1.145$$

Solving for n in Equation 10.7, we find that:

EQUATION 10.9

$$n = \cos^{-1}\left(-\frac{1}{e}\right) = \cos^{-1}\left(-\frac{1}{1.144}\right) = 151°$$

Note that it is not necessary for the spacecraft to depart the Earth in the plane of the ecliptic to intercept Mars! This means you can fly to Mars from any inclination orbit around the Earth. There is actually a locus of possible injection points which forms a circle on the Earth and a cone in space, as illustrated in Figure 10.6, where $V_{injection}$ may occur. At any of these injection points, if you prograde the spacecraft and accelerate to $V_{injection}$ velocity, the spacecraft will be hurled into the plane of the ecliptic!

The problem, then, is how to determine when the spacecraft intersects the side of the cone? If you knew the components of the Earth's velocity vector $\mathbf{V_{Earth}}$ and the spacecraft's $\mathbf{R_{injection}}$ vector components, you could use the dot product equality $\mathbf{R_{injection}}$ dot $\mathbf{V_{Earth}} = |\mathbf{R_{injection}}| \times |\mathbf{V_{Earth}}| \times \cos 151°$.

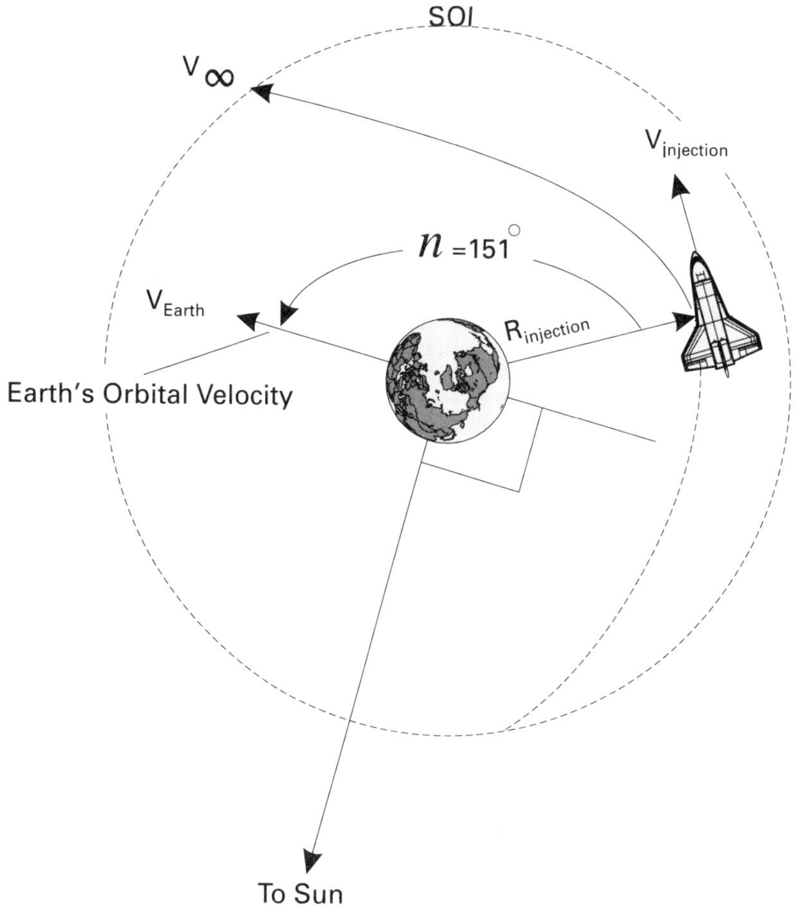

FIGURE 10.5 *Geometry of the departure hyperbola*

Unfortunately, Space Simulator does not provide you with vector components, so you cannot use this method. Fortunately, you can use the geocentric Top Map view to visually estimate the angle *n*.

Before figuring out *n*, let's place the spacecraft in a 320 km altitude equatorial orbit around the Earth:

1. Open the Autopilot, make sure the Earth is selected as your destination, and then click the Orbit button.
2. Type in an orbital altitude of **320 km**.

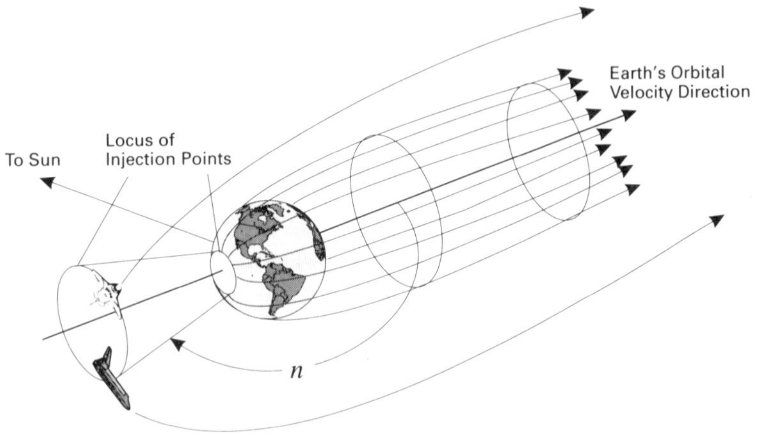

FIGURE 10.6 *The spacecraft doesn't need to be in the same orbital plane as the target planet. Here is the locus of possible injection points.*

3 Type in an orbital inclination angle of **0**°, then click the Execute button to return to the simulation.

The Autopilot will now place the spacecraft in a 320 km altitude equatorial parking orbit.

Now, to estimate the angle *n* needed for the Mars $V_{injection}$ burn, follow these steps:

1 Using the Time and Date controls, set the date and time that is ideal for the proper planetary phase angle. For Mars, this is **03 Mar 2001** at **00:45:00** UT.

2 Open the geocentric Top Map view. Zoom out until you see where the Sun's position is in relation to the Earth.

3 Draw an imaginary line from the Sun to the Earth, and then draw a second line through the center of the Earth which is perpendicular to the first line. This second line is the direction along which the Earth's velocity vector is directed. As shown in Figure 10.5, the angle *n* can be determined from this second line.

4 Accelerate time until the spacecraft crosses the line which forms the angle *n* with the perpendicular line to the Sun.

Injecting Your Spacecraft into the Mars Hohmann Orbit Your spacecraft is now ready for departure from the Earth! Simply prograde the spacecraft and then fire your thrusters until $V_{injection}$= 11.297 km/sec is achieved. Accelerate time to watch as your spacecraft escapes the confines of the Earth and arcs out towards its rendezvous with Mars. You should switch from a geocentric to a heliocentric Top Map view after your spacecraft is 600,000 km from the Earth (notice the heliocentric orbit is elliptical). When your spacecraft nears Mars, switch to an aerocentric Top Map view to better observe the spacecraft's hyperbolic approach to the planet.

Applying the Second Patch: Arrival at Mars' SOI

The spacecraft on a Hohmann trajectory to a planet can enter the planet's SOI at one of three positions: inside, outside, or right in the middle of the planet's heliocentric orbit. Using the impact parameter b and the approach distance d, you can calculate whether the spacecraft will impact or flyby the planet, according to the following rules:

1. If $d < b$, the spacecraft impacts the planet's surface.
2. If $d = b$, the spacecraft penetrates the atmosphere of the planet or, if no atmosphere exists, grazes the planet's surface.
3. If $d > b$, the spacecraft executes a hyperbolic flyby.

In Figure 10.7, we see a spacecraft entering the SOI of Mars on the inside of the planet's heliocentric orbit. If the spacecraft's $\mathbf{V_{aphelion}}$ velocity vector is pointed in the same direction as $\mathbf{V_{Mars}}$ (which would be the case for a Hohmann transfer), the spacecraft's $\mathbf{V_\infty}$ velocity with respect to Mars is given by:

EQUATION 10.10

$$V_\infty = V_{aphelion} - V_{Mars} = 21.483\ km/sec - 24.140\ km/sec = -2.657\ km/sec$$

where $\mathbf{V_{aphelion}}$ = 21.483 km/sec is the Hohmann aphelion velocity from the transfer orbit from Earth, and $\mathbf{V_{Mars}}$ = 24.140 km/sec is the planetary velocity of Mars. Because $\mathbf{V_\infty}$ is negative, it means that the spacecraft will eventually recede from Mars, unless the spacecraft is captured by Mars' SOI.

The following rule applies to any outer planet passage from an inner planet: *If the spacecraft's approach to the outer planet's SOI is from the inside of that planet's heliocentric orbit, the hyperbolic trajectory will turn counterclockwise around the planet. If the spacecraft's approach to the outer planet's SOI is from outside of that planet's heliocentric orbit, the hyperbolic trajectory will turn clockwise around the planet.*

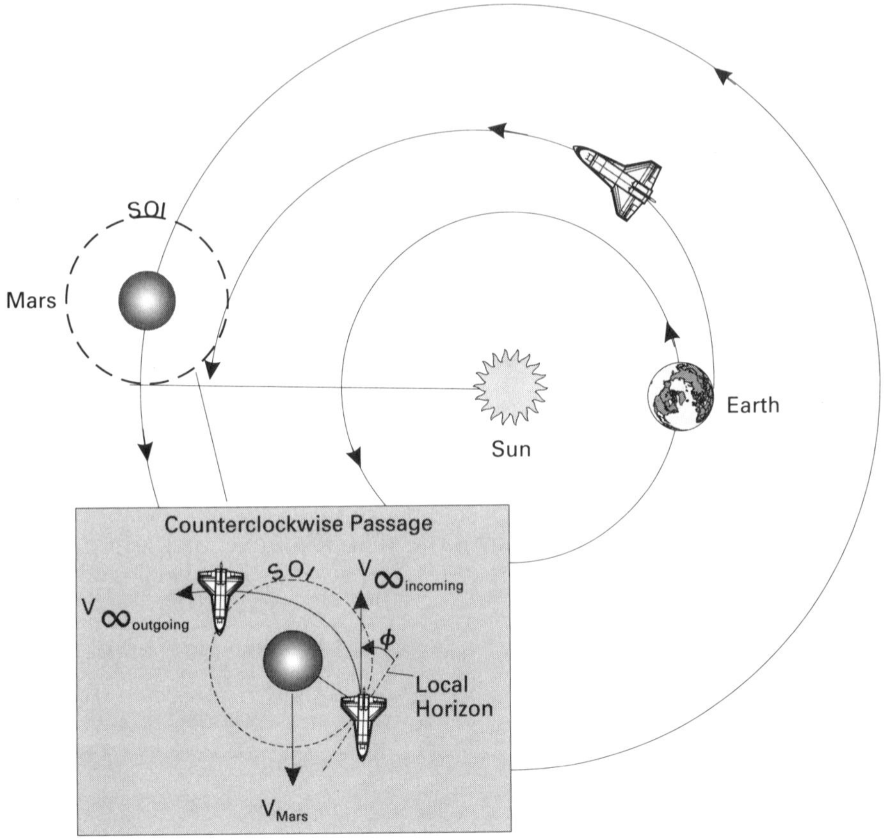

FIGURE 10.7 *Entering Mars' SOI from inside its heliocentric orbit causes counterclockwise planetocentric trajectory*

The impact parameter b can be calculated as follows:

EQUATION 10.11

$$b = R_{Mars}\sqrt{1+\frac{V_{esc}^2}{V_\infty^2}} = 7250\ km$$

where R_{Mars} = 3380 km, and V_{esc} from the surface of Mars is given by:

EQUATION 10.12

Mars' Surface Escape Velocity

$$V_{esc} = \sqrt{\frac{2u_{Mars}}{R_{Mars}}} = \sqrt{\frac{2\times 4.297\times 10^4\ km^3 / sec^2}{3380\ km}} = 5.042\ km / sec$$

Note that the smaller the spacecraft's arrival V_∞ is, the greater b is, which means that the spacecraft has a greater chance of impacting or grazing Mars.

Before we can calculate the approach distance d and therefore determine whether impact will occur, we need to figure out the flight path angle $\phi_{\text{relative to Mars}}$. To simplify matters, let's assume that we have measured $\phi_{\text{relative to Mars}} = 88°$, using the HUD.

To find out if the spacecraft will impact on Mars, solve for d and then compare it to b:

EQUATION 10.13

$$d = R_{SOI}\cos\phi_{relative\ to\ Mars} = 330{,}000\ km \times \cos 88° = 11{,}517\ km$$

Since $d > b$ (11,517 km > 7250 km), the spacecraft executes a hyperbolic flyby of Mars.

After the spacecraft has entered Mars' SOI, the arrival hyperbola parameters can be calculated as follows:

$$\underline{Arrival\ \ Hyperbola\ \ Inside\ \ Mars'\ \ SOI}$$

$$V_\infty = -2.657\ km/sec$$

$$R_{SOI} = 330{,}000\ km$$

$$\phi_{relative\ to\ Mars} = 88^\circ$$

$$E = \frac{V_\infty^2}{2} - \frac{u_{Mars}}{R_{SOI}} = 3.400\ km^2\ /\ sec^2$$

$$h = \left|V_\infty\right| R_{SOI} \cos\phi_{relative\ to\ Mars} = 30{,}600\ km^2\ /\ sec$$

$$p = \frac{h^2}{u_{Mars}} = 21{,}791\ km$$

$$e = \sqrt{1 + \frac{2Eh^2}{u_{Mars}^2}} = 2.109$$

$$R_{periapsis} = \frac{p}{1+e} = 7009\ km$$

$$V_{periapsis} = \frac{h}{R_{periapsis}} = 4.366\ km/sec$$

The spacecraft's altitude at closest approach will be $R_{periapsis} - R_{Mars} =$ 7009 km – 3380 km = 3629 km.

APPENDICES

Mathematics Review

APPENDIX A

APPENDIX A

This appendix is intended to give you a quick review of some basic mathematical concepts that are used in this book.

EXPONENTS

If a number is raised to a power, it is multiplied by itself the number of times indicated by the power or exponent. Thus, two raised to the power of 3 is notated like this: $2^3 = 2 \times 2 \times 2$. Exponents can be positive or negative integers or fractional numbers, such as, for example, $3^{0.44}$ and $7^{-4.5}$, but you can't evaluate them as you would 2^3; instead you should use a calculator. Any number raised to the power of zero equals one, as for example $4^0 = 1$ or $6.888^0 = 1$.

The negative power of a number is the reciprocal of the same positive power, as is illustrated below:

EQUATION A.1

$$a^{-n} = \frac{1}{a^n}; \qquad 2^{-2} = \frac{1}{2^2} = \frac{1}{4}; \qquad 5^{-1/2} = \frac{1}{5^{1/2}} = \frac{1}{\sqrt{5}}$$

n A.1

Some other rules of exponents are shown below.

EQUATION A.2

$$a^0 = 1; \qquad 3^0 = 1$$

$$a^1 = a; \qquad 3^1 = 3$$

$$a^n a^m = a^{n+m}; \qquad 3^4 3^2 = 3^{4+2} = 3^6$$

$$\frac{a^n}{a^m} = a^{n-m}; \qquad \frac{3^4}{3^2} = 3^{4-2} = 3^2$$

$$a^{1/n} = \sqrt[n]{a}; \qquad 3^{1/3} = \sqrt[3]{3}$$

$$(a^n)^m = a^{nm}; \qquad (3^2)^3 = 3^{2\times 3} = 3^6$$

SCIENTIFIC NOTATION

Scientific notation is used to express very large or very small numbers. For example, the Earth's distance to the Sun is 149,000,000,000 meters, and the speed of light is 300,000,000 m/sec. Instead of writing and carrying so many zeros, the numbers are written as a figure between 1 and 10 multiplied by the power of 10 which equals the number of zeros. The number of zeros corresponds to the power to which 10 is raised. For example, the speed of light, 300,000,000 m/sec, becomes 3×10^8 m/sec and 0.00000567 becomes 5.67×10^{-6}.

When numbers expressed in scientific notation are multiplied, the following rule should be applied.

EQUATION A.3

$$10^n \times 10^m = 10^{n+m}$$

Example

$$\begin{aligned}(5.3\times10^3)(4.34\times10^{-7}) &= (5.3\times4.34)(10^3\times10^{-7})\\ &= 23.002\times10^{3+(-7)}\\ &= 23.002\times10^{-4}\\ &= 0.0023002\end{aligned}$$

When dividing numbers in scientific notation, use this rule:

EQUATION A.4

$$\frac{10^n}{10^m} = 10^n \times 10^{-m} = 10^{n-m}$$

Example

$$\begin{aligned}\frac{5.5\times10^2}{3\times10^{-4}} &= \left(\frac{5.5}{3}\right)\left(10^2\times10^{-(-4)}\right) = \left(\frac{5.5}{3}\right)\left(10^{2-(-4)}\right) = \left(\frac{5.5}{3}\right)\left(10^{2+4}\right)\\ &= 1.83\overline{3}\times10^6\\ &= 1{,}833{,}333.3\overline{3}\end{aligned}$$

ANGULAR MEASURE

Angular measurements used to measure astronomical events are based on units of time (for example, Greenwich Hour Angles and right ascension angles are measured using Hours-Minutes-Seconds (HMS) of angular measure), degree arc measure, or radian arc measure. The following units are equivalent.

- One Circle = 360° = 24 hours HMS = 2π radians
- 15° = 900′ = 54,000″ = 1 hour HMS = 0.2618 radians
- 1° = 60′ = 3600″ = 4 minutes HMS = 0.01745 radians
- 1′ = 60″ = 4 seconds HMS = 0.0002909 radians

Time is a useful measure of angular displacement when figuring Greenwich Hour Angles to the vernal equinox. Since the Earth rotates 15° every sidereal hour, and 360° every 24 hours, you can easily plot planet and star positions by the sidereal time and declination angle to the equator. This is how the Right-Ascension-Declination coordinate system works, and if you have an ephemeris, you can quickly determine where an object in the sky should appear in relation to the rotating Earth for a given time and date.

TRIGONOMETRY

The three basic trigonometric functions are defined as follows:

EQUATION A.5

$$\sin\theta = \frac{a}{c}$$

$$\cos\theta = \frac{b}{c}$$

$$\tan\theta = \frac{a}{b}$$

where the sides *a, b,* and *c* of the right triangle used to measure these functions are shown in Figure A.1. The angle Θ is measured in degrees or radians, but you must be sure to set your calculator to either degree or radian mode when using the trigonometric functions and then be consistent in using only those units of angular measure.

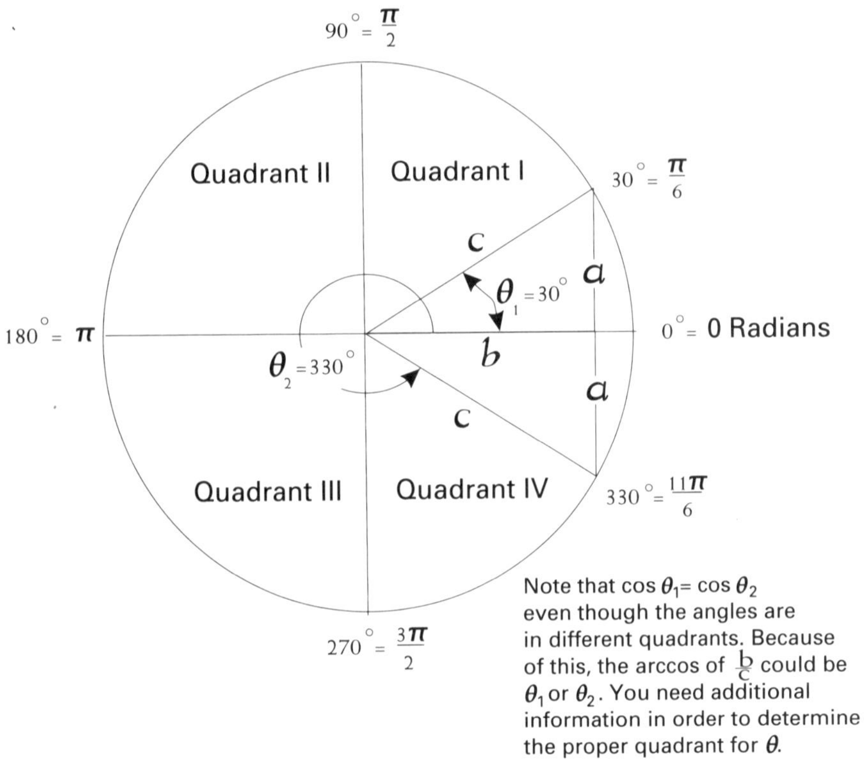

FIGURE A.1 *The trigonometric functions are derived from the right triangle.*

The inverse trigonometric functions are defined as follows:

EQUATION A.6

$$y = \sin^{-1} x = \arcsin x \quad \textit{if and only if} \quad \sin y = x$$
$$\textit{where } -1 \le x \le 1 \textit{ and } -\frac{\pi}{2} \le y \le \frac{\pi}{2}$$

$$y = \cos^{-1} x = \arccos x \quad \textit{if and only if} \quad \cos y = x$$
$$\textit{where } -1 \le x \le 1 \textit{ and } 0 \le y \le \pi$$

$$y = \tan^{-1} x = \arctan x \quad \textit{if and only if} \quad \tan y = x$$
$$\textit{where } x \textit{ is any real number and } -\frac{\pi}{2} \le y \le \frac{\pi}{2}$$

Note that because of the way the inverse trigonometric functions are defined, you won't be able to determine the correct quadrant that the angle y is in without additional information. For example, if x is 0, the arcsin x could be 0 radians (0°) or it could be π radians (180°). For this reason, you need additional information to resolve the correct quadrant.

The Pythagorean Theorem provides the following relationship between the sides of a right triangle:

EQUATION A.7

$$c^2 = a^2 + b^2$$

$$\sin^2\theta + \cos^2\theta = 1$$

In addition, the Law of Cosines can be applied to any triangle, as shown in Figure A.2:

EQUATION A.8

$$a^2 = b^2 + c^2 - 2bc\cos\alpha$$

$$b^2 = a^2 + c^2 - 2ac\cos\beta$$

$$c^2 = a^2 + b^2 - 2ab\cos\gamma$$

The sum of the angles inside any triangle always equals 180° (except spherical trigonometry triangles).

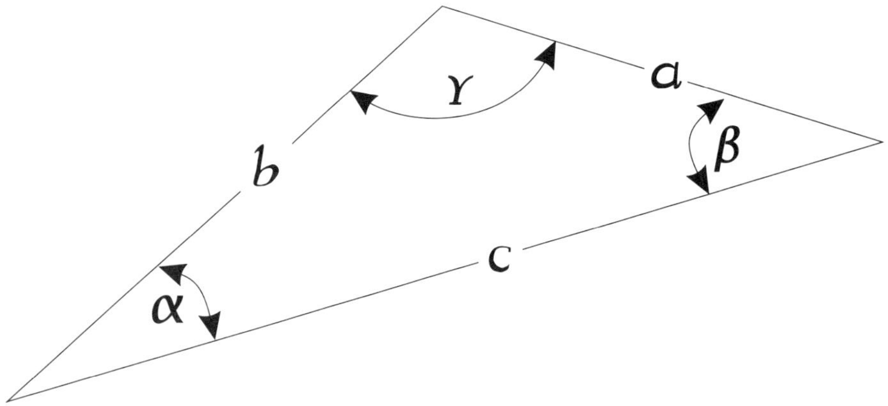

FIGURE A.2 *The Law of Cosines*

VECTORS

The dot product of two vectors **A** $<A_x, A_y, A_z>$ and **B** $<B_x, B_y, B_z>$ is a scalar quantity defined by:

EQUATION A.9

$$A \bullet B = |A||B|\cos\theta = \left(\sqrt{A_x^2 + A_y^2 + A_z^2}\right)\left(\sqrt{B_x^2 + B_y^2 + B_z^2}\right)\cos\theta$$

where Θ is the angle between the two vectors. However, the dot product of two vectors is also equal to:

EQUATION A.10

$$A \bullet B = A_x B_x + A_y B_y + A_z B_z$$

Thus, if you know the components of two vectors, you can find the angle between them by using this equation:

EQUATION A.11

$$\theta = \cos^{-1}\left[\frac{(A_1 \cdot B_2)}{|A_1||B_2|}\right] = \cos^{-1}\left[\frac{A_x B_x + A_y B_y + A_z B_z}{\sqrt{A_x^2 + A_y^2 + A_z^2}\sqrt{B_x^2 + B_y^2 + B_z^2}}\right]$$

Note that when the two vectors **A** and **B** are perpendicular to each other, $\Theta = 90°$ (or $\pi/2$) and the dot product is equal to zero (~;q could also equal 270° or $3\pi/2$ if the vectors are perpendicular—which is again a quadrant resolution problem).

The vector cross product of two vectors **A** and **B** is another vector **C** that is perpendicular to both **A** and **B**, as shown in Figure A.3. The cross product it is defined as follows:

EQUATION A.12

$$A \times B = (A_y B_z - A_z B_y)\mathbf{I} + (A_z B_x - A_x B_z)\mathbf{J} + (A_x B_y - A_y B_x)\mathbf{K}$$

where the new vector $\mathbf{C} = <(A_yB_z - A_zB_y)\mathbf{I}, (A_zB_x - A_xB_z)\mathbf{J}, (A_xB_y - A_yB_x)\mathbf{K}>$.

The magnitude of the cross product is defined as:

EQUATION A.13

$$|A \times B| = |A||B|\sin\theta$$

where θ is the angle between the vectors **A** and **B**.

Note that when the two vectors **A** and **B** are parallel to each other, $\theta = 0°$, and the cross product is equal to zero.

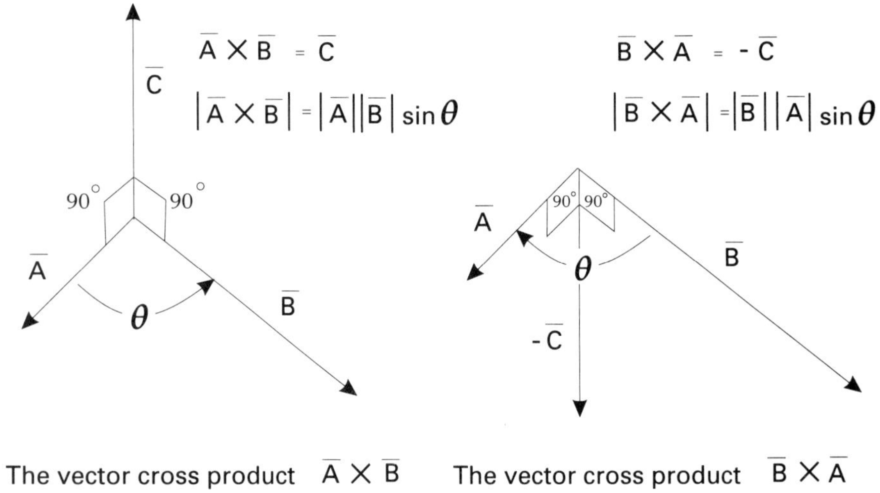

FIGURE A.3 *The cross product*

Miscellaneous Constants and Conversions

APPENDIX B

APPENDIX B

TABLE B.1:

Miscellaneous Constants and Conversions		
Speed		
1 mile/hr (mph)	= 1.47 ft/sec = 0.447 m/sec = 1.61 km/hr	
1 m/sec	= 3.281 ft/sec = 3.600 km/hr = 2.237 mph	
1 km/sec	= 1000 m/sec = 3281 ft/sec = 0.6214 mile/sec = 3600 km/hr = 2237 mph	
Speed of Light	= 299,792,458 m/sec = 299,792 km/sec = 186,282 mile/sec = 1,079,252,848 km/hr = 670,616,629 mph = 7.21 AU/hr	
Acceleration		
Surface Acceleration of Gravity at Earth's Equator	9.75	m/sec^2 = 31.99 ft/sec^2
Surface Acceleration of Gravity at Earth's Poles	9.851	m/sec^2 = 32.32 ft/sec^2
1*g*	9.8	m/sec^2
2*g*	19.6	m/sec^2
3*g*	29.4	m/sec^2
4*g*	39.2	m/sec^2
1 m/sec^2	3.28	ft/sec^2
Length		
1 m	3.281	ft
1 km	0.261	mile
1 km	1000	m
1 ft	0.3048	m
1 mile	1.609	km
1 mile	5280	ft
1 nautical mile	1.15	mile (statute)
1 nautical mile	1852	m
60 nautical miles	1	Degree of Longitude at Earth Equator
1 Astronomical Unit (AU)	= 1.495979×10^{8} km = 92,955,825 miles = Earth Orbital Radius around Sun	
1 light year	= 9.461×10^{15} m = 9.461×10^{12} km = 5.8785×10^{12} miles = 63,240 AU	
1 parsec	= 206,265 AU = 3.262 light years	
1 megaparsec	3,260,000	light years
Mass		
1 metric ton	1000	kg
1 kg	2.2046	lbs. (at Earth's surface only)
1 English ton	2000	lbs.
1 lb	0.4536	kg (at Earth's surface only)
1 slug	14.59	kg
Force		
1 Newton	0.2248	lb
1 Newton	1	kg m/sec^2 F=mxa
1 lb	4.448	Newtons
1 lb	1	slug ft/sec^2 F=mxa
Time		
1 Tropical Year [1]	= 365.2422 Solar Days = 31,556,926 Solar Seconds	
1 Sidereal Year [2]	= 365.2564 Solar Days = 31,558,152 Solar Seconds	
1 Year [3]	= 365 Solar Days = 31,536,000 Solar Seconds	
1 Sidereal Day	= 23h 56m 4s of Solar Time = 0.997269 Solar Days = 86,164 Solar Seconds	
1 Sidereal Hour	= 3600 Sidereal Seconds =3590 Solar Seconds = 0.997269 Solar Hours	
1 Solar Day	= 24 hours = 86,400 seconds of Solar Time = 1.002737 Sidereal Days = 24h 3m 56s Sidereal Time = 86,636 Sidereal Seconds	
1 Solar Hour	= 3600 Solar Seconds = 3609 Sidereal Seconds = 1.002737 Sidereal Hours	
Angular Measure		
=	3.141592654	radians
1 =	0.017453293	radians
1 radian =	57.29577951	
Constant of Gravitation		
G = $6.6725985 \times 10^{-20}$		$km^3/(kg\ sec^2)$

Notes

[1] A tropical year is the period for 1 revolution of the Earth around the Sun with respect to the vernal equinox (e.g., the moment at which the Sun crosses the equatorial plane on March 21st).

[2] A sidereal year is the period for 1 revolution of the Earth around the Sun with respect to the fixed stars.

[3] To make our 365 day/year calender fit the tropical year of 365.2422 days, we have adopted the Gregorian calender which stipulates that we add a leap day every 4 years but skip leap days for those years ending in 00 (e.g. 1700, 1800, 1900) that are not divisible by 400. This brings the Gregorian year = 365.2425 solar days, which is a fairly close approximation of the tropical year = 365.2422 solar days.

Physical and Orbital Data for the Planets, Moons, and Stars

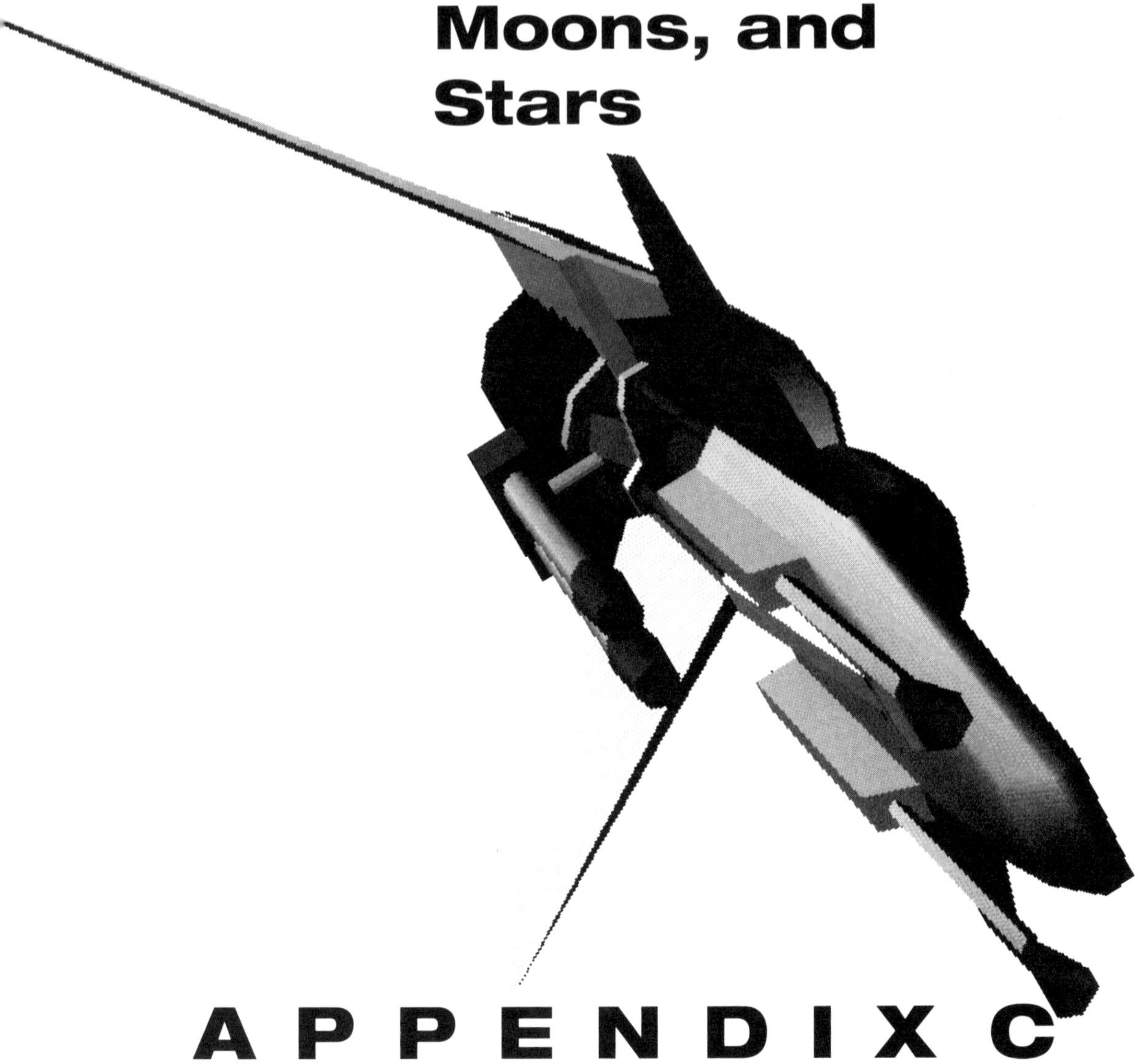

APPENDIX C

APPENDIX C

Physical Data for the Planets and Moons

Body	Radius of Body (km)	Gravitational Parameter u (km^3/sec^2)	Mass (kg)	Units of Earth Mass	Density (gm/cm^3)	Surface Gravity in g's (Earth=1)	V_{esc} (km/sec) from Surface	Equatorial Rotation Period (Sidereal)	Inclination of Equator to Orbit (Degrees)
Sun	695,950	1.327E+11	1.99E+30	332,899.99517	1.40	27.959	617.522	24 days 14h 16m 40s (2,125,000 sec)	N/A
Mercury	2439	2.168E+04	3.25E+23	0.05440	5.43	0.372	4.217	58 days 15h 42m 30s (5,067,750 sec)	0.0
Venus	6052	3.248E+05	4.87E+24	0.81490	5.24	0.905	10.361	243 days 22h 5m (21,074,700 sec) [1]	177.4 [2]
Earth	6378	3.986E+05	5.97E+24	1.00000	5.52	1.000	11.180	23h 56m 04s (86,164 sec)	23.4
Earth's Moon	1738	4.903E+03	7.35E+22	0.01230	3.30	0.166	2.375	27 days 7h 43m 11s (2,360,591 sec)	6.7
Mars	3380	4.297E+04	6.44E+23	0.10780	3.90	0.381	5.042	24h 37m 22s (88,642 sec)	25.2
Phobos	12	6.672E-04	1.00E+16	1.68E-09	2.00	4.73E-04	0.011		
Deimos	7	1.221E-04	1.83E+15	3.06E-10	1.70	2.95E-04	0.006		
Jupiter	71,398	1.267E+08	1.90E+27	317.80000	1.30	2.536	59.569	9h 50m 30s (35,430 sec)	3.1
Io	1815	5.965E+03	8.94E+22	0.01497	3.60	0.185	2.564		
Europa	1569	3.190E+03	4.78E+22	0.00800	3.00	0.132	2.016		
Ganymede	2631	1.028E+04	1.54E+23	0.02578	1.90	0.151	2.795		
Callisto	2400	7.186E+03	1.08E+23	0.01810	1.90	0.127	2.447		
Amalthea	100	N/A	N/A	N/A	N/A	N/A	N/A		
Himalia	90	N/A	N/A	N/A	N/A	N/A	N/A		
Saturn	60,369	3.791E+07	5.68E+26	95.11000	0.70	1.062	35.440	10h 14m (36,840 sec)	26.7
Mimas	197	2.469E+00	3.70E+19	0.00001	1.20	0.006	0.158		
Enceladus	251	4.938E+00	7.40E+19	0.00001	1.20	0.008	0.198		
Tethys	524	5.004E+01	7.50E+20	0.00013	1.30	0.019	0.437		
Dione	560	7.340E+01	1.10E+21	0.00018	1.40	0.024	0.512		
Rhea	765	1.668E+02	2.50E+21	0.00042	1.30	0.029	0.660		
Titan	2575	8.981E+03	1.35E+23	0.02253	1.90	0.138	2.641		
Hyperion	135	4.537E+00	6.80E+19	0.00001	N/A	0.025	0.259		
Iapetus	718	1.268E+02	1.90E+21	0.00032	1.20	0.025	0.594		
Phoebe	110	1.268E+00	1.90E+19	0.00000	N/A	0.011	0.152		
Uranus	25,400	5.788E+06	8.67E+25	14.52000	1.30	0.916	21.348	10h 46m 48s (38,808 sec)	-97.9 [4]
Miranda	243	5.338E+00	8.00E+19	0.00001	1.30	0.009	0.547		
Ariel	580	8.674E+01	1.30E+21	0.00022	1.60	0.026	0.463		
Umbriel	595	8.674E+01	1.30E+21	0.00022	1.40	0.025	0.540		
Oberon	775	1.935E+02	2.90E+21	0.00049	1.50	0.033	0.707		
Titania	805	2.335E+02	3.50E+21	0.00059	1.60	0.037	0.762		
Neptune	24,300	6.806E+06	1.02E+26	17.14000	1.50	1.761	23.668	15h 44m 12s (56,652 sec)	29.0
Triton[3]	1360	1.468E+03	2.20E+22	0.00368	2.10	0.081	1.469		
Nereid	170	3.336E+00	5.00E+19	0.00001	N/A	0.018	0.222		
Proteus	200	N/A	N/A	N/A	N/A	N/A	N/A		
Larissa	100	N/A	N/A	N/A	N/A	N/A	N/A		
Pluto	1155	9.976E+02	1.50E+22	0.00250	2.10	0.076	1.314	6 days 9h 25m 20s (552,320 sec)	118.0
Charon	600	N/A	N/A	N/A	N/A	N/A	N/A		

Notes

For this table, power of ten scientific notation is expressed as "E+12" instead of $x10^{12}$

N/A= Not Available

[1] The rotation period of Venus is 19 days longer than its period of revolution about the Sun. Because of this, the length of a Venus day --the time between successive noons -- is equivalent to 117 Earth days.

[2] Venus rotates from east to west -- in the reverse direction from the rotation of most other planets.

[3] Triton is the only major satellite in a retrograde orbit (meaning that it revolves from east to west around Neptune).

[4] Uranus rotates on an axis that is tilted on its side. During part of its orbit, one pole is pointed directly at the Sun, and the other pole experiences constant darkness.

TABLE C.1: *Physical Data for the Planets and Moons*

Orbital Elements and Data for the Planets and Moons

Body	Semi-Major Axis a			Eccentricity	Inclination of Orbit to Ecliptic Plane	Heliocentric Longitude of the Ascending Node	Heliocentric Argument of Periapsis	True Anomaly at Epoch of June 28th, 00:00 UT, 1969	Orbital Velocity	Sidereal Period		
	AU	10^6 km	10^3 km	e	i (°)	Ω (°)	ω (°)	ν (°)	km/sec	Around Sun (Tropical Years)	Around Sun (Solar Days)	Around Planet (Solar Days)
Mercury	0.3871	57.9		0.2056	7.0040	48.0	29.0	264.1	47.87	0.24085	87.97	
Venus	0.7233	108.2		0.0068	3.3940	76.4	54.7	195.3	35.05	0.61521	224.70	
Earth	1.0000	149.6		0.0167	0.0000	Undefined	102.4	173.7	29.79	1.000039 [1]	365.2564 [1]	
Earth's Moon			384.4	0.0549					1.0176			27.32166 [2]
Mars	1.5237	227.9		0.0934	1.8500	49.3	286.2	289.6	24.14	1.88089	686.98	
Phobos			9.4						0.6739			0.32
Deimos			23.5						0.4268			1.26
Ceres	2.7671	414.0		0.0770	10.6000	N/A	N/A	N/A	17.9	4.603	1681.21	
Jupiter	5.2028	778.3		0.0482	1.3060	100.1	273.5	174.9	13.06	11.86	4332	
Amalthea			181						26.414			0.5
Io			422						17.32			1.77
Europa			671						13.732			3.55
Ganymede			1070						10.871			7.16
Callisto			1883						8.194			16.69
Himalia			11,480						3.332			251
Saturn	9.5380	1426.9		0.0539	2.4890	113.4	340.4	297.2	9.65	29.46	10,760	
Mimas			186						14.436			0.94
Enceladus			238						12.573			1.37
Tethys			295						11.322			1.89
Dione			377						10.004			2.74
Rhea			527						8.4628			4.52
Titan			1222						5.5536			15.95
Hyperion			1481						5.0442			21.3
Iapetus			3561						3.2554			79.3
Phoebe			12,950						1.7073			550
Uranus	19.1910	2870.8		0.0471	0.7730	73.9	97.6	11.7	6.8	84.07	30,690	
Miranda			130						6.6837			1.41
Ariel			191						5.4898			2.52
Umbriel			266						4.6512			4.14
Titania			436						3.6304			8.71
Oberon			583						3.1405			13.5
Neptune	30.0610	4497.1		0.0050	1.7730	131.4	280.9	185.3	5.49	164.82	60,190	
Larissa			74						N/A			0.55
Proteus			118						N/A			1.12
Triton			355						4.4006			5.88
Nereid			5511						1.0765			360
Pluto	39.5290	5913.5		0.2583	17.1360	109.9	113.0	312.6	4.74	248.6	90,460	
Charon			19.7	N/A					N/A			6.39

Notes

N/A Not Applicable or Unknown

[1] The period of the Earth around the Sun, with respect to the vernal equinox is 365.2422 solar days. However, the vernal equinox shifts west (retrograde to the Earth's orbit) due to perturbations of the Sun and Moon which cause the Earth's poles to precess (this motion is called precession of the equinoxes -- and this amounts to 50" of arc each year). Because of this motion, the sidereal period of the Earth with respect to the fixed stars (365.2564 days) is longer than the tropical year (365.2422 days) by about 20 minutes of time.

[2] Due to solar perturbations, the sidereal period of the Moon around the Earth may vary by as much as 7 hours or 0.29166 days per revolution.

TABLE C.2: *Orbital Elements and Data for the Planets and Moons*

Finding Your Orbit Around the Earth

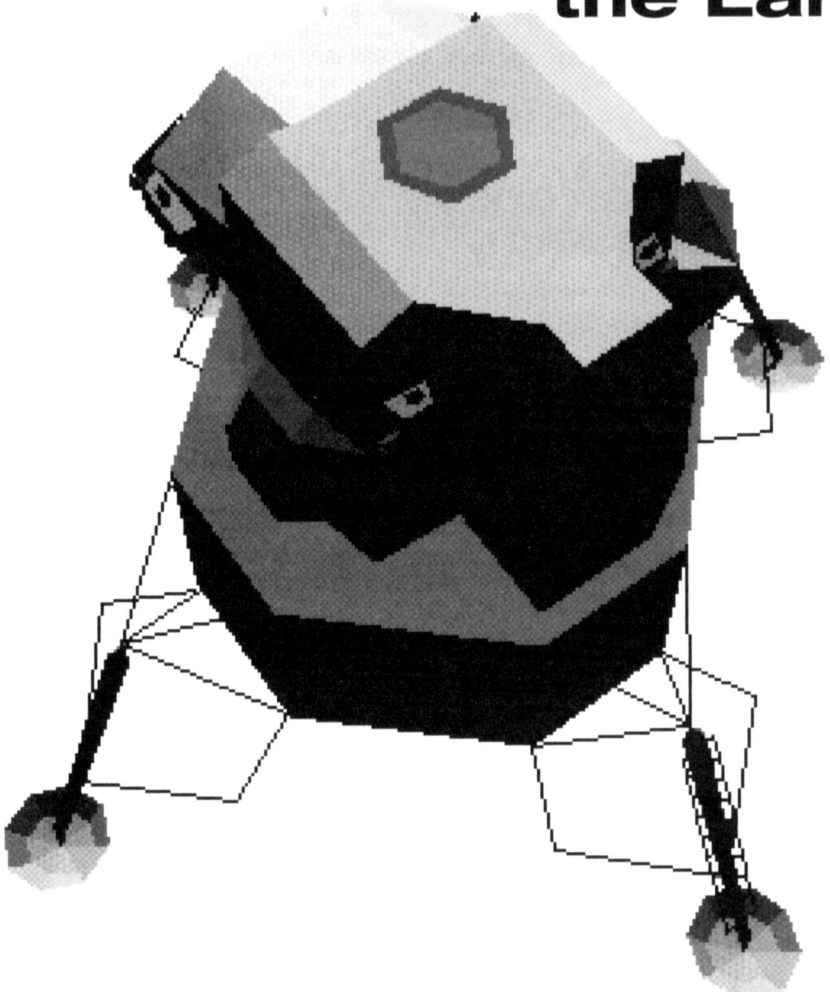

APPENDIX D

The next section introduces you to an original method for figuring out position and velocity vector components, as well as the classical orbital elements. This is the best and most precise method for determining your orbit's characteristics.

FINDING YOUR VECTOR COMPONENTS FOR ORBIT DETERMINATION

Unfortunately Space Simulator does not provide you with the position vector components $\mathbf{R_x}$, $\mathbf{R_y}$, $\mathbf{R_z}$, or the velocity components $\mathbf{V_x}$, $\mathbf{V_y}$, $\mathbf{V_z}$. If you had this information, you could determine all six of the classical orbital elements with ease, using the methods described in Chapter 7. This would allow you to precisely determine your spacecraft's orbit.

I have developed a novel method of figuring out the vector components for **R** and **V** from data that are displayed in Space Simulator. The method is not simple but it works, and it allows you to find out everything you might want to know about a spacecraft's orbit around the Earth. Note that because this method relies on the Earth's latitude/longitude coordinate system for its frame of reference, you cannot use it to describe orbits around the Sun or other planets.

To use this method, you must have a scientific calculator, or a spreadsheet such as Microsoft's Excel, that has built-in trigonometric functions. Also, you must make sure that the calculator is being run in radian mode, not degree display mode, for your trigonometric entries and calculations. Excel's built-in trigonometric functions assume radian values, so you must convert your latitude/longitude degree measurements to radian values before plugging them into the functions. Radians are arc measurements made in units of π and they are related to the 360 degrees of arc around a circle by this formula: radians = $(2\pi \times \text{degrees}) / 360$. To convert 45° to radians, you would multiply $(2\pi \times 45°) / 360 = 0.7854$ radians. Of course, your calculator or spreadsheet will have a built-in radian-to-degree conversion function which you can also use. Since latitude and longitude are expressed in degrees, minutes, and seconds format, you'll first need to convert positions to decimal latitude/longitude before converting them to radians.

EQUATION D.1

$$\text{Convert Latitude/ Longitude to Decimal Degree} = \text{HHH}+\frac{\text{MM}}{60}+\frac{\text{SS}}{3600}$$

To convert latitude/longitude to decimal degree format, follow this formula:

where

HHH =	Degrees of latitude/longitude
MM =	Minutes of latitude/longitude
SS =	Seconds latitude/longitude

For example, to convert a starting longitude coordinate of 39° 28′ 57″ W to decimal degree format, add

EQUATION D.2

$$39+\frac{28}{60}+\frac{57}{3600}=39.4825°$$

You would then convert the 39.4825° to radians by multiplying $(2\pi 39.4825°) / 360 = 0.6891$ radians.

This conversion of the latitude/longitude coordinates is greatly simplified if you have a scientific calculator that converts degrees in the hour-minutes-seconds format to the decimal-hours format. On a Hewlett Packard Scientific Calculator 48G, for example, you would use the HMS→ function by entering the latitude or longitude as HHH.MMSS, where the HHH represents the degrees, the MM represents the minutes, and the SS represents the seconds. Thus to convert the 39° 28′ 57″ W, you would enter 39.2857 and then press the HMS→ function key on the menu display to have the number converted to 39.4825°.

Let's use the Galactic Explorer's orbit, as found in the **Flight** situation, to demonstrate how the method works. First, you'll need to take two positions in your orbit, separated by some time interval. In the example that is given, we'll use a starting time of 12:07 UT and an ending time of 15:24 UT. Next, you should write down the Universal Time, date, distance to the center of the Earth, your speed, and latitude/longitude coordinates at both positions (latitude/longitude is displayed in the Set Location menu command dialog box). Then, using information found in Tables D.1 through D.5, you'll calculate the angle between the Greenwich Prime Meridian and the constellation of Aries, which marks the vernal equinox direction, as well as the **IJK**'s **I**-axis point in the Geocentric-Equatorial coordinate system (which is also the X-axis for the **R** and **V** vectors).

Since the Earth moves about the Sun, this angle changes for each day of the year and needs to be initialized for a given Greenwich Hour Angle (GHA) for January 1 of each year. Furthermore, as the Earth revolves around its own axis the Greenwich Prime Meridian is displaced eastwards by 15° each hour, and this also affects the measured angle. By correcting for the UT, the day of the year, and the year, it is possible to determine the exact angle in radians from the Greenwich Prime Meridian to the vernal equinox. This angle is called the Greenwich Hour Angle, or *GHA*. Then all you need to do is figure out the spacecraft's current longitude in radians and add or subtract it from this corrected *GHA* (for West longitudes, you subtract; for East longitudes, you add).

The result of this is the spacecraft's angle to the vernal equinox, called θ, which is measured in radians. Equation D.3 describes how the spacecraft's θ angle to Aries is calculated. In the equation, GHA_{Jan01} is the proper *GHA* angle for the current year, *Days* is the number of days since the beginning of the year on January 1, UT_{Decimal} is the decimal Universal Time (use the same decimal conversion method for latitude/longitude), and $\lambda_{\text{Spacecraft Longitude in Radians}}$ is the spacecraft's current longitude measured in radians. For West longitudes, the $\lambda_{\text{Spacecraft Longitude in Radians}}$ should be negative. The GHA_{Jan01} for the year 2000 is 1.7447 radians, as can be seen in Table D.2.

EQUATION D.3

$$\theta_{\text{Spacecraft Angle to Aries}} = GHA_{Jan\ 01} + (1.0027379093 \times Days) + (UT_{Decimal} \times 15 \times \frac{2\pi}{360}) + \lambda_{\text{Spacecraft Longitude in Radians}}$$

Through a spherical coordinate to rectangular coordinate transformation (R, ϕ, and θ) $\rightarrow$ (x,y,z), you can then use θ (from the above equation) and the spacecraft's latitude, called ϕ in radians, to compute $\mathbf{R_{x1}}$, $\mathbf{R_{y1}}$, $\mathbf{R_{z1}}$, for position vector $\mathbf{R_1}$. At the second position $\mathbf{R_2}$, you would use the new latitude and longitude to recompute R, ϕ, and θ to obtain $\mathbf{R_{x2}}$, $\mathbf{R_{y2}}$, $\mathbf{R_{z2}}$. In the equation below, the spacecraft's latitude ϕ should be changed to a negative number if it is a South latitude. Use the following spherical coordinate transformation equations to convert the distance R (taken from your Distance readout), θ, and ϕ to rectangular vector coordinates:

EQUATION D.4

$$\mathbf{R_x} = R\cos\phi\ \cos\theta$$

$$\mathbf{R_y} = R\cos\phi\ \sin\theta$$

$$\mathbf{R_z} = R\sin\phi$$

After you have determined both $\mathbf{R_1}$ and $\mathbf{R_2}$, you'll need to calculate the velocity vector $\mathbf{V_1}$, which is the velocity of your spacecraft at position $\mathbf{R_1}$. $\mathbf{V_1}$ has vector components $\mathbf{V_x}$, $\mathbf{V_y}$, and $\mathbf{V_z}$, which are based on the **IJK** Geocentric-Equatorial coordinate system.

But how do you calculate $\mathbf{V_1}$? The answer is to use the Gauss method, so called because this method was first derived by the great nineteenth-century mathematician Karl Friedrich Gauss. Around 1781, astronomers had discovered the seventh planet, Uranus, and were looking for more distant members of the solar system since Bode's Law predicted their existence. A plan was formed to search the sky for evidence of these predicted planets. In 1801, an astronomer by the name Piazzi discovered Ceres, the first of a swarm of asteroids circling the Sun between Mars and Jupiter. Was it a comet or a planet? Nobody knew how to figure this out quickly, since the science of celestial dynamics was in its infancy. Gauss decided to undertake the problem, so he calculated and calculated until he arrived at a solution. Ceres had long since disappeared behind the Sun's blinding glare, and so astronomers had no way of observing it. Gauss, proclaimed to an astonished world that he knew where Ceres was and predicted exactly where it should be one year later. Ceres was rediscovered on New Year's Day in 1802, exactly 1 year later, precisely where Gauss had predicted it must be found.

To understand and appreciate Gauss' achievement, you must realize that at the time astronomers had meager data and virtually no means of measuring distance or velocity, except line-of-sight directions at each sighting. Gauss had to determine the orbit by observing two positions of the asteroid and recording the time between sightings. This was all he had to work with! The method he derived is defined as follows: given two position vectors $\mathbf{R_1}$ and $\mathbf{R_2}$ of an orbiting object and the time of flight between these points, find $\mathbf{V_1}$ and $\mathbf{V_2}$. Once $\mathbf{V_1}$ has been determined, you can figure out all the orbital elements and completely describe the orbit. You can then predict where the object will be in its orbit for any time in the future!

Gauss developed two special functions *f* and *g*, which he used to calculate $\mathbf{V_1}$ and $\mathbf{V_2}$. The basis for his method makes use of a fundamental linear algebra theorem concerning coplanar vectors: *If* **A**, **B**, *and* **C** *are coplanar vectors, and* **A** *and* **B** *are not collinear, it is possible to express* **C** *as a linear combination of* **A** *and* **B** (e.g., $\mathbf{C} = k_1\mathbf{A} + k_2\mathbf{B}$, where k_1 and k_2 are two separate constants). Coplanar vectors are vectors which lie in the same plane, while collinear vectors are vectors which can be expressed as a scalar multiple of one another (e.g., if **A** and **B** are collinear then $\mathbf{A} = k\mathbf{B}$, where *k* is some scalar constant).

Since $\mathbf{R_1}$, $\mathbf{R_2}$, $\mathbf{V_1}$ are all in the same orbital plane they are coplanar, and since $\mathbf{R_1}$ and $\mathbf{R_2}$ are not collinear, you can use this law to find special functions *f* and *g* that will allow this linear combination to exist. The relationship between $\mathbf{R_1}$, $\mathbf{R_2}$, $\mathbf{V_1}$ is summarized in vector equation D.5. Note that *f* and *g* are scalar functions, having a single discrete value (in other words a constant, like the k_1 and k_2 discussed above), while the vectors $\mathbf{R_1}$, $\mathbf{R_2}$, $\mathbf{V_1}$ have vector components. Thus to solve for $\mathbf{V_1}$ you would need to separate out each x, y, and z vector component and solve Equation D.5 three times;

once for each vector component. Thus, for example, $\mathbf{V_x} = (\mathbf{R_{x2}} - f\,\mathbf{R_{x1}}) / g$, $\mathbf{V_y} = (\mathbf{R_{y2}} - f\,\mathbf{R_{y1}}) / g$, and $\mathbf{V_z} = (\mathbf{R_{z2}} - f\,\mathbf{R_{z1}}) / g$.

EQUATION D.5

$$\mathbf{R}_2 = f\mathbf{R}_1 + g\mathbf{V}_1$$

and rearranging terms

$$\mathbf{V}_1 = \frac{\mathbf{R}_2 - f\mathbf{R}_1}{g}$$

Equation D.6 shows both the f and g functions, where Δv is the angle between the two vectors $\mathbf{R_1}$ and $\mathbf{R_2}$. (Don't confuse Δv with the change in velocity variable ΔV used in earlier chapters; they are not the same quantity.) The variable p is the semi-latus rectum, and the constant u is the gravitational parameter for the Earth, which has the value of 3.986×10^5 km^3/sec^2. You can figure out the value of p from the equation $p = h^2 \times u$, where $h = R_1 \times V_1 \times$ cos(flight path angle in radians). In the latter equation, R_1 is the distance taken from your Distance readout, and V_1 is the velocity taken from your Total Velocity readout (don't use vector components!).

EQUATION D.6

$$f = 1 - \frac{R_2}{p}(1 - \cos \Delta v)$$

$$g = \frac{R_1 R_2 \sin \Delta v}{\sqrt{up}}$$

From the dot product Δv can be determined by the following equation:

EQUATION D.7

$$\mathbf{R}_1 \cdot \mathbf{R}_2 = |\mathrm{R}_1||\mathrm{R}_2| \cos \Delta \mathrm{v}$$

and rearranging terms

$$\Delta \mathrm{v} = \cos^{-1}\left[\frac{(\mathbf{R}_1 \cdot \mathbf{R}_2)}{|\mathrm{R}_1||\mathrm{R}_2|}\right] = \cos^{-1}\left[\frac{\mathrm{R}_{x1}\mathrm{R}_{x2} + \mathrm{R}_{y1}\mathrm{R}_{y2} + \mathrm{R}_{z1}\mathrm{R}_{z2}}{\mathrm{R}_1\mathrm{R}_2}\right]$$

After you have determined the velocity vector $\mathbf{V_1}$ from Equation D.5, you can use the methods described earlier in this chapter to determine the six classical elements a, e, i, Ω, ω, and v_0.

EXAMPLE: FINDING THE GALACTIC EXPLORER'S VECTOR COMPONENTS

To demonstrate the method, let's determine the vector components for two positions and the initial velocity vector components for the Galactic Explorer in the flight situation. Using this information we can then determine all of the orbital elements. Note that in the procedure that follows you'll find radian angles that fall outside the range of 0 to 2π. These angles should be converted to their angular counterpart that falls within the range of 0 to 2π. To do this, simply divide the radian angle by 2π, then take the fractional remainder (discard the integer portion to the left of the decimal in the quotient) and multiply this by 2π. Thus, for example, 6000 radians is the equivalent of 5.8412 radians, since 6000 $\times 2\pi = 954.9296$ radians, and discarding the integer portion of 954 leaves $0.9296 \times 2\pi = 5.8412$ radians.

1 Start the **Flight** situation.

2 Write down the date August 31, 2000, and the time (we'll use a UT of 12:07 for the first vector position). Pause the simulation and figure out the number of days since January 1, 2000, using the information found in Table D.1. Since 2000 is a leap year, you'll use the second column. Because the date is August 31, you'll add 31 days to the number 213. This gives you a total day count of 244 days from January 1.

3 Write down the distance to the Earth's center from the Distance display, *and* the total velocity from the Total Velocity display. We'll assign the variable names R_1 for the distance, and V_1 for the velocity.

TABLE D.1: *Number of Days from Beginning of Year*

Number of Days From Beginning of Year	Ordinary Year (365 Days)	Leap Year (366 Days)
Jan	0	0
Feb	31	31
Mar	59	60
Apr	90	91
May	120	121
Jun	151	152
Jul	181	182
Aug	212	213
Sep	243	244
Oct	273	274
Nov	304	305
Dec	334	335

4 Open the Set Location dialog box and write down the spacecraft's current latitude and longitude. South latitudes and West longitudes should be changed to negative numbers.

5 Resume the simulation and advance the rate of time until 15:24:00 UT. Don't set the clock via the Time dialog box, you must use the Time Acceleration button. The spacecraft will be in a new location over the Earth. Note that the UT you use for the second position will be different for other orbits.

6 Repeat Steps 3 and 4 above for the second position vector, but don't repeat Step 5. We will call this position $R2$ and velocity $V2$. Write down the data.

7 Convert the latitude and longitude for each of the recorded positions to decimal latitude and longitude, as described in Equation D.1. Remember that in the calculations to follow, South latitudes and West longitudes need to be entered as negative numbers. Then convert each of these angles to radians. We'll give the spacecraft's longitude at R_1 the variable name $\lambda_{1\,\text{Spacecraft Longitude in Radians}}$, and at R_2 we'll call it $\lambda_{2\,\text{Spacecraft Longitude in Radians}}$. The latitude angles for R_1 and R_2, will be given the variable names ϕ_1 and ϕ_2 (not to be confused with the flight path angle ϕ used in previous chapters).

8 Find the year 2000 in Table D.2. Using the proper GHA_{Jan01} for Jan 01 of the year 2000, write down the radian angle 1.7447. If your orbit occurred in a different year you would write down the appropriate radian angle from the table entry for that year.

9 Convert the UT for both positions into decimal UT. To do this, simply divide the minutes by 60, the seconds by 3600, and then add these two numbers to the hours. Thus 12:07:00 UT becomes 12.1166 hours UT_{Decimal} for position R_1, and 15:24:00 UT becomes 15.4 hours UT_{Decimal} for position R_2. Table D.3 shows the entries for Decimal UT.

10 Using Equation D.3, figure out the angle $\theta_{\text{Spacecraft Angle to Aries}}$ at R_1, being sure to plug in the number of days variable ($Days = 244$, from step 2 above), the UT_{Decimal} at R_1 from step 9, and $\lambda_{1\,\text{Spacecraft Longitude in Radians}}$ at R_1. To convert the resulting angle so that it is between 0 and 2π, simply divide it by 2π, discard the integer part of the quotient, and multiply the fractional decimal remainder by 2π. We'll call this longitude angle θ_1 ($\theta_1 = 2.1420$ radians $= 122.7280°$).

11 Using Equation D.3, figure out the angle $\theta_{\textit{Spacecraft Angle to Aries}}$ at R_2, being sure to plug in the number of days variable ($Days = 244$, from step 2 above), the UT_{Decimal} at R_2, and $\lambda_{2\,\text{Spacecraft Longitude in Radians}}$ at R_2. If you want to convert the radian angle so that it is between 0 and 2π, simply divide it by 2π, discard the integer part of the quotient, and multiply the fractional decimal remainder by 2π. We'll call this longitude angle θ_2 ($\theta_2 = 2.8898$ radians $= 165.5760°$).

TABLE D.2: *Finding the GHA Angle for the Years 1968–2010*

Greenwich Hour Angle to Aries ($GHA_{Jan\ 01}$) for the Years 1968-2010					
Year	Month-Day	Universal Time (UT)	Sidereal Time $GHA_{Jan\ 01}$ in Hours-Minutes-Seconds	$GHA_{Jan\ 01}$ in Radians	$GHA_{Jan\ 01}$ in Decimal Degrees
1968 (Leap)	Jan-01	00:00:00 UT	6h 38' 53"	1.7405	99.7208
1969	Jan-01	00:00:00 UT	6h 41' 52"	1.7535	100.4667
1970	Jan-01	00:00:00 UT	6h 40' 55"	1.7493	100.2292
1971	Jan-01	00:00:00 UT	6h 39' 58"	1.7452	99.9917
1972 (Leap)	Jan-01	00:00:00 UT	6h 39' 00"	1.7410	99.7500
1973	Jan-01	00:00:00 UT	6h 42' 01"	1.7541	100.5042
1974	Jan-01	00:00:00 UT	6h 41' 04"	1.7500	100.2667
1975	Jan-01	00:00:00 UT	6h 40' 06"	1.7458	100.0250
1976 (Leap)	Jan-01	00:00:00 UT	6h 39' 09"	1.7416	99.7875
1977	Jan-01	00:00:00 UT	6h 42' 08"	1.7546	100.5333
1978	Jan-01	00:00:00 UT	6h 41' 10"	1.7504	100.2917
1979	Jan-01	00:00:00 UT	6h 40' 12"	1.7462	100.0500
1980 (Leap)	Jan-01	00:00:00 UT	6h 39' 15"	1.7421	99.8125
1981	Jan-01	00:00:00 UT	6h 42' 14"	1.7551	100.5583
1982	Jan-01	00:00:00 UT	6h 41' 16"	1.7509	100.3167
1983	Jan-01	00:00:00 UT	6h 40' 19"	1.7467	100.0792
1984 (Leap)	Jan-01	00:00:00 UT	6h 39' 22"	1.7426	99.8417
1985	Jan-01	00:00:00 UT	6h 42' 21"	1.7556	100.5875
1986	Jan-01	00:00:00 UT	6h 41' 24"	1.7514	100.3500
1987	Jan-01	00:00:00 UT	6h 40' 27"	1.7473	100.1125
1988 (Leap)	Jan-01	00:00:00 UT	6h 39' 30"	1.7431	99.8750
1989	Jan-01	00:00:00 UT	6h 42' 30"	1.7562	100.6250
1990	Jan-01	00:00:00 UT	6h 41' 33"	1.7535	100.4667
1991	Jan-01	00:00:00 UT	6h 40' 36"	1.7479	100.1500
1992 (Leap)	Jan-01	00:00:00 UT	6h 39' 38"	1.7437	99.9083
1993	Jan-01	00:00:00 UT	6h 42' 38"	1.7568	100.6583
1994	Jan-01	00:00:00 UT	6h 41' 40"	1.7526	100.4167
1995	Jan-01	00:00:00 UT	6h 40' 43"	1.7485	100.1792
1996 (Leap)	Jan-01	00:00:00 UT	6h 39' 45"	1.7442	99.9375
1997	Jan-01	00:00:00 UT	6h 42' 44"	1.7573	100.6833
1998	Jan-01	00:00:00 UT	6h 41' 47"	1.7531	100.4458
1999	Jan-01	00:00:00 UT	6h 40' 49"	1.7489	100.2042
2000 (Leap)	Jan-01	00:00:00 UT	6h 39' 51"	1.7447	99.9625
2001	Jan-01	00:00:00 UT	6h 42' 50"	1.7577	100.7083
2002	Jan-01	00:00:00 UT	6h 41' 53"	1.7535	100.4708
2003	Jan-01	00:00:00 UT	6h 40' 56"	1.7494	100.2333
2004 (Leap)	Jan-01	00:00:00 UT	6h 39' 59"	1.7453	99.9958
2005	Jan-01	00:00:00 UT	6h 42' 58"	1.7583	100.7417
2006	Jan-01	00:00:00 UT	6h 42' 01"	1.7541	100.5042
2007	Jan-01	00:00:00 UT	6h 41' 04"	1.7500	100.2667
2008 (Leap)	Jan-01	00:00:00 UT	6h 40' 08"	1.7459	100.0333
2009	Jan-01	00:00:00 UT	6h 43' 07"	1.7589	100.7792
2010	Jan-01	00:00:00 UT	6h 42' 10"	1.7548	100.5417

12 Using Equation D.4, compute the $\mathbf{R_{x1}}$, $\mathbf{R_{y1}}$, $\mathbf{R_{z1}}$ vector components for position vector $\mathbf{R_1}$ using the latitude ϕ_1 and longitude θ_1 angles for $\mathbf{R_1}$.

TABLE D.3: *Figuring out the Angle Between the Greenwich Prime Meridian and Aries, Corrected for Date and Time*

Corrected GHA for Date and Time = GHA_{JAN01} + ($1.0027379093 \times 2\pi \times$ Days) + ($15 \times$ Decimal UT Hours $\times 2\pi/360$)				
Year and Date Correction for Greenwich Meridian Angle to Aries				
	Angle from Aries to Greenwich Prime Meridian In Radians	Angle from Aries to Greenwich Prime Meridian in Degrees	**Explanation**	
$GHA_{Jan\ 01}$	1.7447	99.9625	GHA for Jan 01, 2000 at 00:00:00 UT	
$GHA_{Jan\ 01}$ + ($1.0027379093 \times 2\pi \times$ 244 Days)	5.9422	340.4605	This GHA is corrected for August 31, and is only Applicable for the Year 2000	
Time Correction for Greenwich Meridian Angle to Aries for UT Time at Position Vector $\mathbf{R_1}$ (GHA_1)				
	Universal Time For Spacecraft at Position Vector $\mathbf{R_1}$			
	Hours	Minutes		
UT Time	12	7		
Decimal UT Time=UT Hours + Minutes/60	12.1167			
			Corrected GHA_1 for Date and Time = GHA_{JAN01} + ($1.0027379093 \times 2\pi \times$ 244 Days) + (15×12.1167 UT Hours $\times 2\pi/360$)	
			Radians	Degrees
Corrected GHA_1 Angle for 12h 7m UT Time			2.8311	162.2105
Time Correction for Greenwich Meridian Angle to Aries for UT Time at Position Vector $\mathbf{R_2}$ (GHA_2)				
	Universal Time For Spacecraft at Position Vector $\mathbf{R_2}$			
	Hours	Minutes		
UT Time	15	24		
Decimal UT Time =UT Hours + Minutes/60	15.4000			
			Corrected GHA_2 for Date and Time = GHA_{JAN01} + ($1.0027379093 \times 2\pi \times$ 244 Days) + (15×15.4000 UT Hours $\times 2\pi/360$)	
			Radians	Degrees
Corrected GHA_2 Angle for 15h 4m UT Time			3.6907	211.4605

13 Repeat Step 12, this time for $\mathbf{R_2}$ but using the latitude ϕ_2 and longitude θ_2 angles. You should get results close to what is shown in Table D.4. You now have two vector positions for your spacecraft that are quite accurate. Quite an accomplishment!

Now we must find the velocity vector for the first $\mathbf{R_1}$ position. Before we can do this we must compute the functions f and g and several other ancillary variables. The variables you need to solve first include the flight path angle, the semi-latus rectum p, and the angular momentum h. For this orbit, we'll assume that the flight path angle turns out to be 1.02°. For other orbits, use the method described in Chapter 6.

To solve for these variables and figure out your orbital elements:

1. Solve for the angular momentum h, by using the equation $h = R_1 \times V_1 \times \cos$ (flight path angle in radians). R_1 is your distance taken from the Distance readout, and V_1 is the velocity taken from your Total Velocity readout.
2. Solve for the semi-latus rectum p, by using the equation $p = h^2 \times u$, where u is the gravitational parameter for the Earth (3.986×10^5), and h is from the previous step. Table D.5 shows the results of these calculations.
3. Before computing the f and g functions, you need to figure out the angle Δv between vectors $\mathbf{R_1}$ and $\mathbf{R_2}$. To do this you use Equation D.7. For this particular orbit, this calculation yields a $\Delta v = 1.4041$ radians or 80.448°. In other words, the two spacecraft positions are separated by an angular distance of 80.448° on a great circle drawn around the Earth.
4. Now you have all the variables you need to solve the f and g functions, shown in Equation D.6. Once you have solved these equations, you should have two separate values: one for the f function, and another for the g function, as shown in Table D.5.
5. Plug the f and g values into Equation D.5 and solve for each component of the velocity vector $\mathbf{V_1}$ (i.e., $\mathbf{V_{x1}}$, $\mathbf{V_{x2}}$, $\mathbf{V_{x3}}$), being sure to use the correct $\mathbf{R_2}$ and $\mathbf{R_1}$ vector component in Equation D.5 (if you are solving for $\mathbf{V_{x1}}$, use $\mathbf{R_{x2}}$ and $\mathbf{R_{x1}}$ in Equation D.5). You now have the vector components for the spacecraft's velocity at $\mathbf{R_1}$!
6. Using the methods described in Chapter 7, you can now use $\mathbf{R_1}$ and $\mathbf{V_1}$ to figure out all the classical orbital elements, as is shown in Table D.5!

I will be posting to the SYBEX CompuServe forum an Excel spreadsheet that does all the calculations for you. All you'll need to do is download the spreadsheet and enter the latitude/longitude data, time, date,

TABLE D.4: *Calculating Position Vector Components for Your Spacecraft Using the Angle to Aries*

Finding R_{x1}, R_{y1}, and R_{z1}		
Date	August 31, 2000	
Calculated Number of Days Since Jan 01 (From Table D-1)=		244
	Hour	Minute
UT Time	12	7
Current Spacecraft Decimal Latitude (Enter Negative Number for S Latitude)		-42.1572
Current Spacecraft Decimal Longitude (Enter Negative Number for W Longitude)		-39.4825
Spacecraft Velocity Magnitude at $\mathbf{R_1}$ Vector Position	3.544	km/sec
	Radians	Degrees
Time & Date Corrected GHA_1 Angle to Aries (Vernal Equinox) from Previous Table	2.8311	162.2105
$_1$ Spacecraft's Current Longitude	-0.6891	-39.4825
$_1$ Spacecraft's Current Latitude	-0.7358	-42.1572
$_1$ = Spacecraft's Angle to Aries (Vernal Equinox) = Corrected GHA_1 + $_1$	2.1420	122.7280
R_1 Spacecraft Distance to Center of Earth	31,696	km
$R_{x1} = R_1 \cos\ _1 \cos\ _1$	-12,703	km
$R_{y1} = R_1 \cos\ _1 \sin\ _1$	19,766	km
$R_{z1} = R_1 \sin\ _1$	-21,273	km

Finding R_{x2}, R_{y2}, and R_{z2}		
Date	August 31, 2000	
Calculated Number of Days Since Jan 01 (From Table D-1)=		244
	Hour	Minute
UT Time	15	24
Current Spacecraft Decimal Latitude (Enter Negative Number for S Latitude)		27.9217
Current Spacecraft Decimal Longitude (Enter Negative Number for W Longitude)		-45.8844
Spacecraft Velocity Magnitude at $\mathbf{R_2}$ Vector Position	3.556	km/sec
	Radians	Degrees
Time & Date Corrected GHA_2 Angle to Aries (Vernal Equinox) from Previous Table	3.6907	211.4605
$_2$ Spacecraft's Current Longitude	-0.8008	-45.8844
$_2$ Spacecraft's Current Latitude	0.4873	27.9217
$_2$ = Spacecraft's Angle to Aries (Vernal Equinox) = Corrected GHA_2 + $_2$	2.8898	165.5760
R_2 Spacecraft Distance to Center of Earth	31,579	km
$R_{x2} = R_2 \cos\ _2 \cos\ _2$	-27,023	km
$R_{y2} = R_2 \cos\ _2 \sin\ _2$	6,950	km
$R_{z2} = R_2 \sin\ _2$	14,787	km

distances R_1 and R_2, and velocity V_1. The spreadsheet will also be made available via anonymous ftp on the Internet at `ftp.iup.edu` in the Flight Simulation directory, and in the Flight Simulator/Space Simulator section library on CompuServe.

TABLE D.5: *Calculating Velocity Vector Components and the Classical Orbital Elements*

Calculated Results			
Gravitational Constant for Earth	u=	398,601.2000	
Find angle v between R_1 and R_2 Using Dot Product		In Radians	In Degrees
Dot Product **R_1 dot R_2** = R_1*R_2*cos v	v=	1.4041	80.4480
Now Calculate f and g functions			
First Calculate p. u is gravitational constant for Earth		In Radians	In Degrees
Calculate Flight Path Angle Using Method of Chapter 6		0.0178	1.0200
h = R_1*V_1*cos (Flight Path Angle)	h =	112,312.8243	km^2/sec^2
p= h^2/u	p =	31,646.0927	km
f = 1-((R_2/p)*(1-cos(v)))	f =	0.1677	
g = R_1*R_2*sin(v)/sqrt(u*p)	g =	8,788.4038	

Velocity Vector 1	Calculated Velocity Components		
V_1 = (**R_2**-f***R_1**)/g	**V_{x1}** =	-2.8325	km/sec
	V_{y1} =	0.4137	km/sec
	V_{z1} =	2.0886	km/sec
	$V_{1magnitude}$ =	3.5434	km/sec

Now Calculate the Orbital Elements from R_1 and V_1							
First Calculate **h** vector							
h = **R_1xV_1**		**h_i** =	50,083.0484				
(Cross Product of Two Vectors)		**h_j** =	86,787.5725				
		h_k =	50,732.3964				
		h =	112,312.8243	km^2/sec^2			
Next Calculate **n** vector							
n = Kxh where **K** =<0,0,1>		**n_i** =	-86,787.5725				
(Cross Product of Two Vectors)		**n_j** =	50,083.0484				
		n_k =	0.0000				
		n =	100,201.7688				
Finally Calculate **e** eccentricity vector							
e = 1/u*((V_1^2-u/R_1)**R_1**-(**R1 dot V_1**)**V_1**)		**e_i** =	-0.0014				
		e_j =	-0.0005				
		e_k =	0.0023				
Eccentricity e =		e =	0.0027		0.0027		e = **0.0027**
Angle of Orbital Inclination i							
cos i = **h_k**/h		i =	1.1021	Radians	63.1468	Degrees	i = **63.1468 Degrees**
Longitude of the Ascending Node							
Cos = **n_i**/n		=	2.6182	Radians	150.0118	Degrees	= **150.0118 Degrees**
If **n_j** >= 0 then is less than 180 Degrees							
n_j =	0	Since **n_j** = 0, is less than 180 Degrees					
Argument of Periapsis							
Cos = (**n dot e**)/(n*e)		=	1.2007	Radians	68.7939	Degrees	= **68.7939 Degrees**
If **e_k** > 0 then is less than 180 Degrees							
e_k =	0.0023	Since **e_k** > 0, is less than 180 Degrees					
True Anomaly v_o							
Cos v_o = (**e dot R**)/(e*R)		v_o =	2.0522	Radians	117.5830	Degrees	
If **R dot V** > 0, then v_o is less than 180 Degrees							
R_1 dot V_1 =	-272.1615	Since **R_1 dot V_1** is < 0, v_o > 180 and so you subtract 360 - 117.5830051 = 242.4169949 Degrees					

Note: Don't forget about quadrant resolution! You don't know whether , , or v_o is > 180 Degrees unless you observe the rules given here. The true anomaly v_o in this example illustrates how quadrant resolution changes the computed angle.	At **R_1** v_o = **242.4170 Degrees**

INDEX

Note to the Reader:

Throughout this index **boldfaced** page numbers indicate primary discussions of a topic. *Italicized* page numbers indicate illustrations.

H

I

J

K

L

M

N

O

T

W

X

Y

Z

[1504] Space Simulator Strategies and Secrets

GET A FREE CATALOG JUST FOR EXPRESSING YOUR OPINION.

Help us improve our books and get a ***FREE*** full-color catalog in the bargain. Please complete this form, pull out this page and send it in today. The address is on the reverse side.

Name ____________________ **Company** ____________________

Address ____________________ **City** __________ **State** ____ **Zip** ________

Phone (   ) ____________________

1. How would you rate the overall quality of this book?

- ❑ Excellent
- ❑ Very Good
- ❑ Good
- ❑ Fair
- ❑ Below Average
- ❑ Poor

2. What were the things you liked most about the book? (Check all that apply)

- ❑ Pace
- ❑ Format
- ❑ Writing Style
- ❑ Examples
- ❑ Table of Contents
- ❑ Index
- ❑ Price
- ❑ Illustrations
- ❑ Type Style
- ❑ Cover
- ❑ Depth of Coverage
- ❑ Fast Track Notes

3. What were the things you liked *least* about the book? (Check all that apply)

- ❑ Pace
- ❑ Format
- ❑ Writing Style
- ❑ Examples
- ❑ Table of Contents
- ❑ Index
- ❑ Price
- ❑ Illustrations
- ❑ Type Style
- ❑ Cover
- ❑ Depth of Coverage
- ❑ Fast Track Notes

4. Where did you buy this book?

- ❑ Bookstore chain
- ❑ Small independent bookstore
- ❑ Computer store
- ❑ Wholesale club
- ❑ College bookstore
- ❑ Technical bookstore
- ❑ Other ____________

5. How did you decide to buy this particular book?

- ❑ Recommended by friend
- ❑ Recommended by store personnel
- ❑ Author's reputation
- ❑ Sybex's reputation
- ❑ Read book review in ________
- ❑ Other ____________

6. How did you pay for this book?

- ❑ Used own funds
- ❑ Reimbursed by company
- ❑ Received book as a gift

7. What is your level of experience with the subject covered in this book?

- ❑ Beginner
- ❑ Intermediate
- ❑ Advanced

8. How long have you been using a computer?

years ____________

months ____________

9. Where do you most often use your computer?

- ❑ Home
- ❑ Work
- ❑ Both
- ❑ Other ____________

10. What kind of computer equipment do you have? (Check all that apply)

- ❑ PC Compatible Desktop Computer
- ❑ PC Compatible Laptop Computer
- ❑ Apple/Mac Computer
- ❑ Apple/Mac Laptop Computer
- ❑ CD ROM
- ❑ Fax Modem
- ❑ Data Modem
- ❑ Scanner
- ❑ Sound Card
- ❑ Other ____________

11. What other kinds of software packages do you ordinarily use?

- ❑ Accounting
- ❑ Databases
- ❑ Networks
- ❑ Apple/Mac
- ❑ Desktop Publishing
- ❑ Spreadsheets
- ❑ CAD
- ❑ Games
- ❑ Word Processing
- ❑ Communications
- ❑ Money Management
- ❑ Other ____________

12. What operating systems do you ordinarily use?

- ❑ DOS
- ❑ OS/2
- ❑ Windows
- ❑ Apple/Mac
- ❑ Windows NT
- ❑ Other ____________

13. On what computer-related subject(s) would you like to see more books?

14. Do you have any other comments about this book? (Please feel free to use a separate piece of paper if you need more room)

PLEASE FOLD, SEAL, AND MAIL TO SYBEX

SYBEX INC.
Department M
2021 Challenger Drive
Alameda, CA
94501

SYBEX®

Other Controls

Action	Press
Switch Slew Mode On/Off	Y
Switch between Distance/Radius and Altitude	Alt S
Switch between Vertical/Tangential and Total Velocity	Alt V
Accelerate Time Scale	F1
Decelerate Time Scale	F2
Set Time Scale to 1.1 year/second	Shift F1
Set Time Scale to 1 second/second	Shift F2
Open Autopilot Dialog Box	Alt A
Autopilot On/Off	Z
Vehicle Transfer	Shift T
Undock	Shift U
Space Walk *or* Reboard Craft	Shift W
Deploy *or* Retract Lander	Shift D
Extend *or* Retract Landing Gear	G
Sound On/Off	Q
Calibrate Joystick	J
Head Up Display On/Off	H
Save Situation	;
Pause Simulation	Pause
Reset Simulation	Ctrl Esc
Exit Space Simulator	Ctrl Break